THE CZAR'S BRIT

THE CZAR'S BRITISH SQUADRON

BRYAN PERRETT
and
ANTHONY LORD

Foreword by
HRH The Duke of Edinburgh

WILLIAM KIMBER · LONDON

First published in 1981 by
WILLIAM KIMBER & CO. LIMITED
Godolphin House, 22a Queen Anne's Gate,
London, SW1H 9AE

© Bryan Perrett and Anthony Lord, 1981

ISBN 07183-0268-0

This book is copyright. No part of it may be reproduced in any form without permission in writing from the publishers except by a reviewer who wishes to quote brief passages in connection with a review written for inclusion in a newspaper, magazine, radio or television broadcast.

Typeset by Grove Graphics
and printed in Great Britain by
The Garden City Press Limited,
Letchworth, Hertfordshire, SG6 1JS

Contents

		page
	Foreword by HRH The Duke of Edinburgh	11
	Authors' Note	13
I	The Launching of 'President II'	15
II	Friends in High Places	30
III	Holy Russia	45
IV	'You Have Shaken Death by the Beard!'	58
V	Battle in the Mud	79
VI	The World Turned Upside Down	99
VII	Debacle at Brzezany	113
VIII	Wanted – Dead or Alive	126
IX	Through a Glass Darkly	148
X	Back to Russia	162
	A Postscript	179
	Appendix	183
	Index	185

List of Illustrations

	facing page
Commander Oliver Locker Lampson	32
A Pierce Arrow Heavy Armoured Car *P. A. Vicary*	33
Seabrook Heavy Armoured Car	33
Members of 15 Squadron at Cromer	33
RNAS despatch riders	48
Two of the squadron's Heavy Armoured Cars	48
Locker Lampson supervises the extraction of a Seabrook Heavy Armoured Car *P. A. Vicary*	48
At Alexandrovsk Harbour *P. A. Vicary*	49
The mail party on the ice	49
The troopship *Dvinsk* in the ice *P. A. Vicary*	49
The beginning of the thaw	49
A Russian railway station	64
Petty Officer Don Spencer with 'Miskab', the RNAS mascot *P. A. Vicary*	64
Outside Moscow *S. M. Payne*	64
Disembarking Armoured Cars from Barges	65
Russian line infantry, Cossacks and RNAS men *P. A. Vicary*	65
Cossacks and Bengal Lancers at Tabriz *P. A. Vicary*	65
The sick bay going through the Caucasian mountains *PO Baker*	80
Locker Lampson reconnoitring on the Mush Plain *P. A. Vicary*	80
Maintenance in Trans-Caucasia	80
A German aircraft brought down near Braila *P. A. Vicary*	81
Model T Ford Armoured car	81
3-pounder gun emplacement in Rumania 1917	81
Lt Ingle's car after recovery from No Man's Land	81
Brew up in Galicia *P. A. Vicary*	128
'Home-made' Heavy Armoured with 3-pounder	128

facing page

Damaged Model T Ford Armoured after the Galacian retreat	128
Lieutenant-Commander Smiles	129
Making repairs in Austria	129
The Petrograd garrison after the Revolution	129
Russian Austin Armoured Car	129
The Armoured Car mess	144
The Kursk squadron leaving Russia on trawlers	144
Duncars' officers in Baghdad	144
Duncars' operational base at Hamadan	145
Bicherakov's Cossack cavalry	145
Bicherakov's Cossack infantry	145
Colonel Crawford and Major Wells Hood	160
Austin armoured car bogged down in a ford	160
Assisting an armoured car out of a *Khud*	161
Wheel changing on the Enzeli road	161
Austin armoured car at the Mud Volcano	161
Machinery wagon in trouble	176
Austin Armoured Car bogged down on the Enzeli Road	176
Locker Lampson, his secretary and a young Prince Philip at Cromer	177
Einstein and Locker Lampson at a Peace Rally	177

List of Maps and Drawings

The Kurds' ambush	63
Operations in Trans-Caucasia 1916	67
The Rumanian Campaign, December 1916 to January 1917	93
Area of Operations July 1917	120–1

Foreword by
HRH The Duke of Edinburgh

When I was about 12 years old I joined some cousins for the summer holidays at Cromer. We stayed at the large rambling home of a Commander Locker Lampson. I remember that he was retired from the Royal Navy and that he was a Member of Parliament. I had no idea at the time that he had had such a remarkable career during the first war, but the fact that I remember him so clearly suggests that his personality must have made a deep impression.

This story of Oliver Locker Lampson's experience during the First World War seems to bear out the saying that 'truth is often stranger than fiction'. The idea that a party of sailors should take a number of armoured cars to Russia is fairly remarkable in the first place, but for them then to become involved in the drama and confusion of the Bolshevik revolution turns the story from bizarre adventure into a grim struggle for survival.

The period of history covered by this book is familiar in general terms. This account provides a revealing and an extremely interesting 'inside' view of the events as they developed.

Authors' Note

It is many years now since we first learned that a British naval armoured car unit commanded by a Member of Parliament had fought on the Eastern Front during World War I, and our curiosity was further piqued when we discovered that almost nothing was known of the unit until the official papers were released in 1968. Even then these were far from complete, and it was clear that we were presented with a thoroughly absorbing jigsaw puzzle from which many of the most interesting pieces were missing. We have long since lost count of the time spent or the miles travelled in acquiring those pieces, but when they were assembled we knew that we had not one but two stories to tell, that of the unit itself and that of its commanding officer, Commander Oliver Locker Lampson RNVR MP, since neither one could have existed without the other.

We could never have completed our task had we not received the most generous assistance from many sources, and we are especially grateful to the Locker Lampson family of Rowfant, Sussex, and to Mr Stephen Locker Lampson of New Zealand, who kindly made available his father's unpublished memoirs.

Among the unit's survivors we were able to trace were Messrs G. Babbage, L. Baker, George Bromley, Dick Brown, George Martin, S. M. Payne, Alfred Rodwell, Frank Round MBE, S. Rule, H. A. Sissons and Ted Titterington. To them, and to the following relatives of members of the unit who have passed on, we owe an inestimable debt of gratitude for their advice, for permitting us access to diaries, documents and photographs and, not least, for their warm hospitality: Mrs J. Anderson, Mrs A. S. Boot, Mr J. Bryant, Lady Patricia Fisher, Mrs M. Leek, Mr Roy Munday, Mrs H. Pugh and Mrs D. Simpson.

Thanks are also due to Mr J. D. Brown of the Naval Historical Branch, Ministry of Defence, to the proprietors of *Blackwood's Magazine*, to Mr Robert Crawford of the Imperial War Museum, the late Mr Crawford-Holden of Cromer, David Fisher, Susan Jordan,

Nancy Lines, Major L. McCulloch, Major C. R. M. Messenger, Mr A. J. Poultney, J. Gordon Phillips (archivist at *The Times*), the staff of the Public Record Office, and to Mr and Mrs P. A. Vicary of the Maritime Photo Library, Cromer, for their kind permission to use rare photographs in their possession.

We are most grateful for the efforts of the military attachés of the Austrian, German and Turkish Embassies to produce material from 'the other side of the hill'. We should sincerely have enjoyed thanking the Soviet Embassy in London for their unfailing assistance and enthusiastic support throughout; rather, we must compliment them on their single-minded determination that such a situation would not be permitted to arise.

We must mention at the outset that to avoid confusion the place-names in our text were those in use at the time. Since then, many have changed at least once; for example, Tsaritsyn became Stalingrad, but is now called Volgagrad. These changes tend to reflect fashionable contortions in what is currently acceptable in Communist thinking and are not, we understand, deliberate attempts on the part of the Soviet Government to promote cartography and sign-writing as growth industries.

February 1981　　　　　　　　　　　　　　　　　　BRYAN PERRETT
　　　　　　　　　　　　　　　　　　　　　　　　　ANTHONY LORD

CHAPTER ONE

The Launching of President II

One day someone would drive an ice-pick into the brain of the man whose pen was poised over the detention order, but for the moment he was at the height of his power. He had recently planned the coup which swept away the tottering Provisional Government of Alexander Kerensky and he was already laying the foundations of the Red Army which would emerge victorious from a long and bloody civil war with the more democratic elements in Russian society. His pince-nez suggested the academic rather than the man of action, and indeed during his period as a student of mathematics at the University of Odessa he had revealed that he possessed a first-class mind. He was, in fact, a ruthless and dedicated professional revolutionary whose creed demanded the overthrow of the capitalist system throughout the world, by violent means if necessary. He was of Jewish extraction and had been born on his parents' farm near Odessa in 1879, growing up in a comfortable but not affluent environment. The names which he had been given were Leib David Bronstein, or Lev Davidovich in its Russian form, although he is better known today by his revolutionary name of Leon Trostky.

The detention order bearing his signature related to members of a British naval unit of 600 men which had fought in Russia for two years, first under the Czar's administration and later under Kerensky's. It was known, more or less officially, as the Russian Armoured Car Division, Royal Naval Air Service, and its commanding officer was Commander Oliver Stillingfleet Locker Lampson, Member of Parliament for the constituency of North Huntingdonshire.

A year younger than Trotsky, Locker Lampson had much in common with him. Both had intellectual leanings, were able, ruthless and politically aware, but there the resemblance ended. The latter's background was that of solid if unspectacular wealth and he had been educated privately at Eton and at Trinity College, Cambridge, where he obtained Honours in Modern Languages and History. At school he had once won the shot-put but was not greatly concerned with sport. His features contained a hint of arrogance and would, in later years, assume a forbidding expression even in repose. He wore his clothes well and possessed a presence that would turn heads, particularly female, whenever he entered a room. He also had a very considerable charm, was a good conversationalist and was extremely generous.

His father was the poet Frederick Locker, whose great friend Alfred Lord Tennyson frequently dined at the family's London home, 25 Chesham Street. Frederick's second wife and Oliver's mother was Jane Lampson, the daughter of Sir Curtis Lampson, an American who had been knighted for his services during Queen Victoria's reign. From Lampson Locker inherited two substantial properties, Rowfant in Sussex and New Haven Court near Cromer in Norfolk, on condition that the family names were joined.

As was common at this level of society during the period, the young Oliver saw more of his Nanny, Harriet Lucas, than he did of his parents, and later commented, 'For twenty years I remained more fond of her than of anyone and the same, oddly enough, could be said of Winston Churchill and his nurse Mrs Everest'. He was, however, also fond of his parents and, as his unpublished memoirs relate, was prepared to humour his mother's almost incredible phobias concerning health and hygiene.

> Her main dreads were draughts, drains, thunderstorms, tramps, mad dogs and mumps. She taught me to spit – not furtively, but with ostentation – if I met a smell. I went round muffled to the ear-tips against winds; for her an open window – like an open drain – led straight to the grave. Every cranny of our rooms was sealed against the demon draught. And she would not allow us to handle coppers. They were the coinage of the common, the infected; only gold and silver were safe. I always returned to school copperless: silver in one pocket, gold in the other, and new coins for preference. Against mad dogs and tramps, assumed to infest the lanes, I was armed at the age of twelve with an American revolver. Most parents would think that a boy thus armed was a greater danger to himself – not so my mother.

The revolver accompanied him to Eton, where, by some miracle, it escaped confiscation. So ingrained was the habit that even after his retirement from public life, Oliver Locker Lampson still went about his country walks fully armed against tramps and mad dogs, both of which, he reflected sadly, had been largely eliminated by progress. His mother would have approved.

She most certainly would not have approved of one of his teenage adventures. With the onset of puberty he had listened enviously to the alleged exploits of his friends and one night set off into the West End to discover the truth for himself. He was most fortunate in that he met not a slick professional but the almost legendary tart with a heart of gold. What could have been an unhappy coupling in the seediest surroundings was stopped by the woman herself who, on learning that it was his first experience, put an end to the matter in his own interest, and even refunded his money.

After leaving Cambridge with a degree in Law he worked in chambers for a year and was then called to the bar, subsequently accompanying Mr Justice Bingham (later Lord Mersey) on circuit as Marshal. It was about this period that he became interested in politics and in 1907 was adopted as prospective Unionist candidate for North Huntingdonshire. In 1908 he demonstrated his skill as an organiser by promoting a marathon race 'in the hope that I may thus create a little sporting excitement and encourage long-distance running in England'. The race was run the following year and the proceeds, the largest amount ever received from a sporting event at the time, were presented to the Huntingdonshire County Hospital.

He had also become interested in motoring, with somewhat varied results. Not long after the marathon his Hotchkiss Landaulette burst into flames and burned itself out. In 1910, on his way to speak at a meeting shortly before the General Election, he misjudged the width of a bridge and drove a second car into a river. Undismayed, he continued on his way. The *Peterborough Standard* reported:

> Thus it was that Mr Locker Lampson in a pair of trousers nearer his knees than his ankles, without a collar, with a red scarf and a pair of carpet slippers, addressed an enthusiastic gathering at Broughton, within two hours of the accident. The audience carried him shoulder high.

The electorate liked him. He was young, he had plenty of drive, and he had style. When the result was declared he found that he had taken a Liberal stronghold by a margin of 435 votes.

His career was progressing, but although politics would always be his overriding interest, for the moment something was lacking from his life. He was restless and he craved for adventure, as did most young men of the time, irrespective of their backgrounds. Sociologists are fond of pointing out the glaring inequalities of the period, but forget to mention that these very factors also produced a generation of outstanding mental toughness, self-reliance, energy and confidence, which enabled many to prosper by their unaided efforts not merely at home but in the dominions and colonies as well. Its heroes were men who challenged great odds, frequently at risk to their own lives and, as in the case of Scott's ill-fated Antarctic venture, the merit did not necessarily lie in achieving success, but in having the courage to try. Notwithstanding, it was also an essentially kind, considerate and honest generation with a strong sense of pride in both its local and its national institutions and an instinctive understanding that discipline was the foundation upon which success was built.

When war broke out in August 1914 it was this lust for adventure, coupled with a sense of duty and patriotism, which led men to swamp the recruiting offices. It had been sixty years since Great Britain had fought a Continental enemy, and since the war was expected to be short, no one wanted to miss it.

For Locker Lampson, the question was how best to employ himself. The small, professional British Army was, man for man and battalion for battalion, the most formidable in the field. During its first battles it had mauled von Kluck's 1st German Army again and again, blanketing its advancing columns with bursting shrapnel and then raking them through and through with the terrible sixteen-aimed-rounds-to-the-minute musketry technique perfected during the Boer War. The dense field grey masses had shredded away and finally sunk into the ground. Only the need to conform to their Allies' movements caused the British to withdraw.

Brilliantly as the Army was fighting it was, however, to the Royal Navy that Locker Lampson turned, inspired by a series of unorthodox events in Belgium during the German advance. The launching of the revolutionary battleship HMS *Dreadnought* and the subsequent naval construction race with Germany had made the Navy unquestionably the more technically aware of the two services, with the result that the Admiralty now reacted to change with a speed unequalled in its history. In 1912 it had founded its own air arm, the Royal Naval Air Service, the main function of which was to be scouting for the fleet.

By the end of August 1914 the Eastchurch Squadron RNAS, under Commander C. R. Samson, had established a base near Dunkirk, having previously landed at Ostend to support the Royal Marine Brigade, which was temporarily attached to the Belgian Army. The Belgians had, from the very first days of the war, been using private Minerva and Excelsior touring cars against the enemy. At first, officers had taken pot shots with sporting rifles at the Germans' advance screen of lancers, but it was quickly realised that a great deal more damage could be done if Maxim machine guns were mounted on the cars. A number of dashing raids were carried out, but in one such affray the popular Prince Baudouin de Ligne was killed, and the next step was to add armour plate for the crews' protection, and during the third week of August the first conversions of touring automobiles to fully fledged armoured cars were made at Antwerp.*

Samson, short of aircraft for his reconnaissance missions, decided to supplement them with commandeered cars, which could also be used to rescue pilots who had been forced down between the armies, their general role being defined as 'aeroplane support'. In this they were so successful that Winston Churchill, then First Lord of the Admiralty, decided in October to form an additional wing of the RNAS to be known as the Royal Naval Armoured Car Division.

An efficient organisation was established with commendable speed, including a headquarters at 48 Dover Street, off Piccadilly, and a depot at Wormwood Scrubs. Suitable vehicles, of which Rolls Royces and Lanchesters formed the majority, were commandeered from all over the country, stripped of their coachwork, fitted with strengthened rear axles, and provided with an armoured body and a turret which gave all-round traverse for its machine gun. As originally planned, each armoured car squadron consisted of twelve fighting vehicles, divided into three sections, each of four cars. With considerable foresight, however, it was pointed out that very soon enemy armoured car squadrons would also appear at the front, and that a contest between machine-gun armed vehicles protected by armour and running on solid tyres was likely to prove inconclusive. It was, therefore, decided to develop a Heavy armoured car, based on the Seabrook (and later the Pierce-Arrow) lorry chassis, mounting a 3-pounder gun which could not only destroy enemy vehicles but also knock out machine-gun posts, strongpoints and artillery positions.

This parallels in many respects the relationship between the battle-cruiser and the cruiser, and in theory each armoured car section had the support of one Heavy car. In practice, it seems that, for a time at least, the Heavies were grouped together in their own squadrons for ease of maintenance, and sections were despatched to work with other squadrons as required. Oddly, the Heavy armoured car concept lost

* The Belgian Army was not, however, the first to employ armoured cars in action. The Italians had used one or two in a very limited role during their 1912 war against Turkey in Libya.

favour in the British service between the wars, and was only reintroduced in 1940 with the 2-pounder Daimler.

Naturally, there was an acute shortage of equipment during the early days and for a while gaps in squadron establishments were filled by the Scott-Maxim combination. This consisted of the water-cooled Scott motor-cycle, to which was attached a sidecar mounting a Maxim machine-gun. The machine was phased out as more armoured cars became available, but the Army enthusiastically adopted the idea for its machine-gun battalions – as did the German Army for its reconnaissance troops during the early years of World War II.

The RNACD squadrons' internal support and administrative organisation was also thoroughly thought through and differs only in detail from that of a modern armoured car unit. In addition to the lorries which carried fuel, ammunition, spares and food, each squadron had a mobile workshop with which to deal with breakdowns, a motorised ambulance for the wounded, and a wireless vehicle through which it could maintain contact with the scout aircraft it was supporting, or with the formation headquarters for which it was performing reconnaissance. There was, too, an early appreciation that sections would have to be self-supporting for comparatively long periods, and primus stoves were issued to the fighting vehicles at least, the forerunners of the indispensable brew kits which have sustained the morale of tank and armoured car crews ever since.

Communication between cars was by hand signal, which was extremely dangerous when in contact with the enemy. An alternative was a system of coloured flags, flown from staffs on either side of the turret, but these could be shot away and, moreover, the system suffered from the major disadvantage that up-sun all flags appear to be black. The safest method was to give a clear briefing for a well-defined mission and leave the rest to car commanders' personal common sense and initiative. Once engaged, changes of plan were communicated to sections by motor-cycle despatch riders who, if they were lucky, returned to report the delivery of their orders.

One problem encountered when raising the force was that in 1914 motoring was in its infancy and that very few men could drive, let alone maintain, a motor vehicle. Those that could were well-to-do young men with private means, professional chauffeurs or lorry drivers, or members of the embryonic motor manufacturing industry. Large numbers of drivers, fitters and vehicle electricians were required, and for the few available the RNACD found itself in direct competition with the Army, where the Service Corps was expanding its mechanical transport branch. The Navy's solution was to accept qualified recruits with the minimum rank of Petty Officer Mechanic, together with the appropriate rate of pay, which was infinitely more attractive than the Army's offer of a private's uniform and remuneration.

Financial considerations apart, it seems probable that the Navy would have won the contest anyway. Much of the contemporary desire for adventure was based on recent technological advances. Thus, while today boys might dream of becoming an astronaut, piloting an advanced jet fighter or driving the world's best engineered car, they know their chances of achieving these ambitions vary from the almost impossible to the highly remote; but in 1914 technology had not outgrown average human assistance, and the chance to pilot a primitive aircraft or drive a Rolls Royce armoured car was there for the taking if one had the will and determination for it.

For a maritime nation, too, the Navy had always had an undoubted glamour, and the sight of the armoured cars touring the streets, a White Ensign flying proudly from a jackstaff behind their turrets, the letters RNAS painted large on the hull sides, and the smart blue landing-party rig of their Petty Officer crews, proved for many to be an irresistible lure.* Dover Street always had more potential recruits than it needed and was able to pick the best. Some men lied about their ages to get in, and others about their medical condition: Petty Officer H. A. Sissons, for example, had suffered from mild myopia since childhood and would probably have been rejected had he not taken advantage of the Staff Surgeon's temporary absence to learn the eye-testing chart by heart. Many had travelled from as far afield as Canada, Australia, New Zealand, South Africa, India and elsewhere in the Empire to offer their skills. Others, like Lieutenant Walter Smiles, a qualified pilot who had abandoned his career as a tea planter on the outbreak of war, transferred from the flying branch in search of the action which the current aircraft shortage denied him. In the same category was Chief Petty Officer George Bromley, who had worked his way through the Marconi Wireless School and whose high hopes of spotting for the fleet had been similarly grounded; intolerant of inefficiency at any level, he had bluntly informed his Commander that he wished to transfer to the *proper* Navy, and had

---

* This uniform was replaced shortly after by the Army's harder wearing khaki service dress, which was worn with naval badges of rank and insignia. The RNACD's cap badge was a Rolls Royce armoured car on an oval plate surmounted by a crown. Collar badges were miniature Rolls Royce armoured cars, bronze for everyday use and gilt for parade dress.

suddenly found himself en route to join an armoured car squadron in France.

As the concept of the RNACD had caught the public imagination, the Admiralty had no hesitation in accepting offers from wealthy individuals and groups to pay the cost of raising and equipping armoured car squadrons. The most notable of these benefactors was the Duke of Westminster, believed to be the richest man in the kingdom, who raised and commanded No 2 Squadron, equipped with Rolls Royces.

Locker Lampson decided to do likewise, although there were serious difficulties in his way. He undoubtedly subscribed a great deal of his own money, but the cost of raising a squadron was somewhat in excess of £30,000, an enormous sum in 1914, and this was beyond his means. Again, while he was able to recruit many suitable men from Cromer and elsewhere in East Anglia, from among his Huntingdonshire constituents and his London acquaintances, there were not enough of them. Fortunately, some assistance was available. Immediately prior to the war the Home Rule Bill had polarised opinions in Ireland to such an extent that civil war seemed inevitable. Both sides had armed themselves and collected substantial funds for the coming struggle but had, for reasons of their own, agreed to put aside their differences until the conflict with Germany and her allies had been resolved. The Ulster Volunteer Force had strong ties with Locker Lampson's Unionist Party and, anxious to demonstrate its loyalty to the crown, came to his aid by making good the shortfall in money and men. A great deal of secrecy surrounded the agreement and, probably for the sake of political expediency, Locker Lampson did not disclose the UVF participation. The curious might, perhaps, have wondered why a consignment of Canadian rifles was immediately available for issue; or indeed why the commander of a unit which ostensibly had its roots in the Eastern Counties should insist that three of his armoured cars were named *Ulster, Londonderry* and *Mountjoy*.

Locker Lampson was commissioned as lieutenant-commander RNVR and his squadron, designated No 15 and equipped with Lanchesters, commenced its basic training at Wormwood Scrubs. Regular officers and petty officers were attached to administer the unit and knock the recruits into shape. The regulars soon made it quite clear that they were the genuine article and that the new arrivals, for all their rank, were not. Being volunteers, however, the men were easy to handle and accepted their stint on the barracks square with good humour, although when it came to technical training those with hard-earned skills showed an initial but understandable reluctance to pass on the specialised knowledge upon which their living depended.

It was soon apparent that Locker Lampson was amply endowed with the great gift of leadership. With the ratings he was reserved but friendly, and although he was willing to share a joke or two with them they soon learned that any attempt at familiarity was sharply rebuffed. He also had a knack of setting a man a task slightly beyond his normal abilities and expressing confidence that it could be performed; because of this the man tried harder, succeeded more often than not, and in consequence his opinion of himself and his commanding officer soared when he was complimented on his efforts. During operations, if a petty officer distinguished himself his name was put forward for an award at once and without question. Above all, as PO Sissons recalls, 'His first and main concern was the welfare of his men. In my opinion he was honourable, sincere, kindly and extremely generous.'

With his officers he took a harder line. An excellent administrator and thorough planner himself, he set high standards from the outset, and was impatiently intolerant of mistakes. He demanded, and received, a performance above and beyond the strict requirements of the service but took the view that officers who acted with outstanding courage under fire were merely doing their duty and did not require the additional reward of decoration. This slightly priggish philosophy had its roots in the still-remembered days of commission by purchase, when an officer was automatically assumed to have a greater stake in his country's cause than did his men, but in 1914 it could be regarded as distinctly old-fashioned if not downright unfair. Off duty, Locker Lampson was always affable company in the mess, although slightly given to favouritism. His officers certainly respected him, and the majority even liked him, but their perspective was somewhat different from that of the ratings. In general, however, he demonstrated the truth of the saying that a tight ship is a happy ship.

With the Germans in possession of all but a fraction of the Belgian coast, most of the newly raised RNACD squadrons were sent to East Anglia to counter a possible invasion threat and, ironically, No 15 Squadron found itself based on Cromer. When the threat passed, the squadrons were despatched to their overseas stations. No 1 Squadron was committed to the fighting in German South West Africa (Namibia), overcoming extremely difficult terrain and proving a decisive influence in bringing the campaign to a successful conclusion.

One section was then shipped round the Cape to take part in the protracted struggle for the German East African colony of Tanga (Tanzania). Nos 3 and 4 Squadrons were sent to Gallipoli where, although actively engaged in the fighting, they were unable to demonstrate their true potential. Nos 2, 5, 6, 8, 15 and 17 Squadrons went to Flanders, where they found very different conditions from those which had faced Samson in the early, free-wheeling days of the war.

The trench lines and their barbed wire entanglements had reached the sea in mid-October 1914 and, in the absence of a breakthrough, the armoured cars were unable to carry out their primary role of support for the RNAS aircraft. Instead, they were employed on direct fire support tasks against enemy strongpoints and machine-gun posts, getting as close to their targets as they could during the hours of darkness and opening fire at first light. Since these activities inevitably attracted a storm of shellfire in return, the gratitude of neighbouring Army units lacked something in its warmth. During this period Locker Lampson's No 15 Squadron operated on the Belgian Army's sector of the front, supported by Seabrook Heavies of No 17 Squadron.

Meanwhile, numerous ideas had been put forward as to how to end the deadlock of trench warfare, and of these the caterpillar landship, better known as the tank, seemed to offer the most promise.* A joint naval/military Landships Committee was set up, one of its early members being Commander F. L. M. Boothby, commander of RNACD. The inability of the Western Front squadrons to perform the task for which they had been formed had proved to be a great disappointment to the Admiralty and their continued existence provoked the intense hostility of the Fourth Sea Lord, Commodore Cecil Foley Lambert, within whose sphere of responsibility the RNAS as a whole lay, and who bluntly told Boothby that in his opinion the RNACD officers and men were 'damned idlers'.

The suggestion that the Admiralty in general and the RNACD in particular should play a major part in the development of the tank was the last straw for Foley, who gave vent to an explosive outburst to the effect that 'Caterpillar landships are idiotic and useless. Nobody has asked for them and nobody wants them. Those officers and men

* The term tank arose almost by accident. The first tanks were built under conditions of great secrecy by William Foster & Co of Lincoln, the security cover story being that they were mobile water cisterns, i.e. tanks, for use on the Eastern Front. The term landship remained in use for some time and the prefix HMLS (His Majesty's Landship) could often be seen ahead of individual names given to their vehicles by the first tank crews.

are wasting their time and are not pulling their proper weight in the war. If I had my way I would disband the whole lot of them. Anyhow, I am going to do my best to see that it is done and stop all this armoured car and caterpillar landship nonsense.'

The First and Second Sea Lords, although less assertive in their views, were also of the opinion that the Admiralty had no business developing weapons for land warfare; only the Third Sea Lord, Admiral Sir Frederick Tudor-Tudor, was sympathetic to the wishes of the Landships Committee. A. J. Balfour, who had succeeded Churchill as First Lord of the Admiralty on the latter's fall from grace following the failure of the Dardanelles venture, was also sympathetic, but, confronted by a hostile majority, was forced to give Lambert much of his way.

Starting in July 1915 arrangements were made for squadrons to hand over their cars to the Army, together with such personnel as wished to transfer, while those officers and men who did not returned to the United Kingdom. The Duke of Westminster's No 2 Squadron, always a friendly, almost clubbish unit, transferred almost en bloc and left for Egypt at the end of the year. As Nos 1, 2 and 3 Armoured Motor Batteries, the Duke's cars fought a brilliant campaign in the Western Desert, rescuing the imprisoned survivors of the steamer *Tara* and utterly smashing the power of the warlike Senussi Moslem sect. Subsequently, some of his cars and personnel supported Lawrence and his Arabs, while others formed the basis of the Light Armoured Motor Batteries which served to such good effect with Allenby's cavalry divisions in Palestine; but that is another story.*

It remains doubtful whether Lambert's decision made much difference to the isolated section fighting in Tanga, and it certainly did not apply to No 20 Squadron, which Balfour insisted on retaining since it was deeply involved in the landship construction and trials programme – and here we digress slightly but with good reason. Once the designers had reached agreement on what they wanted from Mother, the prototype for what was to become the Tank Mark I, Foster's built the machine in only 141 days.† The first trials were held around the works and at Burton Park, Lincolnshire, and the first demonstrations for distinguished visitors took place at Hatfield Park, Hertfordshire, on 29th

---

* Some of the Duke's cars were still serving with the Khartoum garrison in the 1930s, a remarkable tribute to the excellence of Rolls Royce engineering.

† PO Sissons' brother, a carpenter by trade serving with No 20 Squadron, built both Little Willie's and Mother's full size wooden pre-production mock-ups to the designers' specifications.

January 1916, when Chief Petty Officer Hill successfully drove the vehicle over an obstacle course consisting of banks, trenches, flooded craters and wire entanglements. Among those present were Balfour himself, Field Marshal Lord Kitchener, General Sir William Robertson, Chief of the Imperial General Staff, and David Lloyd George. A few days later King George V made a personal visit to Hatfield and Hill drove him over the same course.

The tank now firmly became an Army responsibility, and while the vehicles themselves began their production run the problems of how to man them sprang to the fore. These were even more acute than those which had faced the RNACD and were not helped by an initial shortsightedness on the Army's part. Ratings from the disbanded squadrons would, ostensibly, provide an obvious starting point, but an officer sent to persuade them to transfer to the Heavy Section Machine-Gun Corps, as the embryo Tank Corps was then called, was so gagged by security that he was unable to tell them much about the top secret project save the rates of pay they would receive. On his calling for volunteers, 'The front rank swayed, seemed to lean backwards – so rigid it was – and not a man moved!' It was not that they were not interested, but any leap into the dark requires careful consideration, and a drop in rank to private soldier accompanied by a reduction in weekly pay from £2 5s 6d to 13/6d was hardly an attractive proposition.

The same considerations did not apply to officers, who were able to transfer at their nearest equivalent rank, and it is pleasing to note that of the original six tank companies formed, two were commanded by former RNACD officers. Again, because of their specialised experience the personnel of No 20 Squadron were compulsorily transferred with ranks varying from sergeant to warrant officer, forming the central cadre responsible for training future tank driving and maintenance instructors which would be required in large numbers by the new corps. Thus, in spite of the War Office having originally denied itself many very suitable recruits – its policy was ultimately reversed – the RNACD could still lay claims to being the direct lineal ancestor of the Tank Corps and so the modern Royal Armoured Corps.

However, we must now return to 1915 and to a third area in which Lambert's *diktat* had no effect. The very threat of disbandment induced a personal crisis for Locker Lampson. Fiercely patriotic as he was, there was no doubt that his position as commander of an RNACD squadron had a prestige, an aura and even a mystique which was attractive to the electorate, even if they did not fully understand the nature of the fighting on the Western Front. If his squadron was disbanded the alternatives facing him were bleak; should he remain in the Navy, he was unqualified for sea duty and a dull shore appointment seemed likely; had he known of the tank's development, he would very probably have volunteered, but that lay several months ahead and in the meantime the Army seemed unable to offer anything which quite coincided with his rank and comparative inexperience. He genuinely wanted to get into the fighting, and the professional politician in him told him that his personal performance would be carefully watched both by his constituents and by his fellow politicians. Publicity is political lifeblood, and there would be little enough of that for a man ostensibly destined by events for obscure staff duties.

However, a strand of sheer good luck ran throughout Locker Lampson's service career, accompanied by a strong opportunism which quickly enabled him to exploit changing circumstances to his own advantage. To demonstrate their solidarity, the various Allies had sent contingents to fight with each other's armies, and a Russian brigade was serving in France. One evening Locker Lampson found himself dining in company with a senior Russian officer from the Paris military attaché's office and the conversation turned to the Belgians who, finding no further use for their armoured cars in the west, had formed a squadron which had been sent to Russia. The Eastern Front presented far greater scope for armoured car operations than the Western, the Russian pointed out; moreover, his country was buying all the armoured cars she could lay her hands on, and had already placed large orders with Austin's and other companies. Why, he asked, did not Locker Lampson volunteer his own squadron for service with the Czar's armies?

The idea had an immediate appeal. Quite apart from the real adventure and unknown challenges such a venture offered, the very fact of the unit's being a tiny handful of British men and machines fighting in such an alien environment would produce a flow of publicity quite out of proportion to its relative importance. He asked the Russian to put his request in writing,

> and not long afterwards there arrived in an embossed envelope an invitation. swathed in language which was Oriental in its courtesy, welcoming the detachment to Russia's open arms and bosom. Stressful too, was the the summons to speed of the swiftest, since the White Sea was busy freezing over, and unless Archangel was reached within two months, no chance of penetrating Russia was possible until six months later.

Armed with this, Locker Lampson submitted a formal request for his squadron to be transferred to the Eastern Front as a constructive alternative to disbandment. On its own, the case had little merit, but in the prevailing circumstances the Admiralty was forced to give serious consideration to any proposal from its Russian allies. With Turkey's entry into the war on the side of the Central Powers, Russia's all-important economic lifeline through the Dardanelles had been severed. It had been confidently expected in Russia that the all-powerful Royal Navy would find no difficulty in forcing the Narrows and battering Constantinople into surrender, but this had not happened and British naval prestige had sunk accordingly. It was true that a British submarine flotilla was working with the Russian Baltic Fleet and achieving some spectacular successes, but these operations were of little interest to the average Russian. On the other hand, if Locker Lampson's idea was approved, the appearance of a British naval armoured car unit inside Russia would provide evidence that the Royal Navy's arm was still very long indeed. An exchange of views with the Russian Imperial General Headquarters (STAVKA) resulted in an agreement whereby the Admiralty provided the men and equipment while the Russians were responsible for all expenses, including pay at existing rates. Even Lambert could hardly object to this.

Suddenly Locker Lampson found that he had struck gold. The Admiralty did not consider that a single squadron was an economic proposition, and had decided to send a complete division of three squadrons instead. Numbered 1, 2 and 3, they were to be formed from No 15 Squadron and the detachment from No 17 Squadron serving with them, both of which would return to the United Kingdom immediately; the numbers would be made up from the personnel of previously disbanded squadrons and such new volunteers as wished to go. Locker Lampson was appointed to command, and the added responsibilities earned his promotion to commander. His second-in-command was a regular officer, Acting Commander Reginald Gregory who, like Samson, was one of the original four pioneer Royal Navy pilots who had trained at Eastchurch in 1911. After the formation of the Royal Flying Corps in 1912 he took charge of the Naval Wing's Flying School, where he continued to serve until after the outbreak of war.

The unit's actual title was always imprecise. In the United Kingdom it was referred to as the Russian Armoured Car Division RNAS; in Russia as the British Armoured Car Division. While mustering it was known, because of the very high percentage of RNVR officers, as

President II, a reference to the drill-ship moored in the Thames.

Fitting out took six very busy weeks. The internal organisation of the fighting squadrons remained unchanged, and their primary equipment was the Lanchester armoured car. However, as the unit would be operating in isolation from other British troops and with a line of communication stretching hundreds of rail *and* sea miles, particular attention was paid to providing an adequate supply echelon, mobile workshops and medical facilities. CPO Bromley produced an efficient communications section consisting of vans fitted with half-kilowatt spark sets, thus giving Locker Lampson the ability to exercise forward control of his advanced squadrons by radio, an incredibly advanced technical concept for its day.

The Czar had already named January and February as being two of his best generals, and so some consideration had to be given to the supply of clothing suitable for the Russian winter. This was purchased from Gammage's, the London store, and the prospect of the large order seems to have evoked a robust joviality in Mr Gammage himself. Having seen PO North suitably fitted from head to foot in sealskin, he showered him with artificial snow to judge the finished effect, with which he pronounced himself satisfied. North, already late for an appointment with his sweetheart, left the store without bothering to change, and was immediately conscious of understandably curious stares from passers-by. In later life he always felt a certain guilt regarding a number of sensational newspaper reports which claimed that Russians with snow on their boots had been seen in central London, and sixty years later he wrote to the *Daily Mail*, exploding the myth once and for all.

Towards the end of November a short period of embarkation leave was allowed, and then the unit assembled at Euston Station to board the troop train which would take it to Liverpool. As the carriages pulled slowly clear of the platform and the locomotive started belching its way onto the Camden Bank incline, *President II* began a career which was to be unique in British military annals, which would set records that still remain to be broken, and which witnessed at first hand one of the greatest turning points in world history.

CHAPTER TWO

Friends in High Places

Captain H. S. Robertson's SS *Umona* was lying in Liverpool's Hornby Dock. Her lines were pleasing and her layout followed that of the conventional cargo/passenger liner of the day with a high poop and forecastle, fore and aft well-decks containing hatches, and a single tall funnel rising vertically amidships from the central superstructure. In peacetime she had flown the house flag of Bullard King and Company's Natal Line and in addition to her crew of 75 she could accommodate 58 passengers; when the Russian Armoured Car Division came aboard during the afternoon of 1st December over 500 men were stuffed between decks in supreme discomfort which the novelty of hammocks did nothing to alleviate.

The men were grumbling. Their principal complaint was that they had not been fed during the day, a condition relieved by the provision of hot soup and bread during the evening. Again, they were slightly put out by the lack of a good send-off. Families and friends had not been allowed on the quayside and there was no gala atmosphere of bands, flags and streamers as befitted the start of what was being spoken of as The Great Adventure. Instead, the security conscious authorities had limited their recognition of the event to an inspection by Lieutenant General Sir James Hills-Johnes, vc, carried out under a depressingly leaden sky.* Also present was Princess Marie Louise of Schleswig-Holstein who had privately donated one hundred specially designed warm waistcoats for use in Russia, with the promise of more to follow as soon as they could be made.

On the other hand, the King had sent a personal message to Locker Lampson, which was read out to the parade.

* As Lieutenant Hills of the Bengal Horse Artillery, the General had won his Victoria Cross in a vicious hand-to-hand action during the Siege of Delhi in 1857. Aged 83, he was the Army's oldest VC, but was still very much alive and had informally 'adopted' Locker Lampson's unit, visiting it in Flanders and examining the cars with intense interest. He had insisted on touring the Ypres Salient in one, returning quite unperturbed after being 'near-missed' by shells on several occasions.

Tell the men under your command how glad I am that they have been placed at the disposal of His Imperial Majesty the Emperor of Russia. I know that they will uphold that high reputation which they have already earned in the Western Theatre of War.

Rudyard Kipling, too, had written:

One sees and hears of men going off to adventures all over the world, from the Arctic to the desert and one's heart goes with them, and it is just because of this that one can do no more than send one's love and wish them good luck.

At a less elevated level the men displayed their almost total ignorance of ships and their ways as they attempted to settle in and find their way about, getting in each other's and everyone else's way. 'Now then, you fellows,' yelled an Irish PO in an attempt to restore order from chaos, 'Look out for those damned ropes and step over them *before you move!*' The obvious Hibernianism provoked gales of laughter which annoyed him still further.

Having made themselves as snug as possible, many went up on deck. It was a cold night and some chose to show off in their Russian winter clothing. The officers were not amused and the Liverpool dockers were downright rude about it. At 2100 Pipe Down was sounded and all save the regular crew retired below. Shortly after, tugs manoeuvred the *Umona* through the Hornby lock gates and out into the Mersey, where she dropped anchor in mid-stream.

The following morning the river was shrouded in dense fog which, together with a report of U-boat sightings in Liverpool Bay, prevented sailing for a further thirty-six hours. During 4th December the *Umona* steamed north along the Antrim coast with Rathlin Island clearly in view. For the Ulstermen it was an emotional moment and they lined the rails to stare wistfully at the rolling hills, winding lanes and distant whitewashed cottages. For some the occasion seemed to hold more than mere nostalgia.

'Many's the time I've bicycled there!' said a hoarse voice, tinged with the sadness of finality.

'And may you many times again!' commented Locker Lampson crisply from behind.

The man looked strangely at him before turning back to the rail.

'It's goodbye to Ireland all the same, sir.' Twenty months later he was killed in Galicia.

Throughout Sunday 5th December the weather deteriorated steadily until by evening a full gale was raging. It reached cyclonic proportions and lasted for three days, Captain Robertson later admitting that it was the worst thing he had encountered in twenty-five years at sea. He had already turned the *Umona*'s head into the wind when the crisis was reached. A series of gigantic waves, each of which towered fifty feet above the vessel, was rolling in from the Atlantic and the *Umona* was plunging her bows into each as it arrived, slowly shaking herself free and then climbing laboriously up the forward slope. As the crest was reached she hung poised, her screws threshing clear of the water, and the additional vibration from the propeller shafts was transmitted through the entire ship. Then would come the sickening swoop as she bore down into the trough to begin the whole process yet again.

It was, in fact, a slightly smaller wave which almost killed the *Umona*. Her bows remained buried and she did not climb. The next wave, as large as any encountered, smashed right over her, tearing away two lifeboats, the deck latrines, cookhouse and hatch covers. Hundreds of tons of water thundered down into the holds.

The ship staggered and her head fell away. A third wave struck her on the quarter, rolling her inexorably onto her beam ends. Continuous crashing from the holds confirmed that the armoured cars and other vehicles had broken loose. On the bridge Robertson and his officers clung desperately to hand-holds, their world tilted onto its side.

Robertson could not see how his ship could possibly survive. Ten seconds became twenty, twenty became thirty, thirty became forty and then slowly the *Umona* picked herself up, shedding the appalling weight of water which had almost engulfed her.

The improvised troop decks were a shambles. Kit lay strewn everywhere, mingled with vomit and men in the last extremities of seasickness. Stark terror had long since been replaced by a sincere if temporary death-wish. Hot food was out of the question and would not have been eaten had it been available; those who could nibbled at hard tack biscuits. 'Sick Bay packed out,' wrote PO Baker in his diary. 'Only accommodation for 15. 60 patients in at any one time, many more along the corridor.'

On the 8th the weather began to improve and PO Round, less affected than most, made his way forward with his Kodak Vest-Pocket camera. Across the well-deck the *Umona*'s bows were still pitching crazily skywards and plummeting down into the troughs with thunderous force which sent sheets of spume flying back over the bridge. The

Commander Oliver Locker Lampson. A portrait sent by him to his veterans.

A Pierce Arrow Heavy Armoured Car under repair.

Detail of a Seabrook Heavy Armoured Car.

Members of 15 Squadron at Newhaven Court, Cromer.

ship was rolling in a violent corkscrew motion which did nothing for Round's last reserves. Hurriedly he clicked the shutter and went below.

With the return of calmer weather came the chance to take stock. Particularly serious was the loss of the deck latrines, which had resulted in part of the ship's water supply being polluted with human waste; the water ration was immediately reduced to one cup per day. Inside the holds, the vehicles had been so badly damaged that they would require a complete overhaul. Of more immediate importance to Locker Lampson was the need to restore his men's morale, and in this his powers of leadership became apparent at once.

First, they were paraded on the quarter-deck during the morning of 12th December. Ten miles to the south a light could be seen flashing on the horizon which they were told was the North Cape and that they had therefore reached a point further north than any other British Expeditionary Force. The National Anthem was sung to commemorate the event.

Then, the printing press was broken out and the unit's two printers told to produce a ship's newspaper which would serve as a souvenir of the great gale and provide other news which had been received by the *Umona*'s wireless room. The result sold for one penny and was entitled *The Archangel Herald*. Amongst the general information was the latest news of General Townsend's operations against the Turks in Mesopotamia, the award of the Croix de Guerre to Georges Carpentier, the famous boxer, and a telegram from neutral Rumania which significantly reported that interventionist agitation was increasing and that disturbances had taken place in front of the Austrian and Bulgarian Legations; few on board could have imagined that within a year the effects of these disturbances would involve them personally. There was also a great deal of really awful humour, typical of which was: 'Never mind if the lights are out, we still have our Lamps-on!'

Locker Lampson also contributed to the paper, ostensibly to comment on the King's message, in reality to provide a pep talk.

> We have left our shores for the distant land of a great ally on behalf of a cause dear to us both. We shall be the only British troops in a country containing some 140 millions of stranger-souls. Our force, though numerically small, is yet representative of our far-flung Empire, recruited, as it is, not only from the United Kingdom, but from New Zealand, Australia, Canada and South Africa. We are thus called upon to uphold the honour, not of one nation alone, but in fact of all those peoples who make up Greater Britain and who now march,

united under one King, to victory in this war.

Our task, therefore, is no light one. Upon our lonely shoulders falls the duty of maintaining in Russia the prestige of British arms and traditions. And I would ask if there is any effort we would not make to preserve and improve this? Assuredly not. In matters of money, therefore, in our dealings with men and women, in the daily economy of life, let us see that we exercise honour and discretion, courtesy and self-restraint. Even in our conduct towards the enemy we can reveal our origin and prove ourselves sons of an idea as ennobling as any that ever put arms into English hands...

I suppose the leaders of most enterprises promise their followers good times. I scorn to lay before you prospects of ease and cheap success. You would scorn to expect such from me. I will only promise you difficulties, discomforts, wounds, yes and even death. But I ask your loyal service for a sacred cause and hold no doubt as to your reply. So, with the King's message ringing in our ears, let us go forward confidently in the spirit of the motto which heads this journal and which sums up a soldier's duty so well : let us *Fear God and fear nought*.

Today appeals couched in such terms would be regarded as somewhat over-heavy, but the ideals of the men of 1915 had not been jaded by sophisticated cynicism; they expected rousing, noble words from their leaders and they responded to them.

The *Umona* made her way to a small bay on the north Russian coast where her crew repaired the worst of her damage. It was by now bitterly cold and the ship was coated in ice; even below decks the bulkheads were sheathed in condensed breath frozen to a thickness of one inch. Snow flurries scudded through the perpetual darkness which was punctuated briefly about noon when a dull red sun rose just above the horizon for thirty minutes. In contrast, men stood and marvelled at the flickering wonder of the Aurora Borealis.

It was at this point that a message was received from the Senior British Naval Officer at Archangel. The winter was one of unusual severity and the White Sea had frozen over; the *Umona* stood no chance at all of getting through. In London the Admiralty, already seriously alarmed by the discovery of the *Umona*'s drifting lifeboats, wasted no time in issuing fresh orders. The expedition would return to the United Kingdom forthwith, and try again in the spring.

Locker Lampson plainly regarded the order as a death sentence to his aspirations. He considered, with some justification, that once his command returned it would not be permitted to embark again. On the other hand, if he could establish it on Russian soil for a while, time would be gained during which the inevitable thaw would enable him to follow the original plan and proceed to Archangel; and here Fate dealt him a kindly card, for although the *Umona* was officially provisioned for only twelve days, a mistake in her loading had meant that she was carrying two months' provisions for the entire squadron.

It was, of course, one thing to have the physical means at his disposal to defy the Admiralty's order, but quite another to do so. Nor would Their Lordships be likely to consider the matter as a basis for discussion. There was, however, one area in which their writ was not quite absolute.

The Senior Medical Officer, Surgeon-Commander Scott, was sent for and the position explained to him. Locker Lampson abruptly changed the subject to one or two isolated cases of pneumonia which had appeared during the final stages of the voyage.

'Is pneumonia catching?'

'Well, that is hardly a scientific way of putting it, but it spreads.'

'Would men in the same hold get it,'

'Well, men in a hold where there is pneumonia would be more likely to get it than men in other holds.'

'Then there is danger of an epidemic?'

Scott suddenly saw where the conversation was leading and reacted as Locker Lampson hoped he would.

'Undoubtedly.'

'An epidemic which might start at once and before we could get back to England?'

'Certainly.'

'Then, incidentally and leaving other things out of account, you would advise a landing?'

'Of course.'

With Scott's support a report was despatched which grossly exaggerated the extent of the outbreak, requesting permission to make for the ice-free port of Alexandrovsk where those affected could receive essential treatment, rest and warmth ashore. The Admiralty's suspicions may have been aroused by the apparently tragic scale of the *Umona*'s medical problem, but the request was granted and Robertson conned the ship up the Kola Inlet.

Locker Lampson made no secret of what he was doing. He had the gift of taking even the most junior of his subordinates into his confidence and retaining their absolute loyalty. The Sick Berth attendants knew exactly what was going on but it would be sixty years before any of them spoke of it to anyone other than their immediate families. The general opinion on board the *Umona* was one of 'Don't worry, Locker will get us there – he can handle himself!' *

The 'invalids', in fact, had rather a noisy Christmas. The Sick Bay personnel dined well on mutton chops, roast beef, fried vegetables and potatoes, followed by plum pudding, brandy sauce, mince pies and cake. Not all mess decks did quite as well and on one the derisive yell of 'Shoot the cook!' received the traditional chorus in reply – 'You're eating him!' It was all very good humoured and was followed by Hands to Dance and Skylark on deck until one o'clock the next morning.

Alexandrovsk would become better known to a later generation of sailors as Murmansk, but for the moment it consisted only of a cluster of log cabins, some slightly more impressive official buildings, also made of wood, and a large ornate church. There were no wharves and the settlement was virtually isolated from the rest of Russia by dense forests and swamps, although a railway was being driven north through these from Petrograd, the workforce consisting of German and Austrian prisoners-of-war who died in their thousands before it was completed.

Having bargained for accommodation, the men began coming ashore on 1st January 1916, followed by the bulk of their stores. An inventory found among Locker Lampson's papers reveals that $2\frac{3}{4}$ weeks' supply of rabbit was in hand: with 6 weeks' jam and mustard, $6\frac{1}{2}$ weeks' oatmeal, 5 weeks' pickles, 7 weeks' suet and $7\frac{1}{4}$ weeks' flour: of corned beef, salt pork, biscuits, beans, butter, cheese, cocoa, coffee, tinned milk, peas, rice, salmon, sugar, tea and salt there was sufficient to see them through until May if rationed carefully. In addition, reindeer meat was in plentiful supply and could be purchased locally.

The same document provides the only contemporary record of the unit's vehicle strength, which is listed as: 33 armoured cars; 4 heavy 3-pounder armoured cars; 20 transport cars; 3 mobile workshops; 5 wireless vehicles; 4 ambulances; 1 crane lorry; 2 'CO's sleeping cars; 2 mobile field kitchens; 8 staff cars; and 44 motor-cycles. Against the armoured car entry Locker Lampson has written '20 in Russia', which suggests a slightly earlier shipment to Archangel; the 'sleeping cars' were almost certainly what we should call today command vehicles and would have been used as mobile offices when the need arose.

Apart from personal weapons there were 36 Maxim machine-guns

---

* In 1978 I approached George Bromley regarding the vehicles damaged during the gale, and was taken to task for my pains. 'Who told you about that?' I was asked sharply; '*That* is supposed to be Secret!' B. P.

for which there were 1,500,000 rounds of ammunition. Of these, 14 guns and 1,300,000 rounds were still awaiting shipment in England, and four guns were known to have arrived in Archangel. There were also three towed 3-pounders, making a total of seven three-pounder weapons available, for which the wildly excessive figure of 30,000 rounds of high explosive ammunition had been issued.

The unit's strength is given as being 44 officers and 455 men, of whom 21 and 83 respectively were with the rear party in England.

Once disembarkation was complete a barracks routine was established and a training programme commenced. Three motor-cycles, several Maxims and the towed 3-pounders were brought ashore and instructional classes in these set up; one 3-pounder was removed from its carriage and mounted on a sledge to test its mobility in Arctic conditions. Local roads were dug in the snow and a programme of physical training started. The men were kept hard at work from Reveille to Lights Out and many admit that they were never so fit again; some, with bronchial complaints, were completely cured by the healthy exercise in the extremely dry, intense cold.

Duties undertaken to assist the local Russian Governor included salvaging the cargo of a vessel which had run aground and the construction of a gun battery armed with the 3-pounders and Maxims to protect the vital cable station. But, as Locker Lampson later recalled, by far the most unconventional request for help was received shortly after the unit had established itself.

> The officers had just finished a meal in the mess and were seated at the table playing chess when the door opened and there appeared framed in it a magnificent officer, tall, stately, bearded and smothered in medals, who in a voice of thunder asked to know if I was present. He did not wait for an answer, but like a town-crier proceeded to proclaim that he came direct from the Czar of all the Russians with an Imperial *ukase* for myself. He dismissed all offers of hospitality on finding that I was not present and desired to be taken to me, wherever I was, and however distant.

The man announced himself as Commander Rostchavosky of the Imperial Navy. He was apparently incapable of communicating in anything less than a bellow, which Locker Lampson found slightly disconcerting.

> The magnificence of his manners positively abashed me. He proclaimed the author of his mission as melodramatically as he had done in the

mess and produced a document in evidence which, being written in Russian, conveyed nothing to me whatever. Then he unfolded his purpose. He had arrived on a special mission overland by sledge to Kola, forty miles away, and from Kola he had come by ship to Alexandrovsk, hearing that a unit of British men and cars had landed. His mission was transcendant in its importance. There were ships in the harbour with munitions for Russia, and these had failed to get through to Archangel as expected, and he was deputed to try and get the most vital of these landed at Kola in order to carry them thence overland to Petrograd, hundreds of miles away.

His route would lie along that of the projected railway, which did not yet exist, and he had already organised a transport system consisting solely of reindeers to cover the journey from Kola to Petrozavodsk. Hearing of the British unit, he came as one gentleman to another to implore me to lend some of the cars in order to bridge a gap in the communications which he could not fill by reindeer service. He then rose to his feet and in splendid French pictured the needs of the Russian Army, appealing to my patriotism, my qualities as a sportsman, and my sense of duty. I asked him whether there were any roads, and he had to admit that there were none. I asked him whether there was any food or accommodation for the men and he swept the suggestion aside with the declaration that the men must freeze and starve and die in the service of so magnificent a cause, depicting in the most tropical language the agonies of death which certainly awaited volunteers under his leadership.

Locker Lampson could hardly be blamed for thinking he had a lunatic on his hands. He coldly promised to look into the matter and his visitor left, crestfallen. However, enquiries made the following day confirmed that Rostchavosky's mission was genuine and that although the Russian was a notorious eccentric with a flare for over-dramatisation, he was a capable and energetic officer who made things happen.

The damaged cars were still on board the *Umona*, but the Kola Inlet was now being used regularly by Allied shipping and Locker Lampson learned that several motor vehicles had been landed at Kola. Lieutenant-Commander Wells-Hood was sent with a small party to take them over and a reconnaissance confirmed that by driving deep into the interior and then across a frozen lake it was possible to bridge the gap between the port and the assembly point for Rostchavosky's reindeer sledge trains. Rostchavosky was delighted and soon 4,000 rifles a day were being shipped down the route to the rail-head. Wells-Hood and his men were later decorated by the Russians for their efforts, while for their part they were filled with admiration for Rostchavosky's restless energy which steamrollered its way through every sort of opposition.

Meanwhile, senior officers at the Admiralty were taking a fresh look at the Russian Armoured Car Division RNAS. The landing at Alexandrovsk had been tolerated, but the unit's future hung in the balance following receipt of the news that it required a complete and very expensive mechanical refit without even having been in action. The services which it was performing for the Alexandrovsk port authorities were not really considered to be an adequate return on the investment made, since they could just as easily be carried out by men who were not trained armoured car specialists. The Russians were asked if they would object to the cancellation of the whole project. They said they would not. The Imperial Army was at that time the world's largest user of armoured cars and had quite sufficient for its own purposes; moreover, the Belgian squadron already serving in Russia had not settled down, language, equipment and operational differences all combining to make difficulties. STAVKA did not wish to repeat the experience.

At some point someone warned Locker Lampson; to this day it remains unclear who, but Churchill springs most readily to mind. For Locker Lampson the consequences of the expedition being wound up would be a severe blow to both his military and political careers and, understandably, he did not wish to be remembered as the leader of an aborted mission. He had gone too far and spent too much to turn back without a struggle and since both the Admiralty and STAVKA were obviously against him he decided to lobby the Czar personally. Few would dare to question publically a favourable decision from such an exalted source.

For a mere Commander in the Royal Navy, and indeed for a simple Member of the Commons, this was the most incredible piece of cheek. But once again luck had provided him with the means to lend legitimacy to his actions, for in his possession was a personal letter from the King to his cousin Nicholas which was to be delivered on arrival. As his force had been unavoidedly delayed, Locker Lampson decided that it must be delivered at once and on 25th January left Alexandrovsk for England aboard the SS *Champagne*.

On arrival, he sailed for Norway almost immediately and then travelled by way of Sweden to Petrograd. From there he was forced to make the 24-hour rail journey to Mogilev in central Russia, as Nicholas was rarely in his capital and sent most of his time at STAVKA. It was a fortnight before he was granted an audience and in the meantime was able to observe the various Russian army commanders assembling for a conference.

There was Ivanov with his white beard; here kindly Kuropatkin, who, after commanding whole armies in Manchuria, had offered to lead only a brigade sooner than not serve his country again;* Brusilov, too, thin and incredibly alert in movement; and the Grand Duke Sergei, with his loose knees and spidery legs; and, chief of all, the war's most scientific soldier, Alexeiev – a soldier student whose intelligence and character beamed from his Tartar face and professor's spectacles.†

Then I was summoned to the Czar and left on foot for his quarters. I made my way through the public gardens while on all sides soldiers rose and saluted as I passed. On arrival at the gate my credentials were examined and I was passed through to the house and entered between two lines of magnificent Cossacks who stood at attention, saluting. They were Cossacks of the Emperor's Guard and are recruited in the following way. Each Cossack village chooses one representative for the Guard, of course selecting its best man, and such is the sense of duty of the corps that discipline is a natural product and punishment virtually unknown. The greatest punishment that can befall a Cossack of the Guard is to be returned to the village which selected him as its representative. They wore a red uniform for service with the Czar and their wild accoutrements and savage loyalty struck a note of oriental grandeur even in the simple building where I was received.

Russian officers spoke of their monarch not only as Czar, but as Imperator, and an ADC telling me that the Imperator would soon be free, led me into a small unfurnished room, there to await His Majesty's pleasure. I was shortly summoned and taken across an ante-room which was to become (so) memorable to me later on in the tremendous Kornilov days. Then a door was opened into a study, and, behold! I stood before the Czar of all the Russias, the head of the oldest reigning dynasty in Europe, a monarch whose rule and whose throne seemed then the most firmly established in the world. Here was one who in the year 1916 absolutely controlled the lives and property of nearly 200,000,000 souls, and whose personal power and prestige far outweighed even that of the Kaiser in Germany.

He looked very like our King and stood very simply by the door in high boots, breeches and the ordinary tunic worn by the common soldier. He shook hands frankly and in good English thanked me for coming, and after I had presented the King of England's letter, which

---

* Kuropatkin, it will be recalled, had commanded the Russian field army during the Russo-Japanese War of 1905.

† Not everyone shared LL's unqualified opinion of Alexeiev, who is generally regarded as a brilliant intellectual with limited command abilities; Brusilov, the most successful of the Russian commanders was understandably critical of him.

he read: 'It's awfully kind of you,' he said. Then he enquired of me where I had been and what I had done, and when I outlined some of the hardships in Lapland and the cold, he broke out with the expression, 'Oh, lor!'

He seemed to have the figures of railway distances and army numbers at his finger-tips, and he expressed the determination never to give in. His figure was a sturdy one, and he had a way of standing on one foot and working the heel of his other foot into the floor in front of him as he spoke, which, coupled with his smile, his slow speech and his manner of looking away as he spoke, gave an impression of diffidence and even shyness. It is no exaggeration to say that no Russian I ever met excelled or even equalled the Emperor in charm. It was impossible not to be won over by his evident kindliness, goodwill and courtesy. The only doubt was whether a man so naturally charming could be strong in character and I confess that, even on this occasion, I left with the impression that I could have induced him to agree to many things which he might have felt obliged to withdraw from afterwards.

Locker Lampson could himself charm the birds from the trees and had prodigious powers of persuasion. No doubt he employed an engaging frankness, pointing out that his men were already on Russian soil and were looking forward to fighting alongside the Russian Army, requesting that STAVKA should do everything possible to speed their journey to the front. The impression given is undoubtedly that he won his point with an ease which surprised him.*

At a stroke, he had effectively outflanked both the Admiralty and STAVKA, and returned well satisfied to his quarters. Later, as a further mark of Imperial favour, he was *twice* invited to eat with the Emperor and his personal staff.

> The dishes were on the whole simple and the etiquette less formal than at Court. We would range ourselves round the ante-chamber, chatting until the Czar entered, when we stood at attention. He would go round and speak to everybody whom he had not interviewed already that

---

* Written by LL in 1918 for *Lloyd's Magazine*. If any official record of the interview exists, it is deep in the Russian archives. In an attempt to verify this and various other points I called on the Soviet Embassy in London, requesting their assistance. I was first asked if I was a communist; I replied that I was not. I was then asked why I required this information. I replied that our countries had fought two wars together against a common enemy and that this was an important part of the story. The question was repeated several times and answered accordingly. Some days later I received a plain, unheaded piece of paper informing me that no help would be given. Quite possibly, the Embassy will now deny that the conversation took place and that the letter was ever written! A. L.

day. He would then lead the way into the dining room. Luncheon or dinner was begun by *Sakouski*, which we consumed standing at a side table, and then we would seat ourselves around a large table in the centre of which was the Czar.

His little son usually sat at his side, and no memory is more delightful than the pleasure and pride he found in the boy. The Czarevich must have been about twelve or thirteen, rather delicate-looking, but very lively and keen. He was a regular boy, with strange elfish manners and a great wish to be a man.

Locker Lampson returned to England by the same route he had come and in mid-April boarded the *Umona* once more for the voyage to Alexandrovsk. On this occasion, however, she sailed in company with two Russian liners, the *Czar* and the *Dvinsk*, on board which were the unit's new armoured cars and other vehicles. The journey was uneventful and the three vessels dropped anchor in Kola Inlet on 22nd April.

Alexandrovsk proved a very different harbour to the one I had so recently left. The sun had already melted some of the snow and bared the black basalt rocks in their liveries of yellow and green lichen, and for the first time the huts stood out free from their canopies of white. The work undertaken by the unit had beaten all expectations, and officers and men were cheered with the prospect of an early continuation of the journey to Archangel.

The unit's morale was good. The previous month Lieutenant-Commander Gregory, Locker Lampson's second-in-command, had organised a sledge-athletics meeting which had proved extremely popular. Now it was providing guards and medical care for 1,000 exhausted prisoners whom the Russians had sent north from the rail-head for shipment to Archangel. The condition of these men was wretched, and for some help was administered very much at the eleventh hour. Their sufferings arose not from the deliberate cruelty of their previous guards, who had lived off the same spare rations and in the same harrowing winter conditions, but as a result of Russian administrative incompetence which had failed to provide accommodation or medical facilities; hard physical labour had done the rest. It is said that each sleeper on the line cost a human life, and the whole sorry story bares comparison with that of the infamous Burma Railway.

As the prisoner of war problem was delaying embarkation, the restless Locker Lampson decided to travel overland to Archangel ahead of his command, using the main line from Petrograd. This time he travelled direct from Alexandrovsk to Norway in a small local coaster, but was almost arrested as a spy on arrival. For the rest of the journey across Scandinavia he was forced to assume the alias, first, of a Canadian railway engineer, and later, that of a journalist from Ohio.

Shortly after Easter, news of the Sinn Fein rising in Dublin reached Alexandrovsk. The Irishmen, Catholic and Protestant alike, were naturally enough concerned for the safety of their families at home. A small minority, inflamed by a diet of illegally hoarded rum and barrack-room rhetoric, demanded repatriation at once. When told that this was impossible they became angry, threatening to board the *Umona* and sail her to Ireland themselves. For a while they were beyond their officers' control and Marines were sent for from the British warships lying in Kola Inlet. By the time these arrived the effects of drink had worn off and a more sober reaction set in. The mutiny collapsed bloodlessly under a tongue-lashing from Gregory and Wells-Hood. However, when the *Umona* next returned to the United Kingdom she had on board the ringleaders, various other malcontents, and a few genuine medical cases, a total of 31 men. Quite rightly, Gregory was taking no chances.*

By 23rd May the prisoners had been embarked on board the *Dvinsk* and the RNAS personnel aboard the *Czar*, and both left Kola Inlet. The next day they ran into an ice field which reduced progress to a crawl. On the 25th both vessels were forced to halt and become completely iced in. The *Dvinsk* discovered she was carrying mail for the unit, and a party walked across from the *Czar* to get it. Many took photographs of their friends strolling on the White Sea. The following morning, as PO George Martin recalled, intense efforts were made to free the ships.

'The *Dvinsk* got off during the latter part of the afternoon and entered the sea again, leaving us struggling in the ice. Our difficulty was to get the head of the boat in the right direction, the steering gear being useless. We were heading for land. After supper some of the crew fixed an ice anchor in the ice, and to this a wire rope was attached from the bows to endeavour to swing the head round. This proved successful and during the night we got away.'

The ice was left behind as they steamed steadily south into the wide

---

* It is some measure of the men's pride in their unit's reputation that survivors would only discuss the mutiny with us after they knew we were aware it had taken place. The majority were so disgusted that they avoided any direct reference in their diaries. Thus, PO Martin: 'All the boys upset about the Irish business.' PO Baker: 'Undesirables returned to SS *Umona* for return to England.' When interviewed, CPO Bromley would merely admit that 'There was a drunken Irish crowd, fighting and causing trouble – we got rid of 'em.'

mouth of the Dvina River, and on the morning of the 28th they arrived at Archangel. The journey from Liverpool had taken over five months.

A few men, including George Martin, were granted shore leave, but the magnificent harbour and splendid public buildings held little immediate appeal for them, even after their weeks in the wilderness; the all-important priority was to find an eating house which served something other than corned beef and reindeer meat.

CHAPTER THREE

Holy Russia

At some stage during what is generally called the Crimean War a Royal Naval landing party had raided the Kola Inlet and returned with anything of value that they could find, which in those days and in that latitude was precious little. However, one item looted from a church held more than intrinsic value and its loss was sorely felt by the inhabitants. This was the Icon of St Michael of Archangel and, by coincidence it had been returned as a gesture of goodwill shortly before the outbreak of the Great War. Now, at a dinner given by the civic and military authorities of Archangel for Locker Lampson and his officers, this object of veneration was formally presented to the Russian Armoured Car Division RNAS, for it was the custom for every unit which fought for the Czar to possess some religious article affirming its faith in Holy Russia.

The men came ashore on 30th May. Every ship in the harbour was dressed overall and the streets were hung with the flags of the Allies. The unit marched behind a band to the Municipal Summer Gardens where it was entertained with a speech of welcome from the Mayor and given tea and cakes; the tea, served with lemon in the Russian manner, was a distinct shock to the many who had always considered it to be a beverage to be consumed with milk, but the oatmeal cakes were surprisingly good. The official welcome lacked nothing, but many were aware of an atmosphere of sullen indifference among the people themselves, dismissed for the moment as being part of the temperament of the far north, where men spent half their lives in darkness.

Further impressions of life in Russia were gained when the unit entrained for the south on 1st June to the accompaniment of cheers and the strains of the National Anthem. First there was the wide gauge of the Russian railway system itself, and the fact that so many of the platelaying and maintenance gangs contained a high proportion of women labourers. Then there was the wood-burning locomotive, fitted with a cow-catcher and a wide spark arrester just like those seen in pictures of the American Wild West. The coaches were elderly stock, fitted with hard wooden benches, but it was not these spartan conditions which provided proof of the unsophisticated nature of the Russian Army – it was the complete absence of toilet facilities of any kind, although the journey would be of several days' duration. If a man could not contain himself between the various halts, his dignity vanished as he performed through an open door, his comrades holding his arms and enjoying a great deal of basic mirth at his expense.

The railway passed through a flat landscape in which pockets of ice and snow still lingered. The scenery was monotonous, consisting of interminable coniferous forest cut back several hundred yards from the track. The felled trees had been trimmed, chopped into logs and stacked beside the line, and occasionally the train stopped so that the locomotive's tender could be replenished. Sometimes a sluggish stream meandered into view and sometimes the monotony was broken by the sight of the still, black waters of a lake. Dwelling of any kind were very few and far between. Some found it all new, strange and interesting, others merely depressing.

Only one meal a day was provided, usually in the evening when the train had halted in an area where a Russian garrison was stationed. It consisted of cooked horsemeat, black bread and a millet and potato soup which bore a startling resemblance to hot, greasy water. At the small village stations the population turned out to wave and cheer the train through, but in the larger towns such as Vologda, Jaroslav, Vostoff and Alexandroff a full-scale reception had been prepared. As Locker Lampson later recalled:

> In each case the Mayor, with a band, awaited the train with a welcome unknown outside Russia. 'God Save the King' would be played always three times, and the train would be delayed in the interests of these celebrations, quite regardless of any military or civil passengers who chanced to be on board. On each occasion the Mayor embraced the officer-in-charge and, in my modesty, I deputed somebody else to undertake these obligations, reserving to myself less exacting duties!

The photographs taken on these occasions provide some of the last views of the Old Russia. The station platforms are crowded with military bandsmen, officers with shoulder-boards and swords, the oval Imperial cockade in the caps, long-haired Orthodox priests in their vestments, drosky drivers with distinctive flat-topped hats, respectably suited civic dignitaries, and bearded peasants in their belted blouses. The pictures were taken less than a lifespan ago, yet one feels that one is looking into the world of *Anna Karenina*; the empire of the Czars had a very different concept of time to that of the west.

The train reached Moscow at 0130 on 5th June and here the reception eclipsed anything previously encountered. The men fell in for inspection, which was delayed for the better half of half an hour while the Russian band played every verse of the British National Anthem, including a number previously unsuspected, all attempts to interject orders by the parade commander being stifled by yet another drum roll. What remained of the night was spent sleeping, and the following day local leave was granted.

In the absence of the Imperial Family, Locker Lampson and his officers were formally received by the Grand Duchess Elizabeth, sister of the Czarina, and presented with mementoes of the occasion.

Other members of the detachment also visited the Kremlin, if rather less formally. The clean-shaven, healthy appearance of the British, the superior quality of their uniforms and their unfamiliar rank badges simultaneously attracted both curiosity and confusion. In what is today Red Square Petty Officers Rodwell and Turner were politely requested by a Russian officer to follow him to a saluting base in front of which an infantry regiment was drawn up in review order. Imagining them to be of commissioned rank, one of several senior officers on the rostrum politely asked them in broken English to take the salute when the regiment marched past. A friendly shove in the back from Turner placed a reluctant Rodwell firmly in the place of honour, gravely returning salutes as the companies swung smartly past in column, giving their traditional shout of 'Hurra!' as they reached the saluting base. The business concluded, smiles, handshakes and further salutes were exchanged all round, and the two petty officers disappeared as quickly as possible; Rodwell's achievement may have been unique iu the annals of the Royal Navy, but he had no wish to acquire a reputation for reviewing Russian infantry, and he had a fair idea of what Locker Lampson's reaction might be if the matter became public knowledge.

Elsewhere, too, language difficulties gave rise to problems which could not have been foreseen. Two petty officers were delighted to be approached by a pair of attractive Russian sisters, but it was soon apparent that they were respectable girls from a good background and that nothing more than some friendly conversation was contemplated. The girls' father had business interests in England and, having anticipated that sooner or later Russia was going to be racked by internal strife, had made arrangements for the whole family to move to London in several weeks time. The girls offered to show the two men around

Moscow, paying all expenses and treating them to a meal in the evening, in exchange for help with their English pronunciation; it was an offer which could hardly be refused.

All went well until they took their places in one of the city's smartest restaurants, where one of the men began to feel acute discomfort from the amount of beer he had drunk during the afternoon. He was very young, he had never been out with such girls in his life, and he had never imagined eating in such luxurious surroundings. As he struggled to find exactly the right words his predicament became desperate, and then came inspiration – he asked one of the girls to get a waiter to show him a place where he could 'wash his hands'. Beaming, the waiter led him into the kitchen and proceeded to demonstrate the workings of the establishment's one hot water tap. It was too much. The agonised Petty Officer fled from the kitchen and from the restaurant, dragging his amazed companion with him and leaving the abandoned sisters to puzzle angrily over his strange behaviour.

His chagrin can well be imagined and when, some sixty years later, chance provided him with the address of one of the sisters in England, he wrote to apologise for his *gaucherie*. The answer he received, he reflected ruefully, was more than a little dusty; the ladies were still quite definitely not amused.

Petty Officer Martin and two friends met the English manager of a tea-packing factory, a Mr Bishop, who took them home and generally made them members of his family for the next two days. He was a man of some influence in the British community and had them shown round the dazzling interior of the Kremlin, later taking them out to his *dacha* (weekend cottage) outside Moscow for dinner.

Kindness and hospitality were showered on the squadrons from all sides. A party which attended a special performance at the Moscow Arts Theatre were awarded a standing ovation as soon as they entered the auditorium, being cheered and clapped for fully five minutes until they climbed onto the stage at the actors' request. It was an emotional moment for men far from home, but only one incident among many. As Locker Lampson later recorded, 'Public and private societies and clubs vied with each other in making the visit memorable in every way.'

But there was another side to Moscow life and one which recalled the undercurrents sensed briefly at Archangel. Those who wandered after dark from the main, spacious boulevards into the areas between found themselves in a tortuous, dimly lit world in which the squalor, stink, overcrowding and sheer poverty made a lasting impact; the con-

RNAS despatch riders outside the Talbot Motor Works.

Two of the squadron's Heavy Armoured Cars. Seabrook *Ulster* is on the right; on the left is a Pierce Arrow, probably *Londonderry*.

Commander Locker Lampson supervises the extraction of a 15 Squadron Seabrook Heavy Armoured Car.

At Alexandrovsk Harbour. HMS *Albemarle* is on the extreme left; HMS *Iphigenia* second from bottom right with cargo vessels.

The *Czar* mail party on the ice.

(*Left*) The troopship *Dvinsk* in the ice, viewed from the *Czar*. (*Right*) The beginning of the thaw. Alexandrovsk with some of the sledge dog teams.

ditions in which the poorer people lived were, in the opinion of one Irishman, worse by far than the evils of the worst Dublin tenement. Many slept in doorways or huddled in corners. The sight of the legless Russian soldier lying in the rags of his uniform on the filthy ground was particularly distressing. Soon the apparently affluent British were forced to retreat for their own safety, surrounded by crowds of beggers young and old, sick and lame, the desperately needy and the simply greedy. Coins changed hands, ensuring that a few more miserable lives were prolonged for a few more miserable days.

With the shock of the experience had come anger and resentment that the Russian Government was prepared to tolerate such conditions side by side with the lavish lifestyle of the Establishment and its supporters. The men were little given to political theorising (discussion of politics and religion was intentionally discouraged in the British service because of its potential for internal friction), but they were now aware that in Russia there was virtually no middle ground, and that precious little attempt seemed to have been made to create any. Several tried to put just what they felt into words, but the comment of one will serve for the many: 'You'd think they could do better than *that* for their blokes, wouldn't you?'

The climax of the visit to Moscow was reached on 7th June when the whole detachment marched through the city with bayonets fixed for a service at the English church. The streets and squares were jammed with crowds which Locker Lampson estimated to number between two and three hundred thousand, and the marching ranks were pelted with flowers from balconies, while some of the older citizens openly wept. After the service came an official farewell banquet for which long tables had been laid out in the Summer Gardens, and everyone ate his fill to the strains of band music and songs sung by a ladies' choir. At 1600 the squadrons marched back to the railway station and entrained for what was to be their theatre of war: Trans-Caucasia.

The choice may appear odd, but there was a good reason for it. Having been ordered by the Czar to incorporate Locker Lampson's command into the Russian order of battle had set STAVKA something of a problem. Integration on the main battle front with the Central Powers presented operational difficulties which, it was felt, were unlikely to be overcome. On the other hand, in the remote, difficult and semi-savage country beyond the Caucasus was what is now the least remembered but nonetheless one of the most fiercely contested battlefronts of World War I. Here, Russia shared a common frontier with her ancient enemy Turkey, allied with the Central Powers, and was doing better than in other theatres.

The principal effect of the Turkish Declaration of War in October 1914 was to close the Dardanelles to the much-needed Allied aid which was being poured into Russia; thereafter this was reduced to the trickle that could be handled by the Arctic ports. However, contrary to German advice, Enver Pasha, the Minister of War, launched a winter offensive into the Causasus. This was defeated at Sarikamish in January 1915, where the Turks lost about 30,000 killed. Worse was to follow, for of Enver's original army of 95,000 only 18,000 managed to straggle back across the frontier to Erzerum; the remainder had starved or frozen to death among the Causasus snows in what must be one of the worst managed campaigns in history. For the remainder of the year the front swayed to and fro, the advantage generally resting with the Russians under their capable commander, General Nikolai Yudenich. A Russian offensive commencing in January 1916 rolled across the border to capture Erzerum and Trebizond.

At the very moment the British were being entertained in Moscow the Turks began a counter-offensive which was held without difficulty and which sustained heavy loss. The pattern of fighting was, however, far from straightforward. Vicious massacres carried out by Turkish troops had provoked the population of Armenia into full-scale revolt, while on the Russian side of the lines the perennially ungovernable Kurds, with Turkish encouragement, were busy augmenting their income with a campaign of sniping and ambush. A further complication was that to safeguard their oil interests the Russians had also sent troops into northern Persia, while the British had occupied the southern part of that country for identical reasons.

STAVKA's decision to commit the RNAS armoured cars into this confused situation was almost certainly influenced by the fact that the British were used to soldiering in the remoter parts of the earth, and were notably good at it; there were, after all, numerous similarities between Trans-Caucasia and the North-West Frontier of India. That the unit consisted – nominally at least – of sailors rather than soldiers who had, moreover, never served outside western Europe counted for less than the national reputation.

Bodies like STAVKA tend to dislike being outflanked by comparatively junior officers, and perhaps there was also an element of malicious humour in their decision. The British public had very little interest in the Causasus campaign and the news from that area was scantly reported and little read. For the publicity-seeking politician this wilderness was the back-of-beyond, a limbo in which a potentially heroic reputation could wither and die; but, having gone to such lengths to talk his way into Russia, Locker Lampson now had his orders and, like any other officer, he must obey them.

The journey south from Moscow was very similar to that from Archangel. The train was festooned with British flags and, as the weather became progressively warmer, the passengers climbed onto the roofs of the carriages to enjoy the breeze created by their progress, waving to the crowds which had gathered at the wayside stations. Rostov was reached on 11th June, and another official reception attended; the same day the detachment sustained its first fatal casualty in Russia when Petty Officer Donnelly was drowned swimming in a fast flowing river while the locomotive was taking on wood.

It was now extremely hot and as the train puffed its way steadily southwards throughout the 12th it was noticed that the inhabitants were darker skinned than those of central and northern Russia. To the delight of many, there were brilliantly coloured tropical birds flying free, teams of oxen working and caravans of camels plying their trade, all completely new experiences for the majority of the men. Towards evening someone shouted and pointed ahead. Jagged, snow-capped peaks were rising from the horizon and increasing in size with every mile that passed : it was the Caucasus.

Reveille the following morning was at 0400 and orders to smarten up were given. At 1000 the train steamed into Vladikavkas station and the squadrons marched through the town to an impressive, not to say elegant, barrack set in its own grounds, which was in fact one of the Imperial Army's Military Academies. As a billet the Academy left nothing to be desired; the dormitories contained sprung beds which were more comfortable than some had ever slept in in their lives, although the beautifully polished brown floors soon lost their lustre under the impact of the RNAS hobnailed boot.

> Vladikavkas itself is the home of the Terek and other Cossacks [wrote Locker Lampson] and guards the entrance to the most romantic country left in the world. Within a radius of 100 miles it is alleged that over sixty languages and as many races are to be found, and certainly the villages dotted about in the mountains are often independent self-governing communities. Most of their inhabitants do not talk Russian, and their religions are very mixed. For while many tribes are Christians and others Mohammedan, a few affect a hybrid faith reminiscent of both. In their villages there is little use for money, so instead they covet swords, rifles and horses, and will go to nameless

lengths in order to secure one or the other by theft. They wear the Caucasian *bourka*, a black sheepskin coat; wide-brimmed, black, pointed caps; and, owing to a malady prevalent in the Caucasus, many carry an alarming patch over one of their eyes. Their appearance is consequently villainous, and their habits are horrible.

The town of Vladikavkas itself lies in a damp plain which sweeps up to the magnificent mountains of the Caucasus a few miles distant. You can catch sight of the white pinnacles of Mount Kasbeck, higher than Mont Blanc itself. The River Terek flows through the town, and some beautiful gardens were converted by the Red Cross into recreation grounds.

Locker Lampson's assessment of the tribes was confirmed within days of the British arrival when a Russian cadet was shot and wounded during a night raid. Nor was the uncertain temper of the mountain people the only danger to be faced in Vladikavkas. The detachment was soon affected by an outbreak of dysentery, from which Petty Officer Bendixon died on 23rd June, and Surgeon-Commander Scott issued a warning against eating too much of the local fruit. The outbreak was brought under control but in July Petty Officer Johnson succumbed to an attack of ptomaine poisoning brought on by eating bad fish. Three of the men who had marched through Moscow were now dead, and the only Turk who had been seen was a severely wounded prisoner in leg-irons guarded by a sentry with a fixed bayonet.

The vehicles had last been seen at Archangel, being loaded onto railway flats. In any other country the Staff would have ensured that the train of flat-cars was despatched in the wake of the personnel train. At Vladikavkas, however, there was no news of the vehicles, nor was any expected; all that was known was that the train had left Archangel and was now somewhere in the not inconsiderable area between the Arctic Ocean and the Black Sea. The root of the problem was that the war had placed the Russian railway system under intense pressure, and its officials tended to follow the Establishment line in corruption in that those who were prepared to pay highest in specie, goods or services had their needs met first. The smooth passage of the personnel train had been accomplished because the affair had a great deal of political clout behind it, but the flats held a lower priority and the question of their continued transit now rested fairly well down in someone's pending tray. After waiting with growing anger for several days, Locker Lampson protested directly to General Headquarters Caucasian Front, who despatched a high-powered and well-deserved rocket in the direction of the offenders.

In the meantime the squadrons occupied their time in drill and route marching in intense heat. On 10th July they were able to repay some of the hospitality they had received by staging a concert party at the local theatre in aid of the Russian Red Cross. Locker Lampson and some of his officers attended a dinner which began at 1730 and which no one was permitted to leave until 0400 the following morning, noting that whereas the British tended to become maudlin or quarrelsome in their cups, the Russians became ever more genial and expansive. At one point the Commander faced a situation which required all his diplomatic skill to handle: 'The station commandant's wife, a siren of many summers, confided the bulk of her past history to the back of my neck, imploring me to consider the possibility of marriage in the near future!' Before this knotty question could be resolved, however, the glasses were swept aside and he was tossed repeatedly in the table cloth by the assembled company.

The long awaited train of flat-cars arrived at last on 12th July, bringing with it sixty very welcome bags of mail and the by-now rather lonely escort which had travelled with it. The next few days were spent unloading the cars, guns and support vehicles, checking them over and preparing them for action.

The Russians were intensely interested in the British equipment, but Chief Petty Officer Bromley's radio vehicles drew unfavourable comment and he was tartly told that on no account were these to be used operationally. These vehicles were Bromley's whole raison d'être and without them the entire unit's flexibility would be impaired since forward control of sub-units would have to be exercised by motor-cycle despatch rider. Naturally, he was furious and took his case to Locker Lampson, but the Russians would not relent; they were sympathetic, but the most they were prepared to permit was the establishment of wireless classes in which Bromley could train their own operators.

If the Imperial Army seemed unduly sensitive in the area of radio communications, it had reason to be. During the first weeks of the war STAVKA and other senior formations had made no attempt to encode their transmissions, which were made *in clear*. The infant Austro-German radio intercept service had the coup of its life, listening enrapt as the Russians broadcast every detail of their dispositions. The Germans had reacted accordingly and the result was the disastrous defeat of Tannenberg in which one of Russia's best field armies was all but wiped out. The pendulum governing radio security had now swung too far the other way.

The unit was now ordered forward into the operational zone.

Barracks rumour had it that they were to form part of a force which was going to take Baghdad, and indeed the Russians had made a demonstration in that direction some months earlier in an attempt to relieve pressure on the besieged British garrison of Kut al Amarah, which had been starved into surrender in April.* Locker Lampson himself was unaware of his ultimate destination but was convinced that this was an unlikely alternative, but by a strange twist of fate most of his command would actually reach Baghdad in two years' time, although from a totally different direction.

Locker Lampson's papers contain an interesting account of the journey.

> Our way lay along the Georgian military road, which cuts through the Caucasian range, leaving Vladikavkas in Europe, entering Asia midway, and reaching the heart of Old Georgia at the finish. It consists of nearly 130 miles of metalled road, with many a hairpin bend and precipitous three-verst drop, and a definite time was given us in which to cross it. Armoured cars had never been seen along it before and the villagers on the way poured out in eager interest. As for the scenery, it stood unrivalled. Rugged canyons took up the noise of the car engines; at one point the bare rocks were flung up so grimly and the cliffs had taken on such chaotic shapes that it was as if God had, in the morning of the world, stalked through the valley and suddenly got angry. Such a defile would be quite grassless and treeless, and then a corner would open out and, lo! high in the heavens a shining field, smooth and green and well groomed as a new billiard-table cloth.

A Cossack *sotnia* had been provided as escort, not for the cars' protection, but to ride ahead and clear frequently stubborn civilian traffic off the narrow and frequently dangerous route. South of Tiflis the passable Military Road was replaced by a villainously bad track.

> It ran very bumpy at times and depressions and rocks lay hidden beneath the dust until some accident revealed them. It was a bitter blow to come shortly upon three cars by the roadside stranded within a couple of hundred yards of each other. They had each struck a concealed boulder almost without knowing it, and nothing but a thin, black, oily smear in their tracks had raised suspicions. The ingenuity of the men was beyond praise, and they were seldom delayed long. Any device which could carry them to camp sufficed, and I have

---

* The effect of this disaster on contemporary British public opinion was similar to that of the fall of Singapore in World War II, although less far-reaching in its consequences. In each case the defeat was caused by high-level incompetence and resulted in cruel sufferings inflicted on the unfortunate prisoners.

known petty officers slice off shavings of soap, mix it with jam, and apply it to the oozing hole with a covering of medical plaster; or, again, one petty officer melted down some revolver bullets over his primus stove, made a casting of mud, and poured the lead into place from the inside of the baseplate, which had been taken off.

Not everyone received such praise for using his initiative. The junior officer who had his Lanchester towed into the evening camp site by a team of oxen caused not a little amusement, but was sharply reprimanded for bringing his squadron into disrepute.

Locker Lampson completed the journey without the slightest difficulty in his open Rolls Royce tourer, but for the drivers of the other vehicles it was hard, gruelling work which demanded every ounce of their skill. This was particularly so in the case of the Heavies and the laden Sea Base lorries, which had to be lifted part of the way by rail, as Petty Officer W. P. Baker records in his diary.*

> *July 28th:* Left Vladikavkas for Tiflis. The first car left about 7 a.m. I was in the last and left at 1045 in rear of Sea Base. We went along the roads on the side of the mountains, passing several convoys. On the left hand side it is nothing but a precipice reaching down several thousand feet, and the road proceeds in a zig-zag, in some points gradients of 1 in 8 until the top is reached. At various intervals water issues from the rock, which enabled us to get a good supply for cooling engines. A breakdown occurred which delayed us and at 7.45 p.m. it was now getting dark so we camped the night.
>
> *July 29th:* We continued journey at 5 a.m. and proceeded up the mountains. The journey even more exciting, more zig-zags. After the summit was reached we were able to come down with a free engine. At one point where we went along there was a precipice, 6000 feet, and previous to us passing, a Russian car went over. Along the route are small tunnels built to stop rocks and earth blocking the road. Travelling was still very slow owing to tyre trouble with the Heavy armoured cars. We arrived at a village where we slept in cars beneath the walls of the church.
>
> *July 30th:* We left early in the morning and reached Tiflis about 6 a.m. Stopped in town until 8 a.m. and then went back for the Heavies, who were in difficulties again with tyres. It was decided it was impossible to proceed further. We stopped the night.

* As far as possible the RNACD used naval terminology. Sea Base was the equivalent of Headquarters Squadron in a modern armoured car regiment, and included the unit's transport echelon.

July 31st: Raining like mad, all vehicles sunk into ground. It was found impossible for Sea Base to proceed further by road, so we entrained here for Kars. Assisted loading cars onto train. Left Tiflis about 8 o'clock.

August 2nd: We arrived at Kars in the early hours of the morning and unloaded train. The other cars had arrived the previous night.

August 3rd: Left Kars at 8 a.m. Kars is a very ancient town, the houses rather peculiar, the streets narrow. We went through a village where storks had built their nests on the chimneys. We arrived at Sarikamish during the morning. We have been billeted in a Russian barracks. Slept miserably, the place full of bugs.

By one means or another the Russian Armoured Car Division RNAS had demonstrated its efficiency by arriving at its appointed destination two days earlier than expected. On 4th August it was rewarded by a personal visit from the Grand Duke Nicholas Nicholaievich, Viceroy of the Caucasus and uncle of the Czar. As Commander-in-Chief of the Imperial Army Nicholas had been a popular figure, even though the war was not going well for Russia; but he had bitter enemies at court, including the Czarina herself, who had at length succeeded in persuading her kindly but weak husband to assume the Supreme Command himself and remove the Grand Duke to an area far removed from the centre of power. It was a mistake which would cost the Romanov dynasty dear, but in the meantime Nicholas loyally performed his duty to his nephew, offering advice to Yudenich, his field commander, but never interfering in the conduct of his operations.

Locker Lampson, as usual, has left the best record of the occasion.

He had never inspected English troops before, and I thought how strange the men's bare knees and beardless faces would seem to a soldier of his origin and type. The cars were drawn up in a long line, the men in front, and a wide semi-circle of onlookers was kept at bay by Cossacks. There was a stir at the station as some cars drew near, and before I realised who it was, an enormous man in Cossack uniform of grey material with *kinjal* and skirt complete, had swung his big boots free of the car and was stalking our way. His lofty headgear increased his height and he stood out as a giant among his obsequious followers. I was briefly introduced and then by his side I marched with him towards the British line. He held his huge hand rigidly at the salute as he walked down the line, but did not look for a single second at the men, gazing grimly ahead until the end was reached. Then he turned and shook hands with me. I asked leave to show him the cars, and with increasing interest he accompanied me to the back and front of the fighting squadrons, and was particularly pleased with some trailers for guns, which he declared oxen could usefully manoeuvre in hilly country.* Then he returned to his car and stood up, a colossal figure at the salute as the cars one after another – without a hitch – filed past, until the plain was empty of all save spectators.

This was to be the squadron's last parade together for many months, for their paths would take them in many and divers directions.

---

* These were obviously the towed 3-pounders.

CHAPTER FOUR

'You have shaken Death by the Beard!'

A few days later Locker Lampson went forward to Erzerum to pay his respects to General Yudenich, under whose command he would be working and who

> had won under incredible conditions the victory of Sarikamish, when his troops lacked guns, ammunition, even rifles and when, in the absense of cannon, old mortars were brought from the Tiflis Museum, filled full of black powder and fired off to create the illusion of artillery. His officers adored him and he was said to be the only general who faced the Grand Duke without a flinch.

Yudenich was indeed a hard-fighting, practical officer who owed much of his success to the immense distance which separated him from the Court intrigues of Petrograd, and to the support which he received from the Grand Duke. He had held the Turkish counter-offensive without undue difficulty and the front had now lapsed into relative quiescence. Now that the lines rested so far inside the Turkish hinterland his main problem was supply, the needs of his army being met by endless camel trains which plodded their way steadily south from the railheads.

He made it clear at once that there was virtually no work for the British armoured cars to do in the principal zone of operations and, that being the case, there was little point in keeping the unit concentrated. Part would operate on the army's open left flank, crossing the Mush Plain to Bitlis and supporting the Cossack cavalry which held the ill-defined line as far as Lake Van; and part would cover the right flank of the Russian troops in North Persia, operating south of Lake Urmia. It was also emphasised that the British squadrons could expect no logistic support from the Russians, and would have to carry all their own ammunition, food and petrol.

With three fighting squadrons at his disposal, Locker Lampson was forced to make a choice of priorities, and since North Persia was of secondary importance No 1 Squadron under Lieutenant-Commander F. W. Belt was detached and set in motion for that area, leaving No 2 and 3 Squadrons to tackle whatever difficulties lay ahead on the Mush Plain.

The problems presented by the latter undertaking were not underestimated for one minute. Over 350 miles separated Sarikamish from Bitlis, the majority of which lay through some of the most difficult and dangerous country in the world; and since the long line of communications passed through hostile Kurdish territory, unarmoured vehicles would require an armoured escort, thus effectively limiting the number of operational squadrons actually at the front to one.

An advance base was set up by the lonely bridge at Keupri Keui which, like so many structures between Macedonia and the Hindu Kush, had according to local legend been built by Alexander the Great. From here the forward squadron, No 3, operated under Locker Lampson's personal control, while No 2 Squadron, at Gregory's direction, kept them supplied. 'It was in our system of keeping our communications clear and feeding the cars at every point that we scored over the Russians,' wrote C. J. Smith, one of the officers.

> From railhead to front we had established bases, tiny little camps held by a couple of men, at which precious petrol and other material was dumped to await transport to the next camp, and so on right up to the front. In spite of the bad conditions, the lorries were running almost with the regularity of clockwork. The heavy cars carried the stores from railhead along the made roads to the first base, then the semi-heavies transported the stuff to the second base, whence to a third and subsequent bases light lorries were used. We had established a perfect shuttle service. It was a wonderfully organised system and a glowing tribute to Commander Locker Lampson, who surveyed the terrain, drew up all the plans in detail, and after satisfying himself that they would be carried out to the letter, betook himself to the front.

Locker Lampson has left an account of his own adventures with No 3 Squadron, although dates and several important place names are sadly lacking. What is certain is that the journey across Armenia and into the heart of Asia Minor was not helped by the inadequate – not to say completely inaccurate – information supplied by the Russian staff. Tracks marked as being suitable for motor vehicles were good only for animal transport; fords collapsed under the weight of the cars; and bridges were marked where there were none. In one instance the Commander arrived to find a Cossack bridge guard cooking its evening meal, but no bridge – they had burned it, plank by plank, to keep themselves warm in the chill mountain nights.

Everywhere there were the deserted villages and other dismal reminders of the recent massacres; not that either side was ever disposed to show mercy to the other. A Cossack with whom Locker Lampson was carrying out a route reconnaissance captured a Kurdish woman and offered to share her with him. The Commander, starved of female company, frankly admitted to being tempted but declined, turning in for the night while the man had his way nearby. The Cossack was found the following morning, stabbed through the heart with his own *kinjal*, and the woman had gone.

Mile by mile the squadron pushed on, constructing its own fords, shaping the river banks to permit the passage of the cars, and generally carving its own road through the wilderness, leaving signposts for No 2 Squadron to follow. Much of the going was through deep dust which rain could quickly turn to inches of clinging mud. Hardly a day went by without cars having to be dug out, jacked up, and their running boards removed to provide a tractive surface for the spinning wheels. The crews of the Heavies were particularly hard worked and often a Lanchester would be sent back to help them out of their difficulties. No motor vehicles, let alone armoured cars, had ever been seen in the area before, and this implacable struggle with nature represents one of the unit's finest achievements. The question of failure simply did not arise; Locker Lampson and his men had set off for Bitlis and they intended to get there, very possibly because the Russians doubted that they could do it. The local corps commander, seeing the cars vanish into bandit country and fearing the Grand Duke's wrath if the British were themselves massacred, twice sent up a galloper with orders recalling the squadron : on each occasion Locker Lampson, now an old hand at insubordination, arranged for his Russian liaison officer, Lieutenant Lamkert, to get to a telephone and explain to the anxious general that all was going splendidly and that the objective was almost in sight – further, until the replenishment convoy escorted by No 2 Squadron arrived, the cars had insufficient petrol for the return trip.

Concerning the Kurds, Locker Lampson's views were quite definite.

> They show no sign of civilisation whatever. They are the same as the Carduchi, mentioned by Xenophon in his march of the Ten Thousand and it was indeed strange that we, with our cars, were to come across them along the same route as Xenophon with his hoplites in their retreat. The Kurds have in no wise improved since his day and possess

no single virtue, not even that of courage. Their treachery is their pride, and their cruelty the terror even of the Turks. They are unreclaimed savages: no one has ever tamed them. I was offered poison in case I ever fell into their hands as they took prisoners for one purpose only, that of torture and mutilation.*

For their part, the Kurds had no conception of what an armoured car was. All they could see was that the Cossack escort was few in number and that they seemed to be easy victims. As the squadron harboured for the night in the village of Haskoi they began massing on the hills above and their intentions were all too clear.

They spread out in open order over a wide expanse of hillside and started to descend. Our plan was to allow them to come as far as possible into the plain and then rush them with the cars. Unfortunately there was no exit from the village at the one end, but a track led out of the other and offered concealment right up to the plain's edge, and a dash here with the cars would enfilade the Kurds if only they ventured far enough.

They reached the plain in loose order and some of them entered the village at the foot of the hills. The rest came steadily on, but stopped a few hundred yards out in the plain. We hung on, hoping ... nay, expecting – a further advance, and lying still as mice. But the Cossack officer in charge, who misunderstood his orders, thought the time had come, and gave the signal. Lieutenant de Coninck, a very capable Belgian officer attached to our unit, was in charge of the cars detailed for duty, and at once he leapt forward with them; and since he started some hundreds of yards back in the village, by the time the plain was won he had attained a very high speed. At first the Kurds noticed nothing, but the Maxims opened early, and forthwith they fell upon their faces and disappeared in the grass, while those in the village rushed like insects from the houses and flung themselves into neighbouring ditches. The crisp crepitation of the Maxims seemed ceaseless, but the cars only reached the enemy in time to pick off a few, and the bulk escaped into the hills, where they were safe to give back innocuous and desultory shots. I could see them yet, secure from the cars and gathering in knots to discuss further action.

The Heavies had not yet caught up, although the leading car was bogged down in a ford only some little way back. Locker Lampson had already sent the crew an order to the effect that if the car could not be extricated the 3-pounder was to be manhandled onto a field car-

* Like the Basques, the ethnic Kurds are still divided by international boundaries. Their wish for an autonomous state of their own has resulted in constant unrest in northern Iraq and Iran.

riage and dragged forward, together with a supply of ammunition. At length the gun appeared.

> I sent a messenger to bid them aim at the Kurds far up the mountain side, and I watched for results through the telescope. The first shot fell wide and was not even within the orbit of my glass, but the next struck near, and on its heels flew the third into the very heart of the bunch. Thenceforth the gun searched the bushes and ravines, as most of the enemy had gone to ground, although a white hat could still be picked out every now and again through the telescope.

The first round had undoubtedly gone to the RNAS, but the Kurds were unlikely to let the matter rest. Some days later another Heavy became stuck while crossing a stream and after sending on the rest of the squadron Locker Lampson returned with his tourer and one Lanchester to render assistance. After two hours' work it was clear that the only hope lay in digging a channel which would divert the water round the car, and as this would take time the Commander decided to leave the Lanchester with the Heavy while he pressed on in the wake of the squadron, unescorted. In due course he found himself running along a narrow track which wound its way between low hills.

> The path ran like a white ribbon through the parched yellow grass. Two hawks followed us like baby aeroplanes and a hoopoe kept alighting ahead quite near the car and lifting his gorgeous crest as if to beckon us on. But the wheelway was awful and only at a snail's pace could we advance. We must have covered four hundred yards when it seemed as if a door banged in the hills. The driver, Weller, did not notice, but I saw alarm in our interpreter's eyes and the orderly asked, 'What's that?'
> Before I could reply the bang was repeated not once but a hundred times and the rocks took up the echo and repeated it again and again. We were being fired on, not as yet from very near, but the bullets sang overhead and splashed in the white dust around. In a flash I decided not to turn back for I dare not stop and become a stationary target. So, 'On, on,' I shouted. 'Not madly, but quickly!' And forward we rattled and lurched.
> Our course was neither comfortable nor clear as at every turn we had to slow down for deep splits or dried waterways. This only was certain – that our course inexorably approached a point where the snipers would be broadside on. But I dare not stop; that meant certain death. Nor could I just do nothing. Our sleeping kit was with us and, swiftly stacking this high on the right, I got out my rifle, crouched down and let fly. But my shots were lost in the buzzing of those leaden bees overhead and the rattle in the hills.

'You have shaken Death by the Beard!' 63

'On, on,' I shouted. 'Not madly, but quickly!' 'And forward we rattled and lurched.' An illustration from Locker Lampson's account in Lloyd's Magazine.

Then it occurred to me that this must be a planned ambush and that some felled tree awaited us shortly, so I shouted to the driver to go steady and for everyone to be ready to jump. On we roared. Once the car gave a frightful lurch, hung for a moment helpless, then plunged forward, the lonely target of an increasing fusillade.

There was no artillery in use against us, nor thank God, any Maxims, but hundreds of riflemen were hidden in the hills and potting away. Some had modern rifles and their bullets would whine like wasps and strike the ground with a crisp slap, but most of the bullets were unlike any that I had yet heard in the war. They were out of Martini Henry barrels and droned like cock-chafers and struck with a great fat wallop.

Shortly thereafter a bullet struck the seat under me and made the springs sing, and another smashed the orderly's rifle stock in his hands. We had reached the deadliest section of the defile where the path hugged the hills for over a mile. Yet we dare not, we could not, race. We could only plunge blindly on through the fusillade. It seemed impossible to escape, the firing was too furious. I expected any second to see one of us killed or the engine vitally hit. The snipers were so near, they could not miss. As only game shooters ever seem to remember, you must aim yards ahead of a moving object to hit it and I guessed the Kurds were making no allowance for our forty miles an hour.

Indeed, they must have scuppered us but for something I suddenly remembered – my car was a fine Rolls Royce for those days and before leaving home in 1915 I had fitted it with the latest of lively inventions – I had bought a klaxon horn. Not one of your effete sirens, reduced by present day regulations to a wheezy ghost of former lung force, but one of those early unabashed soul-stirrers connected to a rueful snake. 'Driver,' I yelled, 'Sound your klaxon!' He clapped his hand on the button and the whole hillside rang with the unexpected roar. The effect was magical and it did exactly that for which I had dared not hope. It startled the enemy into anticipating retaliation and, as if at some signal to cease fire, every rifle stopped and for at least two minutes no sound broke from the hills.

We roared on and won open ground before the first sulky shots broke out again, and by the time they were in full swing the bullets had lost their most dangerous direction. But the surface of the track was still pitted, which meant reduced speed, and the tall grass hid whatever might be round the next bend. Clearly we were nearing freer ground and needed only a couple of miles steady going to be safe. And then – we rounded a corner and there, barely 300 yards ahead, ran a river. I stood up and realised that it was the obstacle they had prepared. Not broad, indeed, as rivers go, but of a size to dispirit any Kurd-hunted car. The driver instinctively slowed down, and I felt the wind of redoubled bullets all round.

'Get ready to jump out and swim!' I called and on we ran. I could see the surface of the river flogged white by those murderous bullets.

(*Left*) At a Russian railway station. (*Right*) Petty Officer Don Spencer with 'Miskab', RNAS mascot photographed at Vladikavkas.

Outside Moscow. A photograph from S. M. Payne's album.

RNAS personnel disembarking Armoured Cars from barges.

A group of Russian line infantry, Cossacks and RNAS men.

Cossacks and Bengal Lancers at Tabriz. The latter (left) are the bodyguard of the British consul.

Surely we must succumb.

We reached the water and I strained over the side of the car to direct the driver. I remember the front wheels driving the water before them in little white eddies and I recollect the hiss of the back wheels as they sank in. But not far in – only three or four inches at first, and for fifty feet this depth never varied. Then suddenly we lurched in up to our axles. I looked back and forward – oh, God, we were not even half way.

Then we seemed to take a dive right over our wheels but up, slowly we surged again and crept on with the wavelets foaming like steam against the tyres. We kept this level for ages and the car went grinding on. Then – surely the level was dropping and I craned over the side and measured the distance with my eye. Could it be? We had passed the centre and now the water was falling, We were safe – the whole river had not held fifteen inches of water at its deepest. The bullets were flying still, but very wildly, as we pulled out on the other side, and we had not raced on half-a-mile more before an armoured car shot into view. Oh, the welcome of this sight and the pleasure to find them safe! The entire unit was gathered here and could not credit their eyes when they saw us. They had been violently attacked themselves, and had protected the unarmoured cars by interposing the armoured cars between them and the enemy. But despite this, the lorries were riddled with bullets and several of the men slightly wounded. Lieutenant Turner was wounded in the head, largely owing to his determination to kill a few Kurds before quitting. He had knelt behind his lorry and fired 37 shots from his rifle alone, and there was no doubt that the enemy had suffered considerable loss.

Great credit was due to Weller for his magnificent driving, and again great credit was due to Sholl, who had coolly met the ambush and brought the unit through with no appreciable damage.

The affair did not detract from the men's opinion that their leader was something of a card, and the Cossack escort was visibly impressed. 'Commander,' shouted one of them, 'you have shaken Death by the beard!' Locker Lampson admitted to feeling slightly 'war-worn' at the time, and the remark did much to soothe his jangled nervous system.

The squadron reached its destination, which it called Happy Valley, several days later. The cars were overhauled and a camp established. Active operations were, for the moment, out of the question, since almost all the available fuel had been consumed on the way forward. Rations too were now running low and had to be reduced.

The divisional intelligence staff indicated that the Turks were planning an attack on Happy Valley and instructions were issued to Locker Lampson that in the event of this actually taking place the squadron was to extricate such cars as it could but abandon the rest rather than lose the crews. The Commander indignantly retorted that if the situation was expected to be as serious as that the men would prefer to fight it out in their cars until the issue was decided one way or the other.

He also produced a constructive alternative.

The petrol shortage was so acute that the squadron could no longer be kept as a whole upon its legs, nor could any number of cars be sent out against the enemy. But by skimming every car tank of its residue and getting the last drop left in the tins, we were able to fill up the armoured cars with sustenance for a journey each of, say, a score of miles. We then asked for the loan of some Cossacks and a party of our men accompanied the expedition on foot. Our aim was to enter and circle the plain, ostentatiously making observations, prospecting roads and testing trenches until the enemy could not fail to believe that the Russians contemplated an attack and, what was more, an attack supported by armoured cars for the first time in these regions. For I reckoned that the presence of this new arm on the plain was staggering to the enemy and that, ignoring what the cars could in fact effect, he must hold an exaggerated opinion of their war capacity. We had come, moreover, so scatheless through the ambush that the savage Kurds might credit us with powers not of this world, and even the Turks would be uncertain what hidden horrors lay in store for them.

At any rate, the plan was not only conceived but carried out, and great praise was due to Lieutenant Crossing for his patient piloting of the cars over the plain. He took to a horse where the cars could not pass and rode into great danger, but was luckily never struck although constantly fired upon. The manoeuvres, too, not only drew fire, but undoubted interest, and a prisoner who came in from the Turks admitted that they did not know what to expect. I was for sending him back after allowing him to see vast preparations for an attack, but the Russians would not release him. At any rate, so realistic did our operations become that the Turks withdrew troops from an exposed spur and sent a patrol for the first time for weeks into some outlying villages.

These manoeuvres were conducted the same day as the news of the likely Turkish attack was received, and were timed to precede this attack, which was anticipated at dawn the following morning. After this we settled down in camp and measured up our petrol. There was enough to take each car five miles, and with this we must do our best. The valley head was picketed, officers and men given clear orders, and it remained to sleep well ere the sentry roused us to stand to arms and see dawn and a Turkish attack break simultaneously.

At length day broke and the camp crept out of the darkness sadly and slowly, until outlines stood solid again and the valley lay revealed.

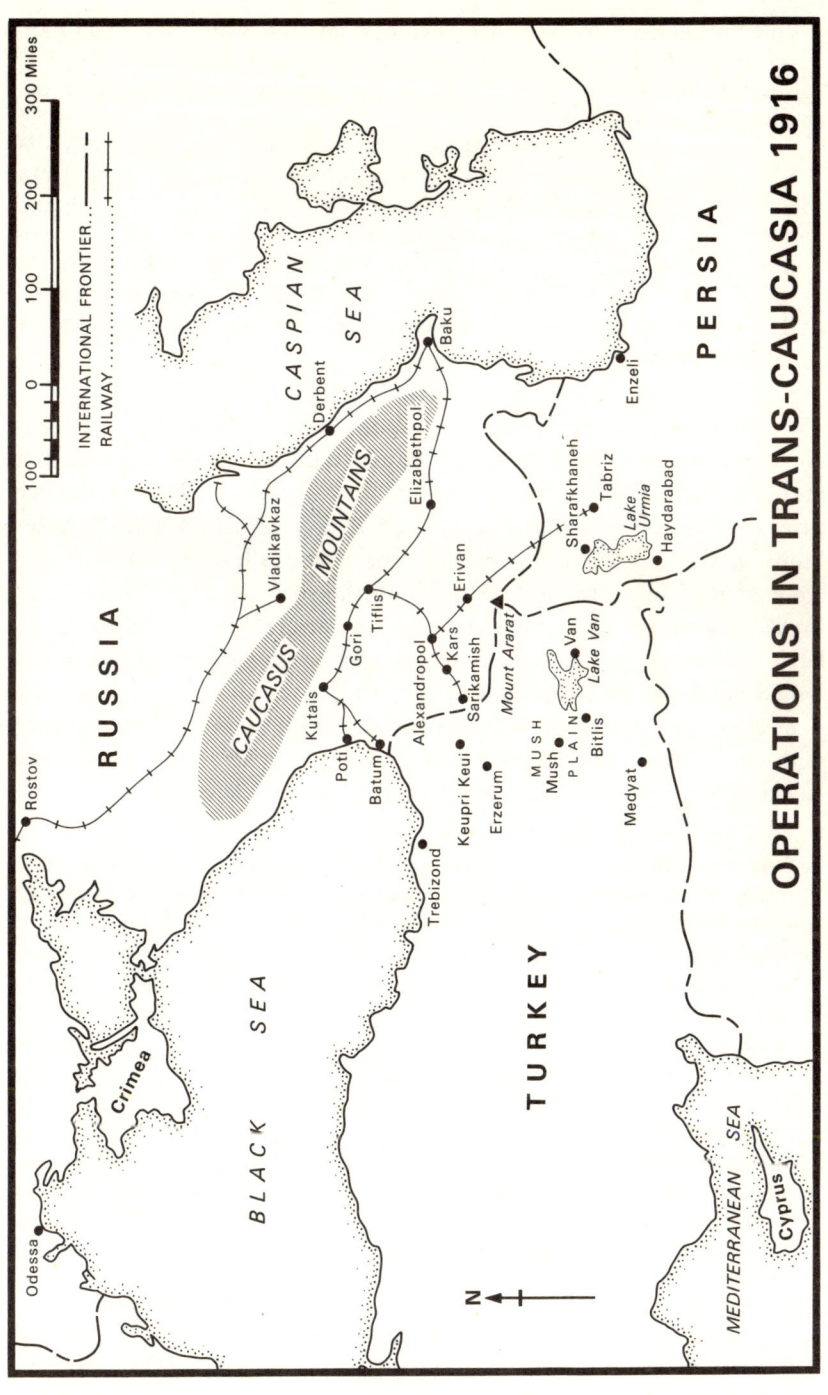

But no sight, no sound which was unusual. We waited yet a full half-hour, standing to arms in the cold light, but the enemy might still be sleeping for all his show of life; and, with hearts not altogether unthankful, we broke off for a glorious morning meal.

Information, subsequently supplied by prisoners, was illuminating as to this night and the previous day's operations. It clearly bore out our belief that the Turks could be bluffed. They had meant to attack and even prepared for the purpose, but the presence of the British unit and in particular the cars' laboured perambulation of the plain the day before had forced them to credit the chance of a Russian advance. They thought twice about attacking, and took up a purely defensive attitude instead.

Two days later a supply convoy got through, escorted by cars from No 2 Squadron. The Kurds had sniped distantly at the column, but had lost the will for a close engagement. But the convoy's experience proved beyond doubt that Locker Lampson was operating at the outer limits of viable logistic support. At one time no less than 20 vehicles were bogged in or broken down along the route, and the hard going involved so much low gear work that 66 per cent of the fuel load had been consumed. As the light lorries would be going back unladen, less would obviously be required, but even so the amount of petrol actually deposited with the forward squadron was only a small fraction of that with which the convoy had set out. It was, however, enough to satisfy Locker Lampson, who was now itching for offensive action.

Our star was now in the ascendant, and every man felt that our improved conditions must be put to speedy and splendid use. I rode over to the staff many miles distant in the hills and got leave to organise and undertake an attack upon some Turkish and Kurdish positions facing us. It was still thought that the enemy might deliver an assault and it was feared, in particular, that a village named 'M' at the foot of the Turkish hills might afford cover for troops and even guns. Finally, even if no attack matured, it was felt that this village should not go unregarded, but should be taken and rendered useless for winter occupation by the enemy.

It was agreed that no considerable attack over a wide front was advisable; but the General guaranteed a bombardment of the Turkish positions higher up the line by way of feint, under cover of which we might launch an attack unexpectedly. Every facility, too, was forthcoming, and several companies of infantry with some *sotnias* of cavalry and two squadrons of frontiersmen, were placed at my disposal.

The village which we were to take did not lend itself to isolated assault and would not normally have been attacked except as part of far wider operations. And this was chiefly because it lay at the foot of opposing hills, so that any troops approaching it must traverse six miles of open plain to reach it. Even though warfare in Turkey was less intensive than in France, trenches less interlocked and artillery far scarcer, yet an advance over open country could hardly be conducted even here by a body of men in isolation and unsupported by operations elsewhere. In fact, it was a proposition so obvious that the Turks would probably not be expecting any direct assault on this village. But although it was true of infantry and cavalry that neither would readily move to such an attack, theoretically there was no reason why armoured cars should not. Firstly, because however difficult it may be for infantry and cavalry quickly to cross an open space under bullet fire, armoured cars may, within reason, neglect both rifle and machine guns when on the move. Secondly, because although armoured cars cannot stand up against artillery the enemy, not expecting such an attack, would not have guns in preparation. Thirdly, because armoured cars on good ground are mobile beyond any other arm, and with luck would dash out across the plain and mop up the intervening six miles in as many minutes.

The village lay at the entrance to a valley, which separated the hills from a detached buttress of cliff, upon the crown of which were dug the advanced Turkish trenches. The distance across the plain was under six miles and midway stood a structure extraordinary in these surroundings. A large circular tower in ruins – all that was left of a far more extensive fabric – offered the soldier a rare post for observation and the antiquary all the delights of research. It was planted in a graveyard of huge tombstones which leaned all ways and upon them, as upon the tower, were traced cabalistic signs and inscriptions, said to be Assyrian. The site of a gallery led from the tower to a pool which was as much a miracle to our men now as it had doubtless been a mystery to generations of worshippers. It formed a complete circle some 300 feet in diameter and from the heart of it, out of depths no line could plumb, there swirled up eternally waters which, whatever the season, were ice-cold and which brimmed over in such volume that three streams took here their being – the rising of great rivers.

The ground around the pool and the tower, with its outcrop of ruins, offered capital car cover. We decided, therefore, to conceal some cars here, after making up the roads leading to the spot; we even thought of reconnoitring and making up the tracks beyond as far as we dared, towards the enemy village. For our plan was to rush the bulk of the cars swiftly forth from their shelter in Happy Valley over the plain against the village, and simultaneously to rip those near the tower from their concealment, and hurl them ahead on the same errand.

But this was not all! A gully ran into the enemy village from the flank, and although this gully was impassable for cars, horsemen could move unperceived along it and enfilade the village. To guard this gully it was necessary to enter some outlying hamlets across the plain, and for many days prior to our attack we sent Cossacks to reconnoitre them, hoping to accustom the enemy to the presence of our patrols there and to allay his fears.

At last the day had come, and away rode the Cossacks and a party of our men under Turner an hour after sun-up. It was not possible for them to adhere rigidly to a time-table, but we allowed them four hours in which to reach their objective and off they trooped. In this space of time, too, we hoped that the village we were to attack would be effectively launched upon its day's work and lost to other considerations.

Turner's party on horseback carried Maxims and moved slowly, but they were in the hamlets some three hours after leaving us, and in another hour we must sally out. During the night we had worked up and concealed near the tower in the plain two armoured cars carrying quick firers (i.e. machine-guns) and one with a three-pounder. These could not be better hidden and there is no question that their whereabouts remained a secret. With the rest of the cars we stood ready in the camp and watched the village fill through our glasses and folk crowded to their duties. The car engines were humming and not a nut out of order. Then, as the signal fell, forth flew the unit under Sholl at top speed, and even the three cars near the tower darted off like wasps over the plain. In five minutes we were level with the tower, the firing had begun and the ceaseless chatter of the Maxims rolled over the hills. The village had not realised its danger until one car was only 600 yards away; and then it was as though someone had lifted a stone from it, exposing black insects in an agony of commotion. From the huts, the houses, the barns, tiny figures, tiny figures of men shot out, until the terraces and fields were crawling with battalions in flight. There seemed no organisation or rallying point. A few tried the road up the valley, some scrambled painfully up the mountainside, and I distinctly heard the Maxims of Turner's horsemen in the gully beating back the escape that way.

Meanwhile, the infantry placed at our disposal were deploying in the plain to protect our left flank, and had entirely mastered these reaches. But, despite this early success and the evident punctuality of the party on horseback, it was not all going our way. A cyclist returned from the cars to say that huge cracks in the dry earth separated them from the village and that the best they had so far been able to do was to fire over this obstruction at long range into the village. It was only what we had feared, if not actually expected, and I at once withdrew a couple of cars and hurried them round to worm a way in from the other flank, while I started the 3-pounders forthwith shelling every exit to the village. One shot completely demolished a circular house which crumpled as if constructed of cards and seemed to vomit forth a score of men, dead, wounded or fleeing. Another brought a huge piece of rock down the cliff side into a gully and blocked all egress at this point. Not a single enemy gun had yet come into play and it became obvious that enemy guns could now only act with the gravest risk of damage to their own people. For the cars had advanced into the very outskirts and were too interlocked with the enemy to be distinguishable any longer. Indeed, Turner with de Connick and his horsemen were past the fringes of the village, had fired into the western end and were busy pouring lead into the streets. And immediately afterwards some of the cars got in, won a terrace of the village, and did the greatest execution. The surprise was such that no organised effort was made to resist, except by those soldiers who had escaped into the hills and started firing back.

We were not to capture prisoners or bring back booty – neither was possible. We aimed merely at a surprise attack and a swift withdrawal; in fact, at a raid, and it was not in keeping with these intentions to delay. So we swept hurriedly through the village from end to end, driving the soldiery out, entering houses and setting fire to ricks, barns and stores. We had no time to consider enemy wounded, or attempt the capture of anyone; but parties were posted at the main issues of the village with Maxims, and many were killed escaping. The wind had been carefully watched and that end of the village was first fired from which the breeze blew, and such was its force and such the dryness of the houses and grass, that in thirty minutes the entire village space was enveloped. Everywhere subsidiary fires leapt forth, and before three-quarters of an hour the village had disappeared in smoke, which rose from it in a great grey plume and streamed down the valley.

It was imperative to cease fire with the 3-pounders, as we now had as much chance of hitting friend as foe. But such was the eagerness of the men that I sought other targets for their zeal and turned a couple of our small guns upon groups of the enemy which had collected up the hillside, out of range of the Maxims. We followed and dispersed these (distant some 3,500 yards) with brilliant effect and prevented an organised descent into and recapture of the village. And then we turned for fresh effort elsewhere.

The valley which led from the village lay deep between its hills, and we had got so far into the mouth that the tops of some houses in a hamlet higher up the valley stood revealed and a cluster of tall trees seemed to promise the presence of another village yet further up. Now our information from Russian headquarters was seldom full and often inaccurate. Moreover, they had been unable to supply a single map of this particular area and were wild with delight when I produced an 18-year-old chart made by an English missionary in these parts. In spite of this we knew little of the configuration of the country held by the Turks. Yet prisoners under examination had agreed that while the valley leading from the village was not of great importance in itself, there was a village 4,000 yards up it, where two battalion headquarters lay and where the enemy had collected a power of munitions for the coming advance.

It was impossible for us now to approach nearer and get a clearer view of the valley, and there was danger in delay. But certainly those poplar tops presupposed a village, and they corresponded strangely in position with the hamlet referred to by the prisoners. Anyhow, it was important to shell the valley against approaching supports, and even a few random shots could do no harm. So we started peppering the valley and I discussed further plots with Chief Petty Officer Benson, an admirable man who was in charge of these operations and who was the first petty officer to win a Commission in the field with our unit. He felt that the far poplars undoubtedly denoted a village and declared that although 3-pounder shells could not be fired on an invisible target with accuracy, he could guarantee reaching this distance if allowed to elevate the gun and lob shells over the intervening promontory.

There were now only a few 3-pounder cartridges left and I put Benson himself onto the gun as No 1 Gunner and marksman. His first shot grazed the promontory top and raised a feathery puff of dust, the second, the third, the fourth, the fifth and the sixth all whopped over and fell in silence on the other side. Then flew the seventh, followed in a twinkling by the eighth, and back bellowed a report which shook the hills and made the air tremble where I stood. In ignorance of what this portended, we finished up the box upon the hill and kept half-a-dozen to see our cars safe out of action. We were to learn later from prisoners, whom these explosions sent flying into the Russian lines, that our shells had struck a magazine and exploded it, and that a large dump had been simultaneously fired, killing over 300 Turks.*

I was getting anxious for Sholl, such was the smoke and confusion, and ordered our cars to return at once and meet me at the tower. The cyclist orderly disappeared as effectually as the rest, but ere long he and the cars returned. Sholl and his crew were nigh stifled from the fumes and tottered fainting from their car; other car crews were similarly exhausted, but the casualties were pronounced among the Cossacks alone. Turner and his party arrived last, longing to linger but unable to remain behind once the controlling presence of the cars was withdrawn.

The precise date of the engagement is not known, but PO Baker of No 2 Squadron heard of it on 27th August and entered some details in his diary, so it could only have taken place a day or so earlier.

The Russians were delighted with No 3 Squadron, which had per-

* This is almost certainly the first recorded instance of a fighting vehicle carrying out a successful fully-indirect shoot with HE ammunition, and Locker Lampson's account suggests that the outcome was not simply a matter of luck. Today such shoots are carried out as a matter of routine, the tank gunner using a clinometer and traverse indicator to apply corrections based on the fall of shot, signalled by radio from an observer who has the target in view. Benson had no such aids and since he was unable to bracket his target, he seems to have applied a degree of elevation with each shot, creeping steadily towards the ammunition dump.

formed every task set with not a little dash, and a certain amount of style as well. The Grand Duke awarded six St George's Crosses and eleven St George's Medals to be distributed to the most deserving, while Locker Lampson – always somewhat parsimonious in the matter of decorations – saw to it that Sholl received a well-earned Distinguished Service Cross for his services throughout.

September marked the effective end of the campaigning season on this sector, where intense high-altitude cold and deep mountain snow made winter operations impossible. Both sides tacitly agreed to live and let live, reducing the front to isolated pickets while most of the troops withdrew into winter quarters. While No 3 Squadron prepared to embark on the long journey back to base, Locker Lampson went on ahead in his tourer, this time escorted by two Lanchesters, and passed through the site of the earlier ambush without a shot being fired; he was greatly amused by a rumour which was circulating around Keupri Keui to the effect that he had recently met with an untimely and tragic end.

Meanwhile, what of No 1 Squadron and its lonely venture into North Persia? After being issued with tropical kit the squadron left Kars by rail on 20th August. The legendary Mount Ararat was sighted the following afternoon, and the credulous invited the incredulous to believe that the Ark was still up there, buried somewhere under the summit's gleaming mantle of snow. The train reached the railhead of Sharafkhaneh on 22nd August and the cars were off-loaded and driven to Tabriz while the stores were shipped by barge down Lake Urmia to Haydarabad.

At Tabriz the car crews were given a meal by the British Consul, whose post was unique in the service in that he had his own bodyguard of Bengal Lancers, the Persian Kurds being no more lovable than their brothers across the border in Turkey.

The squadron then proceeded with difficulty to Haydarabad where it established its advance base. Patrols were pushed out, operating on tracks which were, if anything, worse than those encountered on the Mush plain. The heat was almost unbearable, affecting several men badly, while others contracted a dose of malaria for which a Russian medical officer supplied quinine. They had, however, arrived too late to take part in the fighting, and the crews' only battles were those they fought daily to keep their vehicles moving at all. Even so, every precaution was taken, ammunition bandoliers were worn constantly, and each night the patrols formed a leaguer with the lorries and motorcycles in the centre, an armoured car at each corner and a further car about 200 yards out, facing the hills from which it was expected the Kurds might launch an attack.

Then, in mid-October, Belt received a signal which both astonished and pleased him. His squadron was to be pulled out of North Persia – in fact, the whole Russian Armoured Car Division was being pulled out of Trans-Caucasia and had been ordered to proceed by rail with all speed to Odessa. As the men loaded the cars onto barges which, to save time, were to be towed back up the lake to Sharafkhaneh, some joked that the unit was seeing so much of Russia that it should be re-styled as 'Locker's Tours'. The jest would find sour echoes in the Admiralty's corridors of power a few weeks later.

The train of events leading to this startling development had begun the minute Locker Lampson had driven into Keupri Keui, to be greeted by a breathless Lieutenant Hulls.

> 'Have you heard the news?' said he.
> 'What news?' said I; 'The news of my death?'
> 'No!' said he; 'The news of Rumania. She's declared war!'
> 'On which side?' we all yelled as one man.
> 'On ours!' he shouted.

Locker Lampson could hardly believe his luck. Here was the chance he needed to rescue his unit from the obscurity of the Caucasian front and pitch it into the limelight again. As always, he went straight to the top, leaving the following day for Tiflis, where the Grand Duke granted him an audience and entertained him to lunch.

> I ventured to point out to him that the severe autumn and winter in the Caucasus would prevent the use of the cars for at least eight months, and that as a force we did not feel justified in receiving Russian pay and remaining inactive for so prolonged a spell. He acknowledged the common sense of this plea and of my proposal to try and procure immediate fighting elsewhere, and generously gave me a letter to General Alexeiev suggesting transfer to a more active front. I left Kars on 2nd October and reached Petrograd on the 8th, proceeding at once to the Russian Headquarters at Mogilev. Here on 10th October I had an interview with General Alexeiev in which he expressed his readiness to transfer us to any front we felt most suitable to our work. Rumania having entered the war and a swift Russian advance down the Dobruja even up to Constantinople being the popular expectation, I asked to go to Rumania.
>
> 'You will not get fighting there with armoured cars,' said he.
> 'But the roads are excellent,' said I. 'And ere long the Rumanians

will have entered Transylvania, where the country is ideal for armoured car work.'

'But you will not fight in Transylvania,' said he. 'You will be lucky to fight in Rumania at all.' And he shook his head. 'Fighting in Rumania cannot be sustained.'

'But it has started,' said I. 'The Rumanians are already in Transylvania.'

He did not exactly smile, but his lips curved out sadly.

'Not for long,' said he. 'They will be out of there and back before you can reach them.'

'But the Dobruja! Can't we get a run for our money there?'

'Perhaps, if you are quick; but the roads are few and the swamps plentiful – and you must be quick.'

'But surely a country which enters a war must fight, and to be with the Rumanians will mean that we shall have fighting?'

'Not so,' said he. 'Better for you to go to Galicia, where roads are good, and wait there for a future campaign.'

'But that means waiting months,' said I.

'Yes; many months. But whenever an advance or retreat takes place, it will be registered and felt in Galicia. And here the highways offer scope. Shall I send you to Schmerinke?' And he bent over his map and picked the place out with an unerring forefinger.

'No, sir,' I pleaded politely. 'Not there for a dull winter. But please to Odessa – a halfway house, from where we may turn either to Rumania or Galicia, even as the battle sways.'

'Be it so.'

The appropriate signals were despatched to Gregory and to Belt, and the following day Locker Lampson was again received by the Czar. On 13th October he set off for England, impelled by his political instincts to be seen once more at the centre, using as an excuse the need to re-equip the unit with more suitable vehicles and, at the Grand Duke's suggestion, to explore the possibility of obtaining a flight of aircraft which could perform forward reconnaissance for the squadrons.

Although some of the cars were still on their way down from the Mush plain when the movement order arrived, Gregory did extremely well and managed to get both squadrons entrained at Kars by 17th October. The journey was painfully slow and Odessa was not reached until 31st October; Belt had further to come and did not arrive until 4th November. All rail traffic out of the Caucasus was routed through Baku, where the smell of crude oil hung heavily in the air; it was a place some of the men would return to. Elsewhere, at Derbent station, an attempt to give food to a group of manacled political prisoners awaiting transit to Siberia almost resulted in a confrontation with their Russian guards.

The few documents to survive this period do not mention the fact, but the transit arrangements were almost certainly expedited through the office of the Grand Duke's British Military Attaché, a major of the Black Watch who had lost an eye the previous year at Ypres. He was a thoughtful man who spoke little but then to some point, and was well liked. He was a future Viceroy of India and in another war he would give Britain one of her most resounding victories when her fortunes were at their lowest ebb. His name, he told the RNAS officers, was Archibald Wavell.

At Odessa the unit was given a banquet at the Stock Exchange and then treated to a Gala Performance at the Opera House, reputed to be one of the most splendid in Europe. The programme consisted of excerpts from *The Demon, The Queen of Spades* and *Carmen* and was greatly enjoyed by many to whom Grand Opera had previously been a mystery. On 10th November Gregory and the Acting Consul General, Mr Picton Bagge, gave a return dinner for the civic dignitaries and the senior naval and military officers of the garrison. The following day Gregory was ordered to have the unit ready to entrain for the front; as Alexeiev had feared, the Rumanians had been routed and the Russians were now rushing all the troops they could into the country in an attempt to stabilise the line.

Locker Lampson had fully intended that his stay in London should be a short one, but in the event he was away for three months. Of this period both his articles for *Lloyd's Magazine* and his unpublished memoirs are curiously silent; nor do the unit's papers contain any hint of what took place. He was carrying letters to the King from the Czar, the Grand Duke and Alexeiev, which he no doubt delivered, but the deliberate omission of such a period leads one to the conclusion that he found the visit neither pleasant nor rewarding, and that he may even have been within an ace of losing his command.

It goes almost without saying that there were those at the Admiralty who were only too pleased to have the wandering and wilful Commander within their grasp for once. His deception at Alexandrovsk had been tolerated; that he had, over Their Lordships' heads, obtained the Czar's approval for the continuance of the Russian venture was something which had to be borne but which was unlikely to be either forgiven or forgotten; and now, without even the courtesy of consulting them, he had arranged for the transfer of a British Naval unit from one theatre of war to another. This was a breach of discipline bordering on contempt and was not going to be tolerated.

In defence, Locker Lampson would have pleaded that the urgency of the situation merited the *fait accompli*, which he was now in London to justify. There was also the need to maintain the prestige of British arms in Russian eyes, since there was already talk that the Western Allies were prepared to leave the burden of war to Russia. If the less stuffy were inclined to regard the Commander's impertinence with well concealed humour, he was certainly not going to be allowed to escape unscathed. It would do no harm to let him sweat for a while over his uncertain future; in the meantime the unit could be left in the capable hands of Gregory, a regular officer who knew the rules and would stick to them.

The request for aircraft was rejected immediately; nor were Their Lordships prepared to exchange the Lanchesters for Rolls Royce armoured cars; they had, it was felt, already spent more than enough on this private army and they were not prepared to spend more on a re-equipment programme. Wisely, Locker Lampson did not press the point.

In one area of the equipment field he had, however, been successful. During the early days in the Caucasus Locker Lampson had observed that with the exception of his own Rolls, the vehicles which performed best were the Model T Ford tenders, which had a high ground clearance. The unit still had a home base at Newport, Monmouthshire, and Locker Lampson had issued orders for several of these vehicles to be converted to light armoured cars and shipped out to Russia.

The vehicle was designed by Chief Petty Officer L. Gutteridge, who calculated that even the simple conversion he planned would double the Model T's weight of 10 cwt, and allowed for this by using stronger suspension springs and tie rods on the back axle. The 5mm armour plate was attached to an angle-iron framework which was in turn bolted to the chassis, and consisted of a housing for the engine and radiator, a tall cab for the driver, and an open-topped superstructure at the rear, the suspension being partially protected by wheel discs. The vehicle was armed with a rear-facing Maxim, the crew of which sat behind the driver's cab, protected by a square 9mm gunshield. Quick release clamps permitted the gun to be removed for ground action. A large 10 gallon petrol tank and a patent Stepney Wheel completed the conversion. Nine such vehicles were built by G. Allen and Sons of Tipton, and had already been despatched some time before Locker Lampson arrived back in the United Kingdom.

While Locker Lampson awaited his fate, November drifted into

December and soon the Festive Season opened. On Christmas Day itself the Duty Operator at the Admiralty was startled to receive a signal from Russia :

> BRITISH ARMOURED CARS UNDER MY COMMAND IN ACTION DECR 25th IN RUMANIA FURTHER COMMUNICATION LATER ENDS
> ACTING COMMANDER GREGORY

A second signal was received on Boxing Day :

> BRITISH ARMOURED CAR DIVISION IN ACTION IN RUMANIA DECR 26th STOP NO CARS LOST STOP CASUALTIES LIEUT LUCAS SHADWELL SLIGHTLY WOUNDED LIEUT SMILES SLIGHTLY WOUNDED OPERATIONS STILL PROCEEDING ENDS

It seems unlikely that either was shown to Locker Lampson before the holiday ended. Further signals continued to arrive in a steady stream.

> FOLLOWING ADDITIONAL CASUALTIES BRITISH ARMOURED CAR DIVISION RUMANIA STOP CPO MCFARLANE 2772 PO FEAR 2989 WOUNDED ENDS

and

> BRITISH ARMOURED CAR DIVISION CONTINUOUSLY IN ACTION RUMANIA STOP REPORT LOSS ONE SMALL ARMOURED CAR DESTROYED TO PREVENT FALLING INTO ENEMY'S HANDS STOP GUN SAVED ENDS NUMBER 534
> ACTING COMMANDER GREGORY

For Locker Lampson these signals turned the knife in the wound and threatened his political as well as his military career. He was well aware that some of a politician's bitterest enemies lie within his own party and that the fact that he had spent Christmas peacefully in England while his command was involved in heavy sustained action would inevitably be used against him. It was imperative that he should return to the front at once.

Whether the Admiralty relented of its own accord or whether he used his considerable influence to bring pressure to bear is not known, but he was permitted to remain in command and left England at once. He would return to a unit which had won itself a reputation for hard fighting in which he had had no part. He would not kick over the traces again, but he was angry and resentful; clearly he had made several serious errors of judgement, and the long journey gave him ample time to ponder them.

CHAPTER FIVE

Battle in the Mud

Locker Lampson's principal mistake, in which he was not alone and which he later frankly admitted, lay in imagining that Rumania's entry into the war could in any way benefit the Allies. In fact her participation was a disaster which placed yet further strain on the overburdened Russian war machine and expedited the collapse of the Czar's regime.

For the first two years of the war Rumania, flanked on three sides by the Central Powers, had wisely chosen to remain neutral. A cardinal factor in Rumanian politics, however, was the question of the three million ethnic Rumanians living across the frontier in Austro-Hungarian Transylvania, and public opinion demanded incorporation of this province into a Greater Rumania. The accession of King Ferdinand on the death of his uncle to 1914 encouraged those who souht to resolve the question by open war, although the real driving force behind the movement was his wife, Queen Marie, a granddaughter of Queen Victoria noted for her strong will and ambition. A staunch ally was found in the incredibly convoluted personality of the Prime Minister, M. Bratianu, who nevertheless refused to intervene until victory seemed assured. By the autumn of 1916, however, it seemed that the moment had arrived.

In June the Russian army group commanded by General Alexi Brusilov had launched a surprise offensive on the south-western sector of the front which, by September, had thrown the Austrians back as far as the Carpathian foothills. The line had been stabilised by the arrival of German troops drawn from the Western Front, and by Russian exhaustion. This was to be the swan song of the old Imperial Army, for, although it was its most successful operation of the war, that success was bought at the terrible price of 550,000 casualties, adding fuel to the fires of disillusion and despair which were already burning on the home front. For his part, Brusilov was embittered by the lack of support which he had received from his fellow army group commanders and disgusted by the inefficiencies and graft which kept him starved of vital munitions and reinforcements: the experience drove him firmly into the revolutionary camp.

The view from Bucharest was somewhat different. Bratianu did not care one way or the other for Russia's difficulties, but he knew that Brusilov had inflicted losses amounting to 700,000 men on Austria-Hungary, and it seemed as though the ancient empire of the Habsburgs was incapable of absorbing much further punishment. On 27th August he declared war on Austria and Germany and launched an invasion of Transylvania.

Rumania possessed a large army, but it lacked experience of modern war and its opponents were now veteran troops. It dressed in sky-blue and was regarded by Locker Lampson's men as 'a Chocolate Soldier outfit'. Initially it made some progress against the Austrians and was about to continue its advance when its whole strategy was suddenly unhinged.

Bratianu's declaration of war had not included his southern neighbour, Bulgaria, and few Rumanian troops had been left along the common frontier. Bulgaria was, however, already allied with Austria and Germany and it was naive to assume that she would not take advantage of the situation to strike at her old enemy. The Bulgarians attacked on 1st September and began advancing up the Black Sea coast, capturing the vital port of Constanza on 22nd October. Forced to strip their Transylvanian front of divisions with which to meet this threat, the main Rumanian army was defeated and thrown back across its own border by General Erich von Falkenhayn's German 9th Army. The continued advance of the Bulgarians down the Danube and into the Dobruja compelled the Russians, most unwillingly, to pour troops into this area in order to protect their own southern flank, and it was onto this already stricken field that the British armoured cars had been summoned.

The unit had left Odessa by rail on 14th November, travelling by way of Bolgrad to Reni, where the vehicles were unloaded. It had been intended to motor from here to the front, but the weather had deteriorated, snow alternating with heavy rain, and Gregory did not consider the roads passable. The cars were therefore loaded onto three enormous decked grain barges which were towed upstream by a paddle steamer, passing Galatz and Braila on 25th November and reaching Hirsova on the 27th. For Gregory the journey held echoes of the past, for he was a qualified Danube pilot and had conned HMS *Barham* up the river as far as Galatz during a courtesy visit in 1907.

Hirsova was now occupied by General Sirelius' hard-fighting IVth Siberian Corps, which had recently repulsed elements of the Bulgarian advance guard. As a result of the fighting much of the town lay gutted and in ruins and there was some difficulty in finding weatherproof billets.

Sirelius told Gregory that he did not believe the enemy to be present in large numbers and that he intended to incorporate the cars in a spoiling attack which he hoped would result in a Bulgarian withdrawal towards Constanza and the important Danube crossing at Cernavoda; Numbers 1 and 3 Squadrons, under respectively Lieutenant-Commander Belt and Lieutenant Smiles, would support the attack at Topalul, some fifteen miles to the south, while Lieutenant-Commander Wells-Hood's Number 2 Squadron carried out a similar operation a little further to the east, near the village of Pantilimon Ustin. On 28th November all three squadron commanders went out to reconnoitre the ground they would have to cross; Belt and Smiles, apparently travelling in the same vehicle, were treated to an air-burst by the Bulgarian artillery, and received superficial wounds from small shell splinters.

At Topalul the attack went in on 30th November, supported by the Russian artillery and the fire of Rumanian warships on the river. The scene was picturesque and, as Petty Officer Baker was to recall, the atmosphere was a little unreal. 'At twelve the monitors opened fire together with the batteries. I walked down to the river to watch them but could not realise that the battle was commencing. A band was playing and the surroundings seemed enjoyable until the enemy replied by sending shells back. Even then it was interesting.'

Gregory and the squadron commanders are known to have written a report on the subsequent action, but this is not among the unit's papers and it seems likely that it was removed at a later date by Locker Lampson and its contents incorporated in an account which appears in his memoirs.*

> One Russian and one English car led the attack and ran up the same road in support of the infantry advancing on either side. The enemy trenches were deep and protected by a webbing of barbed wire, but the road defence was less highly organised, and if the cars could conquer the mud they might even reach and enfilade the Bulgarians where they lay. Both cars were powerful and well equipped and, despite a hail of bullets, they kept on. The Russian forged ahead under her higher horse-power, paused in order to back into battle, and then reversed right into a lake of mud and remained locked fast in this slimy

* The details are confirmed by the diaries of Petty Officers Round, Martin, Baker and Spencer.

embrace. Sub-Lieutenant Lefroy in his car was not far behind and, seeing this misadventure, steered clear of the slough and was able, despite the concentration of every enemy Maxim in the neighbourhood upon his car, to reach the first line of wire and pepper the trenches facing him. But to win a really effective vantage point he must also back his car and in turning it too dropped into soft ground. A shell simultaneously exploded at the side, shifting the whole superstructure so that the turret would no longer revolve and dislocating the gears so that only the first speed would work. Seeing this plight, the enemy poured their fire upon the car and put every Maxim out of action.* It is a miracle that she escaped, but after prolonged efforts at swinging her free, Lefroy tore the car out and on one speed she limped back at a snail's pace into safety.

A second Russian car was now in the field and dashing forward to assist the first. But it, too, struck mud and embedded a score of yards from his fellow. At once Sub-Lieutenant Walford swooped out with his car to the rescue, drawing Maxim after Maxim of the enemy as he advanced. He won the flats and got to within forty yards of where the Russian car lay up to the axles against the barbed wire, and searched the trenches near him again and again. But the impact of accumulated metal was terrific. It failed, indeed, to piece the armour, but shattered the bare thought of a continuous frontal attack. In fact, the enemy bullets sprayed against the driver's shield in such numbers that, although harmless in themselves, they threw off nickel splashes in a sort of mist which obscured the driver's view. Walford got the car to reverse and fired uninterruptedly with excellent effect until his car, too, foundered in the mud. Still he stuck to it, keeping the Bulgarians near him deep in their trenches and picking off those who exposed themselves, until a lucky enemy shot ripped up the casing of his Maxim and put it out of action. The feat of extricating the car was prodigious, but she struggled forth after two of the crew had been wounded. As for Walford and the driver, their faces a bleeding rash from the minute pinpoints of nickel flung off by striking bullets.†

The cars first bogged, however, had not stirred and no one had yet managed to reach them. Lieutenant-Commander Belt, therefore, who had been wounded the day previously in the hip and who consequently could not sit but only crouch in the car, gallantly himself ran out to the rescue. But the treachery of the soil was very baffling and the soft

---

* The Maxim, it will be recalled, was a water-cooled weapon. Once the water jacket had been punctured and the coolant drained away the gun rapidly overheated and became unusable. It was some time before fighting vehicle designers adopted air-cooled machine guns as standard.

† Locker Lampson is describing the phenomenon known as Bullet Splash, which had already been noted during the first tank attack on the Western Front, a few weeks earlier. Subsequently, tank crews were issued with slotted metal goggles and a chain-mail face mask, but none of this protective equipment seems to have reached Russia.

ground yielded, clung to his wheels and held them fast. For a quarter of an hour he remained a target for all the available enemy fire, firing himself continuously, and it was not until his driver had tightened the epicyclic gears that he could free the car. He found a further advance impossible, but finished off his ammunition at pointblank range when perforce he must return.

On the way back he met Sub-Lieutenant Gawler running up to assist, but stopped him and ordered him out of action. The condition of the ground was deplorable, the road had become pocked with shell holes, and was now the object of a merciless artillery concentration. Moreover, night was fast approaching and the outlines of the road could no longer be distinguished from the mud flats on each side. With unspeakable difficulty, Belt and Gawler withdrew in the deepening dark, and the cars' work was over for that day. But it is satisfactory to be able to state that the diversion here created by their activity forced an enemy concentration of guns and men upon this sector, which enabled the Russians to take Hill 132 on the left flank and Hill 69 on the right beside the river.

Night passed, a medley of noises and strange lights, and dawn broke upon cars at attention and expectant. Weather checked an early sally again and it was mid-day before Lieutenant Sholl and his unit could leave cover, dash out over the intervening hill and swoop down upon the forward enemy trenches. But the Bulgarians were more than ready, and a murderous first swept the roadway and tore huge holes in the path. It was madness to attempt a passage, and the cars were reluctantly recalled. Attack after attack had been made against the enemy and failed and casualties among the Russians were mounting up every moment. There were no reserves ready or expected, the troops were 'done brown' from fatigue, and the presence of Germans amongst our latest captives promised nothing but an inky outlook for the morrow.

It was 2nd December and an exhausted Russian army found itself too weary to attack and must have a respite for reform. So our cars under Lieutenant-Commander Belt were ordered out that day by way of a blind and to conceal the Russian need for rest and recuperation. Walford got his car right up to the enemy lines and not fifty paces from the wrecked Russian cars. He continued firing with excellent results until his gun jammed irremediably. He was forced to retire and reached safety with a broken baseplate, from which all the grease had run out. Gawler accompanied him; but, in turning to reverse, dropped his front wheels into a shell hole concealed by mud and broke a torque rod. Still he stuck to it, and put a couple of Bulgarian parties out of action before he withdrew.

For Petty Officer Baker, the spectacle of the preliminary bombardment had soon been replaced by a harsher reality. 'The Russians advanced from their trenches, being cut down in hundreds, but it was not until the wounded came in that we realised the full horror of war. Read, Goodier and myself assisted the surgeon. We dressed wounds on men who a few hours earlier were in the prime of life but were now terribly mutilated. They were coming in in a continuous stream. Some were able to reach the dressing station, others were dead on arrival.'

Petty Officer Martin, too, was shaken by what he had seen.

> They are a poor lot of men. They are Siberian regiments, some with no boots on their feet, and they look as though they have had no food for a week. They are very young, or old men. A party of us volunteered to help them with the wounded. As they came in in carts we carried them into dressing rooms set up in old houses. I saw some awful sights. All the wounds were very dirty with shrapnel and bullets still in the flesh, the blood sticking the clothes to the wound. We carried them in, the nurses dressed them and then we carried them to tents and there laid them on straw.

Surgeon-Commander Scott and his brother, Surgeon-Lieutenant Maitland Scott, set up their own casualty clearing station at Topalul. The first wounded began arriving during the evening of 30th November, and from then on the two surgeons and their staff worked incessantly, dealing with 2,000 cases in 24 hours. Their reputation soared, and in the months to come Russians would beg for British medical treatment rather than go to their own clearing stations; in fairness to the latter they were hideously overworked, ill-equipped and under-supplied, and could not hope to compete.

Over at Pantilimon Ustin No 2 Squadron had gone into action on 1st December.

> Wells Hood had bided his chance. It was not for nothing that he had fought already in this war with armoured cars at Antwerp, in South-West Africa, in France, Belgium and Turkey, and he calculated his opportunities with rare patience and fortitude. The enemy infantry had decided to advance rapidly and expected little opposition in this quarter, believing as they did that the British cars were wholly reserved for the other flank. Wells Hood waited until they were far ahead of their trenches and moving up in the open, and then he sprang out to within sixty yards of them before they dreamed of an attack. It was in vain they fell upon their faces or tore back to their trenches; his cars caught them clean and within the radius of hundreds of yards they were stricken and mowed down. The advance as a whole slackened, wavered, then ceased, and before many minutes the Bulgarians to a

man were back under cover. Still Wells Hood pursued them, harrying the trenches.

He had ordered Lieutenants Ingle and Mitchell to follow at intervals of 150 yards and these cars, leaving the main road, struck across country to reach a sector of trench which Wells Hood could not cover. But the going was shocking, and both cars were trapped in the slimy surface many yards from their objective. In vain did Wells Hood struggle to reach them, but the intervening fields were a morass. In fact, as he turned to reverse over a ditch, his power failed him so suddenly that, gazing out of the observation hole, he saw a pool of petrol on the ground whither it had flowed from a couple of bullet holes in the tank. But the car was a Rolls Royce, fitted with a spare gravity tank near the steering gear, and at once he switched this on.* But before the new petrol supply could reach the engine it had stopped and the gunner, Petty Officer Vaughan, pluckily leapt out in front amid a deluge of bullets and started it up. After which the car kept solidly at its excellent work unchecked, and fell back only after three hours' ferocious fighting.

Meanwhile, Ingle and Mitchell were perilously placed. Their cars stood deep in the mire and no swinging or tightening of gears availed an inch. The Bulgarians poured their shells and bullets upon these luckless derelicts until the tyres were ripped to ribbons and the Maxims had become shreds of casing. Mitchell's car was put out of action first and finding it immovable and the Maxim useless, he and his men crawled out at the back, which afforded some shelter, and crept to a shell hole.

Ingle's car was further from the lines and protected by the other, and the mud round it was shallower, but the engine had stopped in one last mighty heave to get free. Ingle, sooner than wait for one of his men, jumped out himself to start her up. He succeeded and was back in the car like a flash. But the car's effort of extrication once more brought the engine to a stop, and Ingle must jump out again to wind her up. A bullet struck him above the knee, shattering his leg, and he fell clinging desperately to the starting handle. In vain he sought to drag himself to the back and regain the car. But the shells crashed all around, tearing the woodwork to pieces; the Maxim simultaneously collapsed, the turret twisted, and both car and armament ceased to function. Ingle shouted to the men to descend and take cover, and dropped himself over the lip of a new-formed crater into comparative shelter within. Even then there was no respite and the exploding shells smothered him with earth and debris, while for upwards of an hour the car was shot at by every gun and rifle for hundreds of yards.

His thigh smashed and in agony, Ingle drifted into unconsciousness for

* In addition to Locker Lampson's Rolls tourer, the unit had one Rolls armoured car. Mitchell and Ingle were in Lanchesters.

long periods. His crew, calling to him from their own shell hole and receiving no answer, assumed him to be dead and crawled over to join Mitchell and his men, one of whom was also wounded. At length the Bulgarians came out to round them up and lead them off, glancing perfunctorily at the half-smothered Ingle on the way.

Ingle came to to find himself on his back, staring up at a cloudless sky, then he passed out again. He had an impression of further shells exploding, small arms fire cracking overhead, the running of many feet and hoarse cries. When he next regained consciousness it was dark. A searchlight was sweeping No Man's Land and there was sporadic splutter of rifle fire. He was dimly aware of the thud of hooves and the sound of muted voices and, looking over the edge of his shell hole, saw a party of men and horses working around Mitchell's car.

Not unnaturally he took them for Bulgarians and decided to try and crawl back to the Russian lines, a mile and a half distant. The only way he could move was by lying on his back and pushing himself along on his hands, having first propped his broken limb on top of his sound leg to prevent it dragging along the ground. Every ten minutes he was forced to rest from this agonising progress. A severe frost had fallen and the ground was frozen hard. Soon his hands were raw and bleeding, but he stuck doggedly to his task until dawn broke. He was now utterly exhausted and was becoming feverish. Glancing over his shoulder he saw that the Russian wire was only 80 yards distant. Using a phrase which had been taught to every man in the unit he used the last of his strength to shout, 'I am an Englishman fighting for Russia and am wounded!' Within minutes a sergeant and six men had run out to carry him in.

Ironically, this tremendous feat of courage and endurance had not been strictly necessary. Very possibly at Wells Hood's urging, Colonel Zavalinshevsky of the 39th Siberian Rifle Regiment had not only mounted a local counter-attack which had pushed the Bulgarians back several hundred yards during the afternoon, but had also provided No 2 Squadron with horse teams and a working party with which to recover the derelict cars, and this had been successfully accomplished under the direction of Lieutenant Hunter shortly after dusk. The party had been exposed by the Bulgarian searchlight and, although sniped at constantly, had completed its tasks without casualties. The Russians had then retired to the trenches which they had held during the morning. As a result, Wells Hood was pleased to be able to recommend the men of the working party for decoration. They were: Second-Lieutenant Paveloff; Peter Gladushoff, mounted scout; Philip Novikoff and

Andre Feodorohen, Maxim gunners, all of 39th Siberian Rifles.

On its own, Sirelius' spoiling attack might well have succeeded in stabilising the Dobruja sector, although IV Corps' success had been bought at the fearful price of 9,000 casualties. Elsewhere, however, the main Rumanian army had been decisively routed at the battle of the Arges River and Bucharest itself fell on 6th December. Sirelius was now in danger of being trapped between the Bulgarians in the Dobruja and the Austro-German forces which were now advancing steadily east and which would soon be bringing pressure to bear on his right flank. Only an immediate withdrawal to the north would extricate his command from the dangerous situation in which it now found itself. Gregory was summoned to the headquarters of 6th Army, under whose control Sirelius was operating, and told that his cars would cover the movement.

> I arrived back at Hirsova at 10 p.m. on 8th December to find that orders had already been given for the evacuation of the town. Lieutenant-Commander Belt had acted very promptly, immediately commandeering two Rumanian barges at the jetty and loading up all our stores, provisions, ammunition, repair staff, broken down cars, etc. One barge had already left for Reni by the time I arrived and the loading up of the second was proceeding rapidly. After reporting to the Chief of Staff IVth Siberian Corps, I was ordered to take over the defence of Hirsova until its complete evacuation.
>
> The British Armoured Car Division, together with the only remaining Russian armoured car and some men of the Russian armoured car section, remained for the defence of the port against hostile attack by monitors and other river craft, from 9th December to 13th December.* During this period the town was completely evacuated with the exception of a small Russian cavalry patrol working in conjunction with us. We had continuous fine rain for some days which, owing to the already bad state of the roads, caused me great anxiety as to our line of retreat.
>
> On 13th December I received orders that I was to leave Hirsova with the British Armoured Car Division at daylight on 14th December for the town of Alebei Chioi. The roads were extremely bad in places and great care had to be taken in driving owing to their pitted condition and the holes being covered with thick mud and water. I arrived at Alebei Chioi at 4 p.m. on 14th December and arranged for the billeting of the force. The first cars of Numbers 1 and 2 Squadrons arrived by daylight on 15th December, and at 4 p.m. on this day No 3 Squadron arrived. By dark all cars had arrived except one transport

---

* To Gregory's disgust the Rumanian monitors gave no assistance at all, disappearing rapidly downstream in a cloud of their own funnel smoke.

lorry, which had got badly bogged and caught fire. This was brought in during the night by a special working party sent out for the purpose.

On the 16th Gregory received a warning order from Sirelius that the cars were required at Braila, fifty miles distant and on the opposite bank of the Danube, and that they should arrive not later than the 19th. This was a tall order, but Lieutenant Lamkert and his fellow liaison officer, Lieutenant Reppmann, who had served with No 1 Squadron in North Persia, were sent out on a route reconnaissance. All plans were, however, thrown out of gear by a Bulgarian breakthrough the following day which threw the whole of the Dobruja into a turmoil. Gregory's thoughts on the Rumanian army, 'a rabble, blocking their own roads and completely disorganised', were sharply interrupted when a mounted orderly galloped up with fresh orders: the unit was to proceed to Tulchea in the Danube delta, where barges would be available for its evacuation.

There is a saying to the effect that no officer really understands war unless he has been involved in a defeat and an enforced retreat. An orderly withdrawal under pressure is the most difficult of operations to execute, but Gregory was equal to the task, calmly and quickly devising a logical method by which the unit's very diverse elements could be evacuated by separate routes but which would still enable his command to function once the river had been crossed.

> At 9 a.m. the whole force left Alebei Chioi and proceeded to Tulchea, arriving at 11.30 a.m. on 17th December. The cars were parked on the quay and the men were billeted pending the arrival of the barges. Great confusion existed at Tulchea, orders having been just received that the town was to be evacuated within 48 hours.
>
> At 10 p.m. I was informed that at 2 a.m. I would be given one barge for the British and Russian armoured cars to take them to Reni, and also that I would be given half another barge to take some of the transport cars to Ismail. The matter being urgent and barge accommodation very limited, and having the additional responsibility of saving the Scottish Women's Hospital cars and nurses,* suddenly thrown on my hands at the last minute, I divided the force into three as follows:
>
> 1. All the light transport and touring cars under Lieutenant-Commander Belt, which I despatched at midnight by road to Isaksha to cross the pontoon bridge at that place and proceed to Bolgrad to await further orders from me.

* This was a privately sponsored organisation formed from volunteer nurses specially for service on the Eastern Front. It operated on some of the most difficult and dangerous sectors of the front and acquired a justly heroic reputation.

2. All the heavy transport including two transport waggons belonging to the Scottish Women's Hospital with the attendant nurses, I placed on the barge proceeding to Ismail under Sub-Lieutenant Turner, with orders to proceed from Ismail to Bolgrad to join Lieutenant-Commander Belt, and await further orders from me.

3. All the fighting cars, ammunition, etc, I took under my command on board the barge with the Russian armoured cars and proceeded to Reni.

We were delayed 24 hours on the way up owing to the non-opening of the pontoon bridge at Isaksha over which refugees and troops were continually passing in an unending stream.

The cars reached Reni during the afternoon of the 19th. Gregory was seriously worried about their condition after the fighting near Hirsova and the wear and tear they had sustained on the road during the withdrawal, and although he was anxious to rejoin the Siberians he could not see how, in the present circumstances, he could help. It would, he reflected, be something of a minor miracle if he could scrape together one serviceable squadron.

The minor miracle was, in fact, already waiting for him in the shape of Chief Petty Officer Gutteridge and the men of the home rear party, who had just completed their rail journey from Archangel bringing with them the converted Ford Armoureds. Lamkert also rejoined at Reni. His opinion was that the roads around Braila were unfit for use by armoured cars, and in this he was supported by Captain Grabovoi, the commander of the Russian cars, who had already obtained leave for his detachment to be withdrawn to Odessa. Gregory was not, however, prepared to accept that the position was as bad as had been described, and took a calculated risk.

> I requested that my transport cars at Bolgrad should be directed to rejoin me at Galatz, and that my two barges with the fighting cars should be removed from Reni to Galatz so as to be nearer the fighting line and not left uselessly exposed to bombardment at Reni. By doing so I fully realised that I was placing the whole of my command in a position from which it was very probable that it would be most difficult to extricate them, as our line of retreat by river to Reni was liable to be cut in a very few days; there were no roads leading to the rear by which we could retreat with armoured cars from Galatz and the railways were completely blocked, either by carelessness or otherwise of the Rumanians. However, to weigh against this, we were a fighting force, the Russian armoured cars had refused to come to the front owing to the existing conditions, and I considered it my duty to uphold the prestige of the British to advance rather than retire. Succeeding events have proved that I decided rightly.

A Special Service Squadron 'A' was formed under the command of Lieutenant W. D. Smiles, consisting of the two Heavies *Ulster* and *Londonderry*, six Ford Armoureds, one Lanchester lorry, two Ford lorries and a Pierce Arrow heavy lorry. This left Reni by barge on 21st December and arrived at Braila the same day.

Smiles immediately pushed out patrols to cover the Russians' open right flank. The enemy was not encountered but the going was vile and he returned to Braila on the 23rd, being ordered to establish the unit at the hamlet of Valei Canepei. The following day Sirelius told him that he would be fighting in support of the 124th Division at Vizurul, and he went forward to report to Colonel Balgramo, commanding the division's 2nd Brigade. The Colonel conducted him through the village and into the trenches, which were under artillery fire from Roobla, reported to contain two batteries and to be full of Bulgarian infantry. While they were observing a shell exploded nearby, killing two Russians, while the splinters nicked Lieutenant Edwards and Chief Petty Officer MacFarlane. With Balgramo's approval, Smiles decided to shoot up the village at dawn with his Heavies, the actual attack being made by Lieutenant Lucas Shadwell in *Ulster* with Sub-Lieutenant Henderson in *Londonderry* in reserve.

> Th car was in action from 7.21 a.m. until 7.35 a.m. [wrote Shadwell]. We fired slowly and deliberately, observing the range carefully and the effect of our shots. No movement of troops was seen, nor was any shot fired at us until we had gone 300 yards on the way back to our lines. We completely destroyed two houses, behind which the enemy's batteries were supposed to be situated. We used about 18 rounds for this purpose and the range was 1,200 yards. Later we fired at longer ranges into the village further behind, and along where we estimated the main road to run.

The outposts confirmed that the enemy had sustained casualties and damage, and Smiles was asked to repeat the dose the next day, 26th December. This was duly done, although *Londonderry* bogged down and had to be towed free, and *Ulster*, commanded by Sub-Lieutenant MacDowell, once again had a successful shoot.

At 0900 the cars were returning through Vizurul when heavy firing broke out all along the trench line and it was clear that the Bulgarians were launching a major attack. At Balgramo's request, Smiles obtained divisional headquarters' permission to bring up the rest of the cars, and ordered Henderson and MacDowell to return at once to Vizurul with the two Heavies and cover the Roobla road.

Both were short of ammunition and a despatch rider was sent back to bring up further supplies. Shadwell was directed to take the right fork in the village and hold the enemy's attack on that flank with his Ford Armoured.

Having completed his written orders, Smiles set off for Vizurul in his own Ford Armoured, arriving to find *Ulster* and *Londonderry* banging away at the enemy down the road. Bullets were cracking past and clanging and whining away off the armour.

'Don't fire unless you've got a target!' he shouted. 'The lorries are on their way up, but don't waste a single round!'

He then took the left fork, leading down to the hamlet of Perlita, and soon came across Balgramo manning the field telephone in his command post. His Siberians had lost heavily and he asked Smiles to go out beyond the barbed wire and hold off the attack.

At first the Ford Armoureds had been considered something of a joke, but Gutteridge had done his work well and the Model T's high ground clearance enabled it to cover the atrocious going rather better than the Lanchesters or the Heavies. However, like any machine subjected to hard usage, it did have its limitations, as Smiles found to his annoyance when his driver informed him that the reverse gear selector was not functioning correctly. This was extremely awkward, for the vehicle's layout was such that it could only engage effectively over the tail.

There was nothing for it but to go in forwards. Smiles passed through the wire and motored on for a further 500 yards before swinging the car across the road. The Maxim was traversed to its limit and fire opened on the advancing lines of infantry. They sank to earth immediately and began to return the fire.

When two belts had snaked their way through the breech of the gun, leaving their residue of hot brass cases littering the floor of the car, Smiles decided that he had achieved his object and that he could afford to retire a little towards the Russian lines.

The driver engaged reverse, let in his clutch, and the engine stalled. Smiles jumped over the side and swung the starting handle. The engine fired, but cut out again after they had covered only 50 yards. Smiles dismounted again and began swinging the handle once more, this time without result.

The car was now the target of every enemy weapon within range and was being struck repeatedly. Smiles was hit in the rump and sent sprawling. He rolled into the shallow road-side ditch where he was joined by his crew Petty Officer Classey and Leading Petty Officer

Graham. Both volunteered to try and start the car but Smiles would not let them, fearing that it would only stall again, and in any event the tyres were being cut to ribbons. Graham was sent back along the ditch to report to Shadwell, with strict instructions that no Russian lives were to be risked in attempts to help or extricate the car.

They remained in the ditch until dusk, Smiles having his wound dressed with difficulty, since any movement attracted concentrated rifle fire and machine-gun fire. The Bulgarian artillery also shelled the car from time to time, but was unable to score a direct hit. When darkness was complete Classey was able to start the engine, but reverse was still unobtainable. The car was bounced forward over the ditch, turned in the field and driven, with muscular assistance from Smiles, back onto the road, regaining the Russian lines without incident.

On the opposite flank Shadwell had reached the barbed wire and opened up with his Maxim. He quickly became the target of every weapon in the area and after firing about 50 rounds was wounded in the neck. The car was driven out of action by Petty Officer Ash.

In the centre the two Heavies had no difficulty in holding the Bulgarians in spite of the ammunition shortage and, as MacDowell's report shows, they eventually became the specific target of the enemy artillery.

> The enemy infantry were advancing in rushes on the Russian advance post. I opened fire on them at 700 yards with the Maxim and checked the advance slightly, but they started to dig themselves in about 400 yards away. I did not open fire with the Maxim until I observed a group of four or five men. I obtained two boxes of 3-pounder ammunition from Sub-Lieutenant Henderson's car, and later six more boxes of 3-pounder ammunition which we went out of action to get from Lieutenant Edwards about 11.30 a.m. I continued in action only firing when I obtained a target until 5 p.m., when the shell fire at the entrance to the village got so intense that I thought it advisable to take the car out of action.

Balgramo was delighted with the results of the day's work. His brigade had suffered 290 casualties, but some 380 Bulgarian rifles were collected during the night in front of the trenches. To the right and left the Russian line had caved in, but Vizurual had been held against all expectations, largely because of Smiles and his cars.

Smiles was one of those rare officers who find complete release in action. He concealed the fact that he had been wounded and next

Battle in the Mud 93

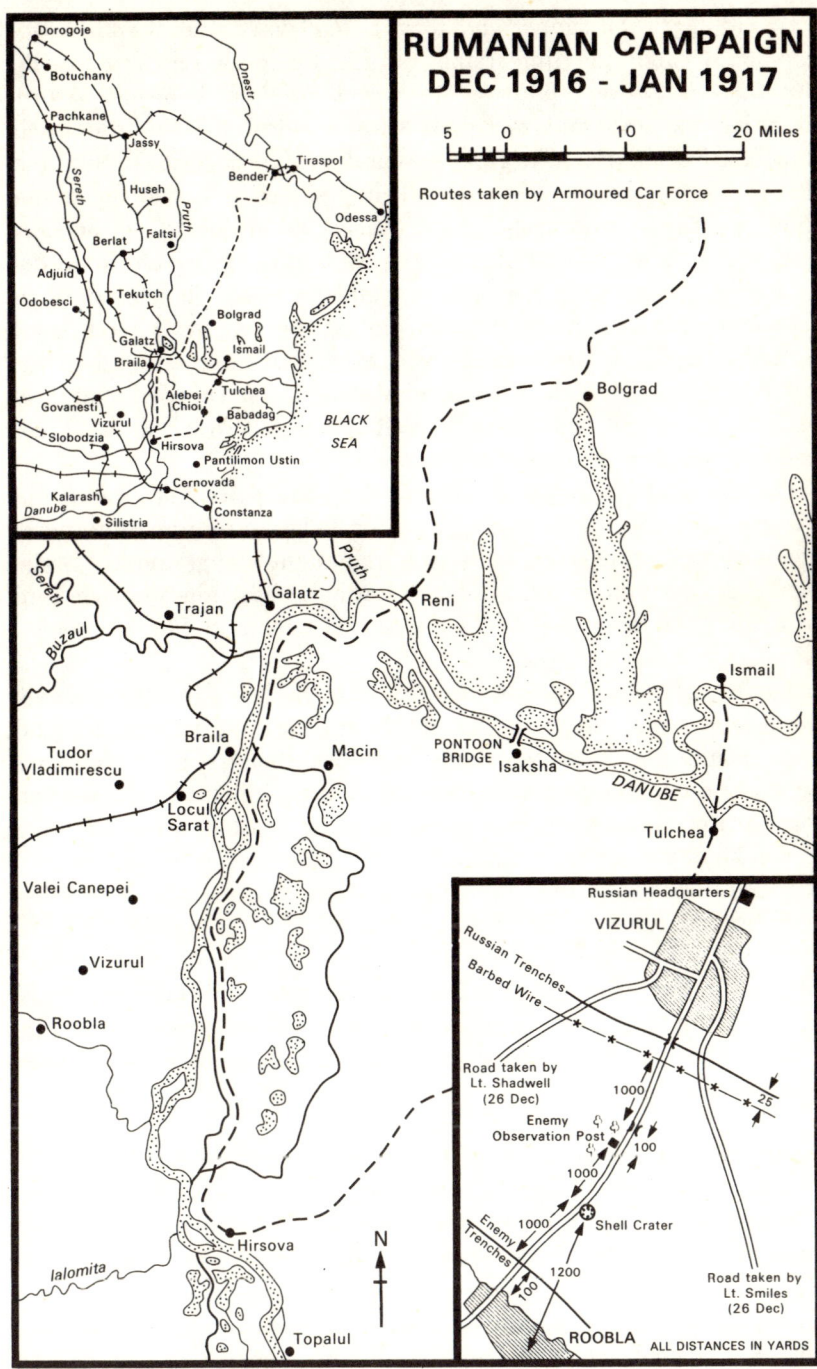

morning (27th December) he took *Ulster* down the Roobla road, hoping to catch the Bulgarians forming up for a renewed assault. But the enemy were prepared to bide their time, knowing Vizurul to be outflanked, and met him with a storm of fire from their trenches. Smiles retired a little way and then, using the Maxim and the 3-pounder, proceeded to rake their positions and shoot up everything in sight, including a house suspected of being an artillery observation post. The Bulgarians turned their guns on him, but whenever the ranging shell-bursts came too close he advanced or retired the car a short distance, frustrating their efforts. He remained in action until his ammunition was exhausted and returned to the village at dusk. By now his wound was common knowledge and, to his embarrassment, he found himself a hero word of whose deeds had even reached the ears of 6th Army Staff.

On the 28th orders were received for the potentially dangerous Vizurul salient to be evacuated and for Balgramo's brigade to retire approximately fifteen miles during the night. Balgramo requested Smiles to cover the withdrawal by creating a diversion and two Ford Armoureds commanded by Lieutenant Hunter and Sub-Lieutenant Kidd were detailed for the task.

Under cover of darkness the cars were pushed silently out along the Roobla road until they were level with the forward trenches, and then opened fire across No Man's Land while the last of the Russians pulled out. Hunter had been ordered to maintain his demonstration for at least half an hour, but stayed for three-quarters before deciding to break contact. In the entrance to the village, however, Kidd's Ford dropped into one of the numerous shell craters, smashing its steering gear beyond repair. The car was abandoned after the Maxim had been stripped out and the engine, radiator and petrol tank destroyed. The party then caught up the Russian rearguard and passed through, reaching the squadron's new headquarters at Locul Sarat at 0230. During the entire operation only one Russian soldier had been wounded.

Meanwhile, at Braila, Gregory had received a surprise visitor in the person of Colonel John Norton-Griffiths. Like Locker Lampson, Norton-Griffiths was a serving Member of Parliament and somewhat larger than life. He had taken part in the Jameson Raid, led a company of scouts during the Boer War, mined gold on the Ivory Coast, built a railway in Angola, and become one of the foremost civil engineering contractors of his day. On the outbreak of war he had raised a cavalry regiment and subsequently been the driving force behind mining operations in the Ypres salient.

When the defeat of its army had become inevitable, the Rumanian Government had promised to destroy the vital Ploesti oil-field and other installations to prevent their use by the Central Powers. Quite rightly, the Allies had no trust in Rumanian promises and had sent for Norton-Griffiths. In a scenario worthy of a thriller he had been told that he must, single-handed, virtually destroy the Rumanian economy, with only his batman for company. He had swept all opposition aside, frequently at the point of his revolver, and wreaked destruction and damage which was valued at £56,000,000. At Braila he was nearing the end of his mission, but Gregory provided him with a working party of twenty men under Sub-Lieutenant Lefroy to complete whatever remained to be done. He was subsequently honoured by the Czar and by his own government, but his engineer's conscience was to trouble him for the rest of his life. Falkenhayn later commented that the effects of his work were worse than a major defeat in the field for the Central Powers.

By 29th December Gregory was able to report to General Zurikoff, the commander of 6th Army, that the rest of the unit was ready for action. Zurikoff asked for a second squadron to cover Sirelius' right flank and Special Service Squadron 'B' was formed under Wells Hood for the purpose, consisting of the Rolls armoured, two Lanchesters, a Pierce Arrow Heavy, three Lanchester lorries, an ambulance and a staff car. It left for Tudor Vladimirescu on 31st December in a heavy snow storm, and during the next few days carried out a series of patrols without contacting the enemy. The roads, already barely negotiable, were carrying 'a continual stream of traffic, consisting of heavy artillery, transport and refugees, night and day, travelling in the direction of Jassy, and the main road was becoming so damaged that it was quite plain to see that if we did not receive orders in a day or two, great difficulty would be experienced in getting our cars over it'.

Smiles was back in action with *Ulster* on 1st January, having been ordered to report the 124th Division's headquarters at 0800.

> They ordered me to shell the village of Cuicei-Bismal and to advance forward from our own trenches with our infantry, who were making a counter-attack. I asked for a Russian officer to accompany me on the car so that he might point out to me the position of the enemy. I started from our own front line trenches at 12 noon. We turned the car and went into action backwards about half a mile from our trenches.

Our own infantry were now on our right flank and advanced against the enemy very bravely parallel with us. The enemy were sighted at 1,000 yards behind a small house and some trees. We immediately opened fire with the 3-pounder on this position, with Chief Petty Officer MacFarlane acting as No 1 Gunner. His first shot was direct on the line but over the house, his second just short, his third through the house. We had no more trouble from there. At the same time, we were firing at 1,000 yards with our Maxim and several of the enemy were observed to drop.

We then turned our attention to the right of the village of Cuicei-Bismal. The Russian officer told me that the range, which he had taken from the map, was three versts. We opened fire at 3,400 yards and reduced the sight down to 1,500 yards before any effect was seen, when MacFarlane put a shot into a large white house, the nearest of the village to us. Having now got the range, we searched the village thoroughly. After we had fired 68 rounds, the enemy's artillery fire got so intense, with shrapnel bursting over us, that I deemed it wise to get out of action and did so without delay, the shell-bursts following us for a mile down the road.

The infantry captain at the telephone box in the front line of trenches ordered me to go into action again, informing me that the village which we had shelled previously was now in the possession of our infantry, so after clearing the car of the empty cases and getting all the ammunition ready I proceeded up the road again. We turned the car round a quarter of a mile from our trenches and reversed towards the enemy. When we got within 50 yards of the position from which we had previously fired, the enemy's artillery opened a very fierce bombardment, the worst I have seen on this front. The house beside which we had previously been in position I saw crumble to pieces before my eyes, and shrapnel was bursting on all sides of us. I therefore ordered the car out of action at once, as I felt it was only a question of seconds before at least one member of the crew would be wounded or the whole car put out of action. On the way back to our trenches we picked up a wounded Russian soldier who had been hit in the head by shrapnel evidently intended for us.

On coming out of action, Smiles retired with his squadron to Braila and loaded his vehicles onto a barge destined for Galatz, following receipt of orders to that effect from Gregory that morning. Sirelius was horrified at the thought of losing the squadron, and telephoned the army commander, who had given his sanction to the orders. At length Zurikoff relented and, with mixed feelings, Smiles and his crews unloaded their charges again.*

* Sirelius told Zurikoff that the presence of the cars had a great moral effect on his men, and that the Bulgarians would never attack when they were present because of the heavy losses they incurred.

Gregory had requested the squadron's withdrawal because of alarming information which he had received from his senior Russian liaison officer, Captain Baron Girard de Contancon of the 10th Novgorod Dragoons, who had replaced Lamkert a few days previously when the latter had injured his leg. Girard had transferred from the cavalry to the armoured car service and was serving on 6th Army's staff when he was posted. He was, therefore, the ideal man for the job, and the records show him to have been urbane, acutely perceptive and highly professional.

He had warned Gregory that the Dobruja sector was on the point of collapse. This meant that the entire eastern bank of the Danube would soon be in enemy hands and that Braila and Galatz would inevitably be shelled from across the river. On 2nd January Gregory was able to verify the accuracy of Girard's forecast for himself.

> The battle raging in the Dobruja could be plainly witnessed from the quayside at Galatz and it was obvious that our troops were everywhere being driven back by superior forces, more especially by superior artillery. The town of Macin, the last in the Dobruja remaining in our hands, fell at 6 p.m. this evening.

The following day Zurikoff announced his intention of removing his headquarters to Bolgrad and gave permission for the unit, less Special Service Squadron 'A', to evacuate Galatz and establish a base for itself at Tiraspol, just over the Russian frontier. The remainder of the fighting vehicles had already been formed into Special Service Squadron 'C' under Lieutenant-Commander Belt, and was available for the defence of the town while the evacuation proceeded. Wells Hood received his recall on the 4th but due to the poor state of the roads did not reach Galatz until twenty-four hours later.

Meanwhile the back-loading of vehicles and stores by barge to Reni and thence by rail through Bolgrad to Tiraspol was continuing under the direction of the adjutant, Lieutenant-Commander Dye and his assistant, Lieutenant Hanna. For the second time Gregory took the Scottish Women's Hospital under his wing and saw them to safety. For a while he was also made responsible for a royal yacht *Prince Ferdinand of Rumania*, for which there was no fuel oil, until relieved of this duty by the Imperial Navy. By the 11th the evacuation was complete and the unit had established itself at Tiraspol.

Up at Braila Smiles had received on 2nd January a further Heavy armoured car, *Mountjoy*, a replacement for *Londonderry*, whose main armament traverse mechanism had given such trouble that the vehicle had had to be withdrawn for the fitters' attention at Repair Base. This addition was most useful, as he was now forced to operate in two directions simultaneously.

Ulster and two Ford Armoureds under Lieutenant Hunter were sent back to cover the withdrawal of 124th Division at Locul Sarat, while Sub-Lieutenant Kidd was sent across the pontoon bridge with *Mountjoy*, commanded by the newly commissioned Sub-Lieutenant Benson, and a further pair of Ford Armoureds to hold a bridgehead on the Macin road while the last Russian troops retreated from the Dobruja into Braila. Both missions were accomplished without incident or pressure from the enemy. At Locul Sarat Hunter went out looking for a German armoured car which had been reported in the area, but failed to provoke its appearance. On 4th January Kidd saw the Cossack cavalry rearguard safely across the river and then crossed himself. The bridge was blown up behind him.

The campaign was now effectively over. Braila could not be defended, and its evacuation began at once, Special Service Squadron 'A' being transported by rail to Galatz on 5th January. Zurikoff intended the town to be the pivot of his winter defence line and Smiles was ordered to place himself under the command of the 10th Division, which had been detailed as garrison; clearly, the Russians still regarded him as too valuable a property to be allowed to return to his own people.

CHAPTER SIX

The World Turned Upside Down

Commander Oliver Locker Lampson did not reach his unit's new base at Tiraspol until 15th January, and by then the campaign was over. His chagrin is understandable, since in Russian eyes the cars had performed prodigies and 6th Army Headquarters had announced the award of no less than 20 St George's Crosses and 26 St George's Medals to non-commissioned personnel.* From a personal viewpoint it seemed to him that the whole object of the Rumanian venture had been missed.

His first task, like that of an errant junior officer, was to prepare a full report concerning the reasons for the unit's move from the Caucasus to the Rumanian front and everything that had taken place since. This contained summaries of reports submitted by Gregory, Smiles and other officers, and these no doubt emphasised his feeling of being left out in the cold; much of what they said, particularly about the later fighting, was omitted. Again, as a leave rota to the United Kingdom had been started, it would soon become general knowledge at home that he had been absent from the front at the critical period, and neither his political opponents nor the electorate were likely to be sympathetic, whatever the reasons. There was, too, the question of re-establishing his own position among his officers and men.

We now see Locker Lampson at his least attractive. Plainly he regarded Gregory and, to a lesser degree, Smiles, as his rivals, and he did not like it. It seems more than likely that he provoked a disagreement with Gregory concerning some aspect of the latter's period of command. Gregory was, however, quite capable of standing up for himself and was entitled to point out, quite tartly, that this already covered most of the unit's history, including the months in the arctic wastes of Alexandrovsk, the move from the Caucasus and the fighting in the Dobruja. Tempers rose and Gregory, deciding that

* The names of the recipients are recorded in the appendix.

for the present it would be best if the two stayed out of each other's way, moved onto the *Prince Ferdinand*, which had been refuelled and handed back and which was now being used to supply Smiles at Galatz.

Clearing the air was not enough for Locker Lampson. On 1st February he wrote to the Secretary of the Admiralty.

> Dear Masterton Smith,
> I have sent in my reports for the First Lord direct to you. I attach the list of officers recommended, as I would like to add a private word regarding them. Firstly as to Commander Gregory. He really has done very well and deserves his promotion to full commander. *He does not want a DSO and I do not wish to recommend him for one.** But he deserves his promotion and I would respectfully ask for this.
>
> Secondly as to Lieut Smiles. This officer cannot very well be refused a decoration as the Russians are giving him a St George's Cross and have said something about asking the English Government to decorate him also.
>
> The other officers are really no less deserving, and in urging their claims, I would point out that I have been on active service with these squadrons for 2½ years and have only asked for one decoration in all that time, namely, that presented to Lieut Sholl.
>
> Lieut Hanna is our best officer and a New Zealander.
> Lieut Ingle has been knocked out for good.†
> Staff Surgeon Scott RN stands very high in Admiralty estimation and deserves every recognition.
> I have avoided putting forward any names but those of officers who really merit reward.

It requires no great powers of perception to recognise that this was a most unpleasant letter. Had Gregory had his acting rank confirmed, he would very probably have been posted away. The grudging reference to Smiles is as unfortunate as the comment that Hanna was the unit's best officer; Hanna, 'an officer whom success does not spoil and whom disappointments can neither embitter nor depress,' had indeed worked himself into the ground in an administrative capacity during the recent campaign, but would have been highly embarrassed to have heard himself so described.

It was the shrewd Captain Girard, the senior Russian liaison officer, who recognised what was troubling Locker Lampson and who sought Sirelius' aid in solving an increasingly awkward problem. Locker

---

* Authors' italics.
† In fact, after a period of convalescence in England, Ingle returned to the unit and stayed with it.

Lampson was to be given a higher award of his own, and since this could obviously not be related to the Dobruja fighting, it would have to be back-dated to the Caucasus, although one might have expected the Grand Duke Nicholas to have raised the subject already had it been his intention to do so. Sirelius agreed to the plan, but was adamant that Smiles was to be rewarded and wrote a suitably worded note to Locker Lampson a few days later.

> On the occasion of your decoration with the Order of St Vladimir of the 4th Class for the fighting done by your division *under you* * in the Caucasus, I take the opportunity of congratulating you upon the Emperor's gracious acknowledgement and I desire to express to you my admiration of the fighting qualities and the conduct of the British armoured cars side by side with the forces of the 4th Siberian Corps.
> The outstanding bravery and unqualified gallantry of Lieut Smiles have written a fine page in British military annals and give me the opportunity of requesting for him the decoration of the highest order, namely the St George of the 4th Class . . .
> I beg you to accept the assurances of my complete respects,
> L. Sirelius,
> General.

Faced with such opposition, Locker Lampson was forced to capitulate and a hastily penned paragraph to Masterton Smith reveals something of a change in attitude.

> This is just to say that since writing to you, I have seen the General in command of the Army under which our force has worked and he tells me that Lieut Smiles is getting a St George's Cross . . . I have also been asked to recommend him for an English decoration equivalent to the Russian one which he has received. I feel under the circumstances it would be rather difficult to refuse Lieut Smiles a DSO. His gallantry has really been quite exceptional. I am very sorry to trouble you but I thought I had better let you know this.

Honours were awarded with a lot less alacrity in the British service than in the Russian and it was August before any announcement was made. By then, for reasons which will soon become apparent, Locker Lampson had more than restored his standing with the Admiralty and his name headed the list of awards for the period October 1916–January 1917 with an appointment as Companion of the Order of St Michael and St George, the citation claiming that

* Authors' italics.

'he was responsible for raising the force in the early days of the war, and has commanded it throughout all its service, both in Belgium and in Russia'.

Staff Surgeon Gilbert Scott and Lieutenant Walter Smiles were admitted to the Distinguished Service Order, and Lieutenant Wright Ingle was awarded the Distinguished Service Cross; Chief Petty Officer MacFarlane and Petty Officers Classey, Graham, Pincott and Vaughan received the Distinguished Service Medal. Acting Commander Reginald Gregory, who had carried the burden of the campaign, received neither an award nor promotion, but was Mentioned in Despatches; as were Lieutenant-Commander Wells Hood, Lieutenant-Commander Dye and Petty Officers Hassan, Whiting, Watson, McIvor, Fear, Bryars, Harris, Husk, Salisbury and Bolton.

In the meantime, Locker Lampson kept his knife into Gregory, and at the end of February an incident occurred which enabled him to give it a particularly vicious twist. The Imperial Army's code of discipline was harsh and officers were allowed to strike their men, who dared not retaliate, in order to drive home some comparatively minor point. This was taken for granted by the Russians themselves, but was viewed with dislike by the RNAS personnel who considered, with not a little justice, that the average Russian soldier was very badly treated. Smoking in public, for example, was a serious crime in the Russian military calendar, whereas the British had always been allowed considerable latitude in the matter; for their part, Russian officers resented what they regarded as an unfair privilege accorded to the British, which set a bad example to their own men.

One evening in Tiraspol a Russian officer approached a member of the unit and ordered him to stop smoking. Either because of incomprehension or truculence, the man failed to obey and the officer struck him. He was roundly thumped in return and the culprit escaped before his identity could be established. Naturally, the Russians complained and requested that disciplinary measures be taken to prevent a recurrence of the incident.

As Locker Lampson was temporarily absent, Gregory was once more in command and on 28th February he issued an order to the effect that identity discs must be worn outside tunics and that smoking was prohibited until further notice in streets and cafés. This was fiercely resented and openly defied by most of the men that same night. The following day the CPOs presented a petition to Gregory, who awarded the entire unit one week's punishment drill and confined it to barracks for the same period, but rescinded the order. This was cheerfully accepted and even the Russians must have been mollified to some degree.

Perhaps the matter could have been dealt with a little more crisply. Certainly, on his return Locker Lampson was not pleased to learn of the problems which had arisen with his neighbours, and wasted no time in writing privately to Masterton Smith.

> In a former letter I suggested that if anything happen to me Commander Gregory might take over command of the force. The extremely hard work which he did in the Dobruja seems to have told on him and it is felt generally that he would not be capable of undertaking these duties. I therefore attach a letter which might be forwarded to the Secretary of the Admiralty. Finally, I think it is generally felt here that it would not be quite fair for Commander Gregory to receive anything like a DSO although I hope he may get his promotion.

The enclosure was equally vindictive.

> I have the honour to request that a former letter of mine requesting that Commander Gregory should take command of this force in the event of anything happening to me might be ignored, as this officer has recently been ill from the hard work he underwent in the Dobruja.
> I would respectfully request that if anything should happen to me, Lieutenant-Commander Belt may take over the command of this force.

Service etiquette demanded that Gregory be shown the correspondence. It also demanded that, having apparently lost his commanding officer's confidence, he should request an immediate transfer. It seems that this was granted and he left for the United Kingdom shortly after. It is pleasing to note that neither Locker Lampson's condemnations with faint praise nor his apparent concern for his former second-in-command's alleged ill health in any way affected Their Lordships' good opinion of Gregory. Nonetheless, having made an enemy of Locker Lampson, he doubtless felt that his best career prospects lay outside the RNAS, and he requested a return to sea duty. He was given command of the Flower Class sloop *Mimosa* in November 1917, joining her in Malta, and was engaged on convoy escort duties between Bizerta and Alexandria until the summer of 1918; he then turned over, with his entire ship's company, to the *Mimosa*'s sister ship, the *Veronica*, at Genoa. From July 1918 until the end of the war the *Veronica* served with the anti-submarine force supporting the Otranto Barrage.

Meanwhile, at Tiraspol Belt had handed over No 1 Squadron to

Lieutenant-Commander Ruston and had assumed the duties of second-in-command. Almost fifty, Belt was the unit's oldest officer, but this in no way inhibited his efficiency nor his capacity for hard work in the extremely trying days to come.

Having disposed of Gregory, Locker Lampson became more his old self and soon developed other interests. A fragment of Rumania remained unoccupied and here the Royal Family were living in their palace at Jassy. He paid a courtesy call and, finding food in very short supply, despatched Petty Officer Martin and a party with rations from the unit's own stores. Subsequently he became a regular visitor and was strongly attracted to Queen Marie, whom he described as 'calm, beautiful, radiant, a wizard in her sense of decoration and dress. The temperature of the room rises when she comes in; all of us feel twice ourselves.' The two possessed very similar temperaments and it seems that the attraction was mutual, enabling Locker Lampson to write of his visits that 'I truly became one of the family.' This deep attachment to the Queen lasted for many years and in 1936 she became godmother to his son Jonathan.

Down at Galatz the front had solidified and Smiles was manning a sector of the Russian trenches. His command, originally forty strong, eventually rose to 158, who were rotated with the personnel at Tiraspol so that everyone had a share of active duty; his heavy equipment consisted of three 3-pounder guns on field carriages, a dozen Maxims and some cars held in reserve.

> Throughout the months of February, March and April [wrote Locker Lampson in a subsequent report] this force was continually in action, under natural conditions of difficulty far greater than any in France, and the conduct of officers and men cannot be too highly praised. Every device possible was employed to hamper and annoy the enemy. Armoured cars covered in white with crews dressed in the same colour, so that they might escape detection in the snow, were mounted on open railway trucks and carried (i.e. pushed) up to the Bulgarian lines, where they inflicted the greatest loss on the enemy. Guns were placed on rafts, ferried across the Sereth, and managed to destroy several observation posts. On one such occasion it took three days and three nights in bitter cold to get each gun into position in the trenches and every conceivable obstacle was overcome. When the snow melted, four feet of water filled the trenches, which became uninhabitable. For a prolonged period our guns were three kilometres nearer than any Russian artillery and proved invaluable in the destruction of *bootkas* (concrete observation posts), haystacks and Maxim

positions. Many complimentary references to their work have been made in both Corps and Divisional orders. During this time the casualties were remarkably small and the cheerful acceptance of hardship and danger by Lieutenant-Commander Smiles, his officers and men was very noteworthy.*

However, while British morale remained high and the Staff applauded the unit's actions, the average Russian infantryman in the trenches was not so enthusiastic. Totally disillusioned and with no further interest in fighting, he simply wanted to live and let live. Unfortunately, every foray by the British provoked a response by the Bulgarian artillery, and it was he and his comrades who suffered. Consequently, he viewed the presence of the RNAS men as a very mixed blessing and relations between the two groups became strained. Eventually, open fraternisation with the enemy became commonplace.

> The Russians would row across the Sereth to embrace fellow fools on the other side. The British unit went its own way and when the troops disobeyed, by its strict discipline succeeded more than once in strengthening the hands of the authorities. We also kept our Maxims and 3-pounders firing regardless of the 'Brotherhood of Nations'. But a bad impression remains with our men, who believe that at least one of our positions was given away to the Bulgarians by a fraterniser and that on another occasion we were fired upon from behind. There is, of course, no proof of this and we mean to forget it anyhow.

A consignment of steel helmets arrived from England and some of these were worn for a short period by the detachment in the trenches. As the Russian Army had not adopted the steel helmet, Locker Lampson no doubt looked on the issue as being slightly bad form and one day attracted a crowd at the Tiraspol base by shooting holes in several with his service revolver. The helmets were withdrawn and went into store.

Relations between Russia and her western allies were now generally at a low ebb, the feeling being that while Russia was making terrible sacrifices neither France nor Great Britain were pulling their weight. About this time a party of twelve men, including Petty Officer Sissons, were sent on local leave to Petrograd, where they acted as ushers at the Embassy during a private showing of the official British film of the Battle of the Somme, given for senior members of the Russian military and political establishment. The film left the audience

---

* The precise date of Smiles' promotion is unknown.

in no doubt as to why the Western Front remained locked in spite of equally terrible sacrifices.

Sissons and his friends were then paid a generous additional allowance by the unit's Petrograd office and ordered to take their meals in the more expensive restaurants, where the British uniforms would be noticed by the Russian élite. To this they had no objection at all and one evening they met a Mr Franklin, an Englishman who had superintended the Czar's livery stables for many years. Franklin entertained them at his family's apartments in the Winter Palace, and since the Czar was absent at Mogilev and the Czarina at Tsarskoe Selo, he was able to take them on a conducted tour of the building and show them its priceless collection of treasures. The sheer splendour of the salons seemed to deny that they were witnesses to the dying days of an era.

On 10th February, after visiting the front, Locker Lampson and Girard left Tiraspol for Petrograd, occupying a suite at the Hotel Astoria. Locker Lampson was evidently still dissatisfied with the performance of his Lanchester cars and transport, and since the Admiralty was disinclined to help, he intended to ask the Russian War Ministry to supply supplementary vehicles with a better ground clearance. The discussions were still in progress when the Revolution broke out and he was thus able to witness it at first hand.

It began quietly enough on Thursday, 8th March. Simple political expediency should have prompted the Czarina's inept administration into seeing that the capital at least was amply stocked with fuel and food, but it had not. During the afternoon several bakers' shops were looted and there was an orderly demonstration down the Nevski Prospekt. The following day, an air of expectation hung over the city and spontaneous crowds began to gather, discussing not only the shortages but also the questions of total withdrawal from the war and the removal of the government from office. There was little violence, although in some incidents the police were stoned. By Saturday the 10th, the crowds had been swelled by thousands of striking workers, the talk had become more inflammatory, and clashes with the police had become more frequent. The authorities had received ample warnings that the working people of Petrograd and other cities were close to desperation and that some disturbance must be regarded as inevitable, and had in fact made some contingency plans. Three courses of action were open: either the storm should be allowed to blow itself out, which many professional revolutionaries believed to be a real possibility; or, deal responsibly with the people's grievances, which would involve some loss of the autocracy's power; or, repress. With unfailing bad judgement, the weapon of repression was chosen.

General Khabalov, the Military Governor of Petrograd, had some 160,000 men at his disposal. His first line of defence consisted of the 3,500 men of the Armed Police, the hated Pharaos, who were capable of defending their stations with machine-guns; if necessary, the police would be reinforced by two regiments of Don Cossacks, the traditional bulwark of the monarchy; but only as a last resort was the Petrograd garrison to be committed, since its loyalties were known to be divided.

On Sunday 11th the crowds gathered again and Khabalov decided to clear the streets. There was some firing, mainly by the police, which resulted in several score deaths, but it was soon clear that the overall situation was beyond their control. The Cossacks were sent in but the majority were in sympathy with the people's aims and some even opened fire on the police themselves.

Even at this eleventh hour Khabalov might have preserved some remnant of the regime had he withdrawn his men to their quarters. Instead, he decided to employ the Army on Monday the 12th and, worse, made known his intention of doing so. The lights burned throughout the night in the barracks of the Imperial Guard regiments as they debated what course they should adopt. After nearly three years of war their ranks consisted mainly of civilians in uniform who knew that they would be ordered the following morning to shoot down their own people, whose demands they considered to be just and reasonable, and this they were not prepared to do. One by one the Footguard Regiments Preobrajenski, Pavlovski, Volinski, Litovski and the Guard Grenadier Regiment Kexholm either confined or shot their less popular officers and marched out at dawn to throw in their lot with the rioters. Together, soldiers and civilians stormed the Arsenal and then the police stations. The fortress of St Peter and St Paul, the Czarist Bastille, surrendered during the afternoon. Khabalov retreated to the Admiralty building, which held out until the 13th. Formations despatched by STAVKA to put down the revolt simply became absorbed into it.

Stripped of all power, the Government collapsed. Hastening back from Mogilev, the Czar got no further than Pskov, where his train was boarded by two delegates from Petrograd. At first, he seemed to believe that he still had the authority to grant constitutional reform, but it was far too late for that. Telephone calls to Alexeiev, Brussilov and the Grand Duke Nicholas confirmed that nothing less than his abdication would suffice. Refusing to be parted from the Czarevitch, he signed the formal deed in the early hours of 15th March, transferring the throne to his brother, the Grand Duke Michael. During the afternoon of the 16th, after discussions with leading political figures, Michael also abdicated, commenting that he would resume the crown if it were to be offered to him by a constituent assembly.

Thus, the most powerful autocracy in the world was brought crashing down in less than a week. This had been achieved with a loss of only 1,500 lives, and was remarkable not only for its spontaneity but also for its tolerance – true, old scores against the police had been brutally paid off and the worst politicians had been roughly handled, but there was common accord between the classes and, for the moment, private property was respected. Even the Czarina, who was universally detested, was permitted to remain with her children at Tsarskoe Selo, and there her husband joined her.

The Hotel Astoria provided the setting for the last act of the drama in Petrograd. A few diehards fired from the roof into the crowd below, which promptly broke in to deal with them, although other guests do not seem to have been molested. Locker Lampson found himself comforting a lady who had swooned with alarm; by a happy series of coincidences, she also happened to be young, pretty and a princess.

As one of very few British officers on the spot, Locker Lampson's importance to the Admiralty had suddenly increased beyond recognition. On 19th March he forwarded a detailed account of events, and in July followed this with a second despatch dealing with later events.

> The state of Russia after the Czar's abdication grew steadily worse. The Provisional Government had failed to find a Czar and springing as it did from a Duma which was out of date and unrepresentative, it soon lost favour and then obedience.
>
> Power fell swiftly into the hands of the Workmen's Committees which were recruited not only from the legitimate ranks of labour but from criminals released in the name of Liberty from prison, and from enemy agents whose interest was to create trouble.
>
> It was inevitable under these influences and in the absence of real rulers that law and order should for a time diminish. In ordinary circumstances all might have worked itself out soon to a satisfactory compromise. But unfortunately a gigantic war was being waged and it was a matter of life and death to an enemy neighbour to promote internal disorder.
>
> German money was never cheaper and German agents were never

more active. Their aim was to undermine the Army and make peace a necessity for Russia. A violent anti-Ally propaganda raged and everywhere the same arguments faced us, obviously struck from the same mint: Why had England forced Russia into the war? Why had England shot down defenceless women in the Boer War. And ceaselessly were reiterated the statements that the war had not been made by Russia but by Russia's deposed Czar, and that peace was the province of a freed people. Moreover, were not the people now a people in arms and without any representation despite all they had achieved and suffered? The military millions must themselves therefore send delegates to Petrograd and voice their views. And a scandalous leaflet, purporting to be an official proclamation, authorised soldiers to disobey their officers unless orders given were approved by the workmen's committees.

From this moment discipline ceased, and the deadly disorder ran riot through the Army. The Cossacks, the cavalry and the artillery did in part withstand the subtle corruption, but how could the infantry resist! For nearly three years they had been mown down in millions: hurled (as they persist in stating) in unarmed masses against magnificently equipped troops, by generals whom they believed were bought by German gold. How could they be expected to want the war to go on! How much preferable the discussions of land and pension problems in committee.

So, they too 'came into their own', and sit in judgement on their superiors, treating their officers terribly. Some officers have been shot, others beaten, and most insulted. In Kronstadt, naval officers have been sweeping the streets and one of them was seen being led along by the beard by one of his men, who struck his face continually. Respect for rank had disappeared. Pushful committee-men force their way into the presence of their generals and demand a complete exposition of the plan of attack before they will allow an advance: and the time of the Staff is divided between reconciling recalcitrant soldiers' councils to the orders given and doing all they can to conceal plans which, once given away, may lose them the Army and ruin an advance. No one can believe the difficulties of commanding officers who now undertake operations uncertain if their men will advance; doubtful whether if they do advance, they are not doing so in order to go over to the enemy; and in fear whether having advanced the men may not return to court-martial their generals for some mistake.

To us at first the Revolution was an assistance. Many restrictions were removed and enthusiasm was epidemic. But soon German propaganda won ground and the ignorant believed that Russia was being compelled to fight for and by England. We were careful to avoid friction but our difficulties were grave. We were asked to appoint delegates from among our men to attend the soldier deputies' council and, by refusing, incurred some unpopularity. Once when some of our ammunition, which was defective, was thrown into the River Dniester at Tiraspol, a great fuss was made. The Jewish Press grew excited; it was alleged that we wanted to blow up a bridge or make a cache for some counter-revolution, and it was only on our claiming an enquiry, which acquitted us, that calm ensued.*

The Revolution was very slow in reaching the Rumanian Armies but shook them as profoundly as any. At first, when the Czar abdicated, leaflets were dropped over our lines by the Germans, stating that the 'beloved Czar' had been removed by the 'brutal' English; a lie which rendered us heroes for several days!

In general, the RNAS personnel were broadly sympathetic to the aims of the Revolution. They were already aware that the structure of Russian society was essentially rotten and that change, if allowed to mature slowly, could only bring good in its wake. Some, like Frank Round, had used their cameras with a skill that would shame a modern documentary maker to illustrate the glaring inequalities. There was, for example, the funeral of the rich man, who travelled to his grave in a magnificent gilded hearse, accompanied by liveried servants, contrasted with that of the peasant who lay swathed in an open plank coffin on a farm cart, while his best friend walked ahead with the lid. There were, too, the glittering vestments and jewelled icons of the clergy to set against the grinding poverty of their superstitious congregations.

Even had a language barrier not existed, the super-heated atmosphere of the Russian soldiers' political meetings was quite alien to the British, and those agitators who approached the unit, burning with apostolic fervour, were politely but firmly shown the door. This very necessary policy of non-involvement, coupled with the belligerent activities of Smiles' command, led to the unit being dubbed as warmongers by the wilder elements in Tiraspol, and an uneasy feeling of isolation grew as the weeks passed.

On several occasions there was unrest in the town and on 23rd April there was a serious possibility that the British would be attacked. The unit stood to all night, manning the Maxims in the cars, and each man was issued with 75 rounds of rifle ammunition. The attack did not materialise, but a few days later the Russian treachery already described by Locker Lampson resulted in two men killed and four

* It should not be imagined from this reference to the Jewish Press that Locker Lampson was in any way anti-Semitic; in fact, in later years he campaigned vigorously against the Nazi persecution of the Jews. In Russia, the Jewish community understandably had less reason than most to love the old regime and its adherents, and was frankly suspicious of British motives.

wounded in the trenches. The atmosphere was now distinctly hostile and on 20th May a serious brawl took place outside the British billets; one Russian was killed and Petty Officer Bunny Smith so seriously injured that he died shortly after.

Locker Lampson returned to Tiraspol on 8th April and ten days later set off again to resume his negotiations, this time with representatives of the new Provisional Government.

> The obstacles, the delays and the confusion which met me need not be enlarged upon. Suffice it that I concluded the most satisfactory arrangements with the new Government. Our status authorising the existence and continuation in Russia of the force at its full strength and pay, together with all due undertakings for supplies, etc, etc, was signed and we now stand on a better official footing than ever before. Moreover, I laid before the authorities our depreciation in cars and material, and they have placed the following at our disposal:
> 8 Fiat armoured cars
> 3 Packard petrol tankers
> 2 Pierce Arrow workshops
> 8 Fiat lorries, $3\frac{1}{2}$ tons
> 6 Fiat lorries, $1\frac{1}{2}$ tons
> 10 Renault touring cars
> 17 motor cycles
> 48 ordinary bicycles
>
> It was then that the authorities at Petrograd confided their troubles and hopes. Discipline, loyalty, patriotism and order had vanished but the summer was nearing, when some military activity on their part was awaited by the Allies and must be attempted. Yet conditions were so grave that all they could hope was that the Army had not yet wholly lost its power to advance. Any reliable men under such circumstances were an asset and they asked me to allow our small force to operate wherever an advance was to be tried, assuring us of the great benefit of our example at such a time.
>
> Of course I agreed. Everybody knew that an advance was contemplated and most people suspected that it would be in Galicia. In Rumania efforts were made by the Russians and Rumanians to keep the British force and in *an open appeal to this effect the name of the front to which we were destined was mentioned eight times.**

The majority of British officers were extremely doubtful as to the Russian capacity to sustain an offensive, and most felt that the venture was bound to end in disaster, if not the total collapse of the Galician front. Because of this Locker Lampson accepted a suggestion of Belt's

* Authors' italics.

that the unit's new base should be located at Proskurov, over forty miles behind the front and well beyond the immediate dangers of an Austro-German breakthrough. A forward operational base would be established at Kozova, west of Tarnopol, close to the headquarters of the Russian 41 Corps, whose divisions the cars would be supporting.

In early June the unit packed up and left Tiraspol for Galicia. The men were not sorry to go, but it was with genuine regret that Sirelius watched them leave, for they were virtually the only troops on whom he had been able to rely, and their steadying influence had acted as a valuable check to the more extreme elements among the soldiers' committees.

CHAPTER SEVEN

Debacle at Brzezany

Austrian Galicia was a pretty country of gently rolling, wooded hills and valleys, still bearing the scars of the previous year's fighting, and it was here that Kerensky decided to locate the epicentre of his own offensive. Immense preparations had been made, but dominating the minds of everyone from the War Minister down was the question of whether or not the ethnic Russian troops would advance when the time came.

It was finally decided that from the vast hordes of soldiers under arms, volunteers should be selected, who would undertake to fight to the end, and these it was determined to form into combative units [wrote Locker Lampson]. They were known as Battalions of Death, and wore two chevrons on their right arms: one red, symbolic of revolution, and the other black, denoting their readiness to die. They proved a magnificent body of men and were only inadequate numerically.

Mr Kerensky then set about strengthening the Russian troops with such foreign troops as could be collected and upon whose resistance to the new doctrines of Bolshevism he could rely. Polish regiments were picked out for the decisive front; a complete Serbian division was withdrawn from near Odessa for special service; and some Czecho-Slovak battalions were raised (from prisoners of war) for particular duty. Squadrons, too, of French aviators and a detachment of Belgian machine gunners and cars were added to this motley army, and last came our unit of armoured cars. As we advanced to the front Tartars jostled Serbians, Poles collided with Belgians, Czecho-Slovak troops strove with Australians along the dusty advance to the lines, and all were aware whither they were going and the why and the wherefore of this babel of tongues. The dates of the attack were not even a surmise, and all these alien elements growled at being made to pick Russian chestnuts out of the fire.

The nearer we approached the front the better the discipline became, until in the trenches we found men even saluting their officers. At any rate, some order and goodwill existed, although the Staff officers made no attempt to conceal their anxiety. They thought that the first line would move and do well, but they founded few hopes on the reserves, and counted for certain upon only 75 per cent of the troops engaged.

They were very anxious days. Traffic was clogged, roads were broken and daily thunderstorms made cross-country going impossible. We felt insecure in our surroundings and found the enemy active everywhere. In the air he was supreme and the day I arrived eight Russian observation balloons were brought down. One fell quite near me – an aeroplane suddenly appeared, hovered a moment and then swooped down upon the captive balloon. Half a dozen rockets shot out from the aeroplane and simultaneously there leapt from the basket of the balloon a man who fell incredibly quickly until his yellow parachute shot open and floated him safely to the ground. The aeroplane rose, and a brown patch appeared, spread, and then started into flame at the tail end of the balloon. The tail tipped as it lost buoyancy and flames ran up the huge body of the balloon until it was entirely enveloped and the basket crashed to earth, leaving of the fabric nothing but an oily discolouration on the open field. This enterprise took barely five minutes to accomplish, without any hindrance from the Russians.

Other balloons took the place of those destroyed and were 'walked' by men on foot for miles to their stations. You could see what looked like a stupendous yellow caterpillar creeping over the ground on legs and the miracle is that so few of them were destroyed by aircraft in transit. The supply seems sufficient, as on one occasion a balloon was sacrificed and sent up as bait with a dummy man in the basket, composed of dynamite. On the approach of the aeroplane the charge was exploded and blew the attacking aviator clean over in the air but without bringing him down.

Preparations otherwise were better than I had yet seen at the front. Roadmakers had been organised; roads screened from observation; and the artillery appeared to be well concealed. It was believed and it may be true that the Russian guns and ammunition far outnumbered those of the enemy and this sense of superiority heartened the troops. The cavalry wanted a fight, the Cossacks smelled loot, and the artillery looked at their big dumps and chafed to let them off. As for the infantry, elements of most regiments could not be trusted, but the general excitement was catching, in the evenings there were gatherings in the streets, the trenches, barracks and bivouacs, and feverish speechmaking and singing prevailed. Little clumps would collect and talk of revolution and war: and I shall never forget the advent of Kerensky's proclamation in orders. This fervent appeal to patriotism was read out everywhere by committee-men, non-commissioned officers and officers, and war-worn veterans round camp fires would take off their caps and cry like children. Whole audiences wept as though physically relaxed by what they heard, and I passed soldiers blubbering their way home in the dark.

Debacle at Brzezany

The average Russian infantryman of the period was a simple, emotional and generally likable soul who was virtually illiterate and quite without any knowledge of the world beyond his own immediate experience. Thus, when Kerensky spoke of Russia's war aims as being a peace without Annexation or Indemnity, there was widespread belief that this statement referred to two towns which the Government was offering to cede to the enemy. The RNAS personnel had long since abandoned explanations as to what British meant. Having strenuously denied being German – a term almost synonymous with foreigner in Russia – or even French, they were on one occasion acclaimed enthusiastically as *Japanese*, these being the only other nationals of whom there was universal recognition!

The South-West Front was now commanded by General Gutor following Brusilov's elevation to Commander-in-Chief, and contained five armies. The 41st Corps, under whom Locker Lampson would be working, formed part of the 7th Army and consisted of seven divisions instead of the normal four since desertion had reduced the average strength of rifle companies from a nominal 250 to a mere 80 men. In the line, from north to south, were the 113th Infantry Division, the 5th Trans-Amur Division, the 3rd Trans-Amur Division and the 74th Siberian Division; in reserve were the 23rd, 108th and Polish Infantry Divisions. The Corps objective was Brzezany, heavily fortified, 'set in a saucer of hills of uninviting steepness,' and held by three German and two Hungarian regiments.* Ony two roads, one on either flank, ran into the objective and it was planned to use the cars along these, No 3 Squadron under Lieutenant-Commander Ruston being based at Doobsche and Nos 1 and 2 Squadrons under respectively Lieutenant-Commander Smiles and Lieutenant-Commander Wells Hood at Lietyatin. The cars' general instructions were to enfilade the enemy's trenches and to keep ahead of the advancing infantry at all times.

The cars, however, represented only a part of the British effort, the full extent of which is described by Locker Lampson.

Brigadier-General Poole, in charge of the British Mission in Petrograd, had hoped to introduce mortars into the Russian Army. He had met with many difficulties, chief of which had been the delay in actually getting the mortars to the front. It had therefore been suggested that our force might take over some mortars, demonstrate their value at the front and so popularise their use with the Russian Army.

Over 60 tons of 2" mortars, Stokes guns and ammunition were

---

* A Continental regiment was equivalent in size to a British brigade.

hurriedly despatched to us from Petrograd and it taxed our insufficient transport to the utmost to bring it in time to the front. The men under Sub-Lieutenant Lefroy worked day and night and in twenty-four hours the whole of it had been transferred from railhead fifty miles to the front. The mortars were accompanied by Captain Hand MC, Captain Gaden and two instructors, and those of our men who had been detailed some weeks previously to learn their use.

The Corps Staff were not only delighted at the presence of the mortars but in the midst of their difficulties begged us to man them ourselves and even asked us to take over Maxim positions at important points in the line to encourage their troops. So that our small force was distributed thinly at intervals along the whole Corps line and occupied itself in running cars, operating Stokes guns, working trench mortars, emplacing 3-pounders and firing Maxims in the trenches. Every spare man was impressed and we went without orderlies and drivers for the purpose. There was not a division engaged within the Corps which had not some of our men fighting with it and we were in such demand that divisions actually gave orders for our men over the heads of the Corps Staff.

On 28th June the general in command of the 74th Division sent for me and explained that a section of the enemy's barbed wire against which his troops must advance could not be reached by his artillery, and he asked if we could mount some 2" mortars and destroy it. We agreed to, but were so short of men that the same crew which operated the Stokes gun had to be employed – like a stage army, for the 2" mortars also. Captain Hand and one instructor under Lieutenant-Commander Smiles undertook this work and Captain Gaden with a similar party of our men was attached to the 5th Trans-Amur Division.

The bombardment was to last two days and to increase in intensity eightfold during the final four hours. It commenced at 0400 on 28th June and news soon reached us that a bridge behind Brzezany was blown up and the enemy trenches levelled to the ground. It continued satisfactorily the next day by which time all our arrangements had been settled, when a message suddenly arrived in the night asking us to shift the mortars at once from the 74th Division to the 3rd Trans-Amur to repel an attack expected here. I was obliged to go up to the trenches in rain and great darkness with Baron Girard, our liaison officer. Our car broke down and we lost the way. The shelling on both sides was very great and we got into some enemy gas which despite our masks made Girard feel very ill but affected me only slightly. With the greatest difficulty we brought a mortar party up, but the trenches where they were to operate could not be reached for the fire. Orders were conflicting and officers in command distraught beyond belief Even the divisional headquarters where we discussed plans was exposed to shells, bullets and gas the whole time and opportunity for calm deliberation was very difficult.

Debacle at Brzezany

The following day 30th June, I visited General Gutor and the War Minister, Mr Kerensky, in the Staff train. Mr Kerensky seemed preoccupied; his clean-shaven, frank, ugly face brightened at the news of the damage done by the bombardment, but his prodigious efforts speaking to the troops and making up by personality for the absence of discipline had worn him out. The rest of the day was spent in receipt of divergent instructions and twice we shifted the Stokes mortars from two rival divisions only to return them with much trouble.

After a night of thunder and rain, 1st July, the day upon which so many hopes and fears were founded, dawned, and the artillery fire rose to a slow crescendo. With the 74th Division alone, which occupied but 1,000 yards, we had two squadrons of armoured cars, a party with 2" mortars and Stokes guns, a party with 3-pounders and two parties with machine-guns in the trenches. Twice the Russian fatigue party detailed to help struck and refused to work under fire, but our officers and men persevered and completed the arrangements themselves. The mortars came into action at 0517, completely destroying the stretch of wire which the artillery could not reach and breaking down enemy earthworks as well.

The cars were due to cross their start-line at 0955 and the infantry to go over the top five minutes later. Watched by Kerensky from a forward observation post, Wells Hood led out his squadron in the Rolls armoured. The cars gathered speed in a cutting and then burst out onto the wastes of No Man's Land. Shells burst alongside the road and copper-nosed bullets clanged off the armour, but within minutes they were level with the first line of enemy trenches and were enfilading them with their fire. Many of the defenders tried to escape above ground and were shot down. While the Russian infantry came up Wells Hood protected the Corps' left flank from interference, and then pressed on down the road to Brzezany until he found it blocked by a barbed wire and sandbag barricade.

Smiles called for volunteers to go forward with him and remove the obstruction. He was joined by Chief Petty Officer MacFarland, Leading Petty Officer Harrison and Petty Officers Gardner and McEwan, and together they crawled up the roadside ditch to the barricade, which was now under such shellfire that Locker Lampson wondered how any of them survived. Dodging shellbursts, they were able at length to dismantle the structure piece by piece, but in the process MacFarland was killed and McEwan badly wounded. The cars passed through and could in all probability have reached Brzezany had not events elsewhere brought the advance to a halt.

On the Corps' right flank Ruston's squadron had also made considerable progress. Ruston had additionally sited two Maxim parties under Lieutenant Turner, a Vickers automatic and a 3-pounder to dominate the enemy trenches. As the day progressed the Germans mounted a local counter-attack in battalion strength; Turner allowed them to advance well beyond the safety of their own trenches and then opened up, doing great execution. His guns then became the target of the enemy artillery. Chief Petty Officer Locke was fatally wounded and several men injured. Turner himself was hit and subsequently gassed but refused evacuation for forty-eight hours, by which time he was also shell-shocked.

Elsewhere along the front one of Sub-Lieutenant de Coninck's two Maxim detachments received a direct hit, killing Petty Officers Mitchell, Pearson and Viane and wounding the remainder. The surviving gun remained in continuous action until mid-afternoon, every Russian Maxim on the sector having in the meantime also been silenced. Sub-Lieutenant Woods' detachments destroyed a number of enemy machine-gun posts and was then subjected to a continuous rain of gas shells against which even the wearing of masks proved ineffective.

The British had accomplished every task they had been set, but on their own they could accomplish nothing. The Staff's forecast as to the performance of the Russian troops had proved to be unhappily accurate. The strange Battalions of Death had indeed gone forward to seek their namesake, and had found him with ease. In 74th Division the two regiments which had armoured car support had also advanced, capturing successive trench lines as the cars reached them, but the rest of the division refused to move. Officers went over the top alone or with but a handful of loyal men, ripping the epaulettes from their tunics in shame, the majority finding a lonely end between the lines. One regiment's priest walked out through the wire, brandishing his cross, but still the men refused to move; he fell, his legs smashed and his body riddled. A powerfully built Australian Petty Officer named Gardiner, serving with one of the Maxim detachments, was so sickened by the spectacle that he launched a personal attack on the nearest platoon, bodily throwing a score of men over the parapet; they merely crawled to the sanctuary of shell holes.

In contrast, the two Trans-Amur divisions had attacked with an astonishing vigour, storming their way through Brzezany Wood and into the outskirts of Brzezany itself. There they halted, waiting for the supporting divisions to arrive and pass through, cooking, resting and playing cards. The supports, however, had refused to advance and the Germans used the gap left by the malcontents of the 76th Division to launch a counter-attack into the flank of the 3rd Trans-Amur, which was forced to fall back to its own lines, swearing to court martial its commander, taking the 5th Trans-Amur with it. The 113th Division also finished the day in a mutinous frame of mind and had to be relieved by the Polish Division, part of which promptly deserted, making for its homes behind the German lines.

Some 2,000 prisoners had been taken during the fighting, of whom several hundred had been shot down as they crossed the lines in the mistaken belief that they were a counter-attack. The prisoners were mostly German and it was some measure of the contempt in which the Russian Army was now held that an officer told Locker Lampson that Brzezany was regarded as a quiet sector on which to rest troops from the Western Front.

Russian casualties had been heavy, particularly among the officers and in the best disciplined regiments; the worst loss, however, was in fighting spirit, which oozed away with the coming of darkness, like the rain which had fallen incessantly throughout. The British suffered five killed and six wounded, the highest single day's total in the unit's history. The dead were buried locally with full military honours on 3rd July; in later years the area became part of Poland and the War Graves Commission erected a monument, inscribed with their names, in the cemetery of the old citadel at Poznan.

On other sectors of South-West Front the Russians had done somewhat better. On 7th Army's right flank General Erdelli's 11th Army was faced with equally disillusioned Austrian formations which surrendered en masse. One regiment, the 81st Czech, marched in as a body and paraded through the streets of Tarnopol, escorted by Cossacks, with their band playing and colours flying. Many of its men were put to work at the RNAS base and on one occasion a deputation requested Locker Lampson to give them some cars so that they could return and fight against their Habsburg masters; he declined. The regiment eventually joined the famous Czech Legion which fought its legendary way home along the Trans-Siberian Railway during the Civil War.

To the south, General Lavr Kornilov's 8th Army had also done well, although elsewhere along the front, particularly on the Guard Corps' sectors, there had been mutinous scenes and a refusal to advance which nullified the value of any gains made. Kerensky's offensive, always a gamble, had failed.

At Brzezany, the Germans had not returned to the trenches cap-

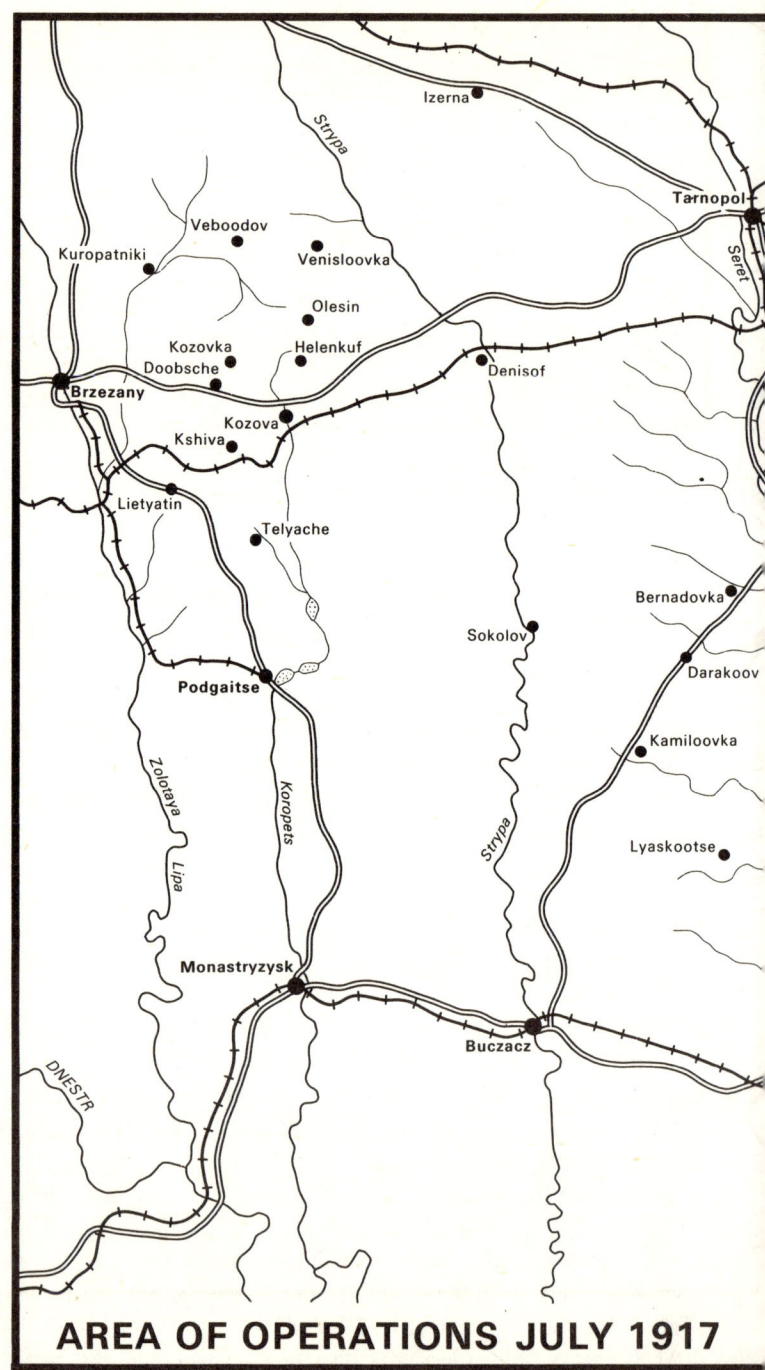

AREA OF OPERATIONS JULY 1917

Debacle at Brzezany

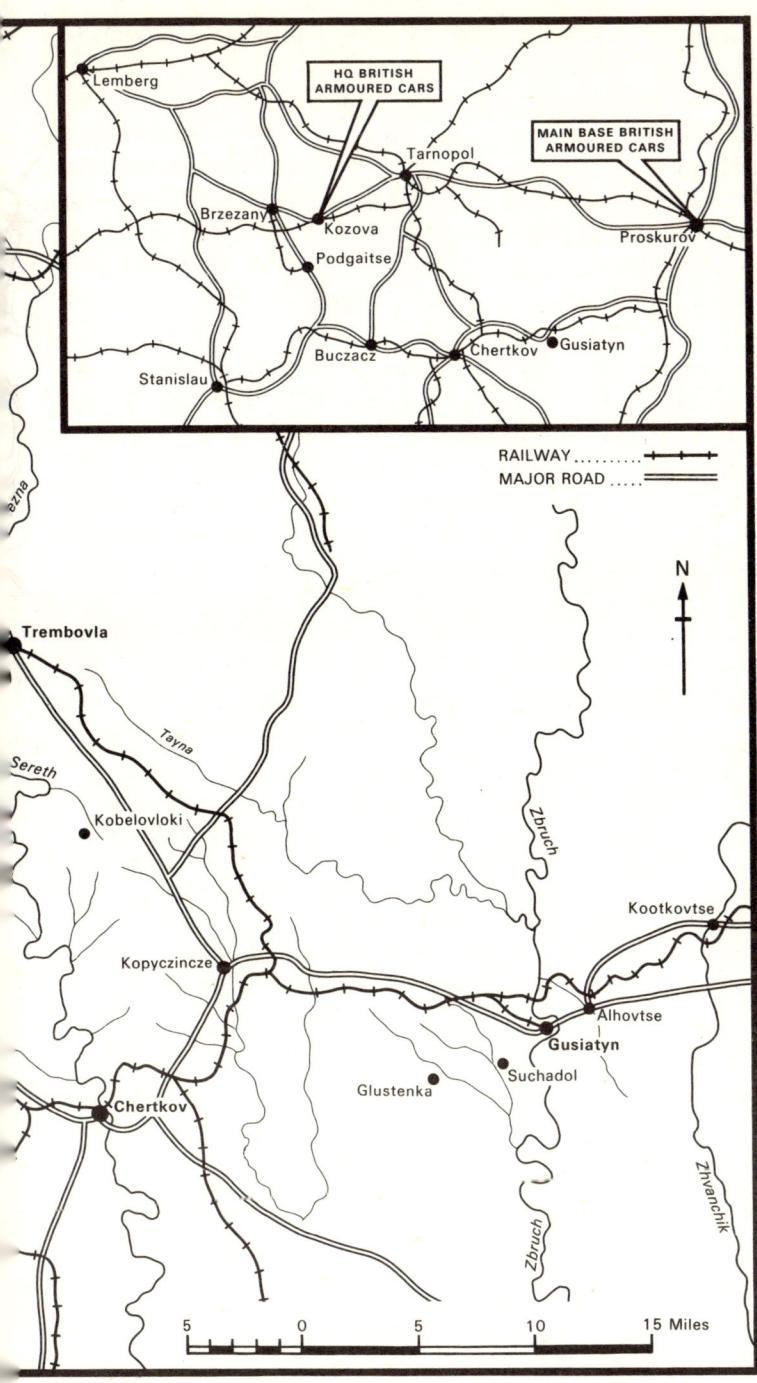

tured on the first morning, and the British cars went out daily to prevent their doing so. The Germans responded by sending out one of their own cars to do battle with Smiles' squadron and an indecisive engagement took place at 600 yards range. A diary note mentions that the German was driven off by 3-pounder fire, presumably from the Heavies, since the towed guns were still emplaced in the Russian line. In spite of this, the Russians refused to come forward to occupy the abandoned trenches, although Locker Lampson had promised that his mortar, Maxim and 3-pounder parties would accompany them and several British officers actually walked across No Man's Land in daylight to demonstrate the absence of the enemy. Worse still, reserve divisions were refusing to spend more than twenty-four hours in the line, and some were even declining to enter it at all; one formation had to be forcibly disarmed after it had been surrounded by Cossacks and a Russian armoured car company. During the night of 4th July the Germans moved back into their old positions and the lines were exactly as they had been before the great attack took place.

The morale of 41st Corps, now barely good for defensive tasks, was to receive a further shattering blow. On 8th July Locker Lampson was in his billet at Kozova, eight miles behind the front, when he heard a shell scream overhead and then explode.

We went out as another shell followed suit, and found the station being shelled and some material already on fire. Behind the station had been laboriously collected weeks and months of food, stores and fodder and beside it were stacked dumps of ammunition to feed the guns for many months. The third shell struck a heap of rockets and star shells, and these flung themselves far and wide setting fire to whatever they touched. The station is situated half a mile behind and above Kozova, which lies in a hollow, and having sent an interpreter to offer our help to the Staff, I took a car and ran out towards the station to see what mischief was likely.

We reached a field about a thousand yards away to find that the fire had already gained strength and ground. A confused crackling sounded and then the clear crepitation of cartridges exploding. Adjoining heaps of stores and ammunition soon got alight and the noise and smoke grew every minute. At the same time shells whizzed over the town and exploded near the station. At length the area of destruction widened so rapidly that no hope of putting the fire out remained and the reply from the Staff refusing our help confirmed the impossibility of interference. A wind had sprung up and was blowing sparks, fragments and smoke over the town. Moreover, the station population had taken alarm and was streaming out over the fields leaving only one engine to pull a number of carriages out and the armoured train to do what it could. The flames mounted up, spread and reached more ammunition and the continuous tumult of explosions deepened, punctuated by loud detonations and the scattering of shells right and left into the air.

We watched fascinatedly and then quite abruptly the full horror fell. It seemed as if the earth had held enchained a giant struggling to be free and that in a last paroxysm he had burst the containing crust. A gigantic body of flame, incredibly red and vivid, leapt into the air, followed by a column of smoke so huge that the entire station with its outhouses in a second disappeared. The column rose quite straight into the air, broadened suddenly at the top into the shape of a tree, and then we were felled to the ground. The concussion and the noise can never be adequately told. It was not one detached detonation but an immense rising roar and we scrambled behind the car against the falling fragments which whistled in hundreds through the air.

The ground was littered with shell fragments, shells and casings, and I walked to where our field hospital was, half a mile distant. Throughout my walk no less than eight crushing explosions occurred, carrying fragments for miles, and I reached the road with its protecting bank to find scores of refugees huddled in the ditch. Two men by my side were wounded by fragments and I got them to our hospital, which Staff Surgeon Scott had already evacuated.

Nothing of the station could now be seen. News came that among the exploding dumps were many gas shells, that half a million tons of dynamite remained to go off, and we were urged to move our ammunition at once. So with the help of some Russian cars and to the tune of continuous explosions and crackling, we transported in four hours every ounce of ammunition to some outlying fields. Here we slept the night and were awakened by aeroplane bombs in the morning.

The town of Kozova itself escaped by a miracle. The river which divides it saved the lower and larger half, and the dynamite did not explode. But the effect upon a dispirited corps and army can be understood. Ammunition is a rare commodity in Russia and the army's supply for a long period had vanished, consisting in part of big shells from England which could not be replaced for many months. It had been concentrated at Kozova in bulk upon the expectation of a successful advance which would leave the town out of reach of enemy guns, and practically the whole stock had gone up. Cossacks, seeing in this the unseen hand of spies, killed several Jews the same night and we were asked to patrol the town and keep order; but not desiring to come into contact with any Russian elements, I not unnaturally refused, and this duty was undertaken instead by a Polish squadron.

A few days after this incident Kerensky returned to Petrograd, but made a point of thanking Locker Lampson for the squadron's services during the offensive. A Mortar and Stokes Gun School was set up for the Russians and detachments from each of 41st Corps' divisions were trained in the use of these weapons.

On 18th July Brusilov was replaced by Kornilov as Commander-in-Chief, and two days later Kerensky took over from Prince Lvov as Prime Minister. Kerensky was a sincere, if emotional, man with honest socialist principles. His new appointment had not, however, been given him because of a universal trust in his abilities to steer the ship of state through the troubled waters of Russian politics without grounding on the shoals of extremism. In fact he was neither well liked nor especially trusted, and lacked both the foresight and the essential ruthlessness required in high office; but he was the one individual to whom political parties of all shades had least objection.

Since its inception, the Provisional Government had been forced to work in parallel, if not actual competition, with the Petrograd Workers' and Soldiers' Soviet, and no measures passed by the former could receive effect until they had been approved by the latter, although the *original* objective of both was the ultimate democratic election of a Constituent Assembly. In more normal times the Government could have sharply curtailed the Soviet's power, but its own existence depended on the goodwill of the Petrograd garrison and the People's Militia which had been substituted for the police, and in these areas the influence of the Soviet was dominant. The Soviet was, however, soon infiltrated by Bolsheviks and a power struggle with the Government became inevitable.

This was accelerated by the arrival from Switzerland, with German assistance, of the veteran revolutionary and agitator Vladimir Ilyich Ulyanov, better known as Lenin. Born at Simbursk in 1870, Lenin had a middle class background, his father being a Provincial Schools Inspector with an official status equivalent to that of Major-General and the right to be addressed as Excellency. But in 1887 Lenin's brother Alexander was hung following his implication in a bomb plot against the Czar, and the family were ostracized by their neighbours and former friends; it is thought by many that Lenin's loathing for the middle class, its property and values, stems directly from this period. It was inevitable that he should follow in his brother's revolutionary footsteps, and that much of his subsequent life should be spent in prison or in exile; inevitable, too, that he should be drawn to the extremist left wing of revolutionary politics and into the Bolshevik Party with its creed of class hatred, its internationalism and its burning desire to apply a nineteenth-century economic dogma to twentieth-century problems.

Although its title meant Majority, the Party never achieved anything like such popularity and for this reason disliked the democratic process although paying lip-service to its principles; the intention was that once power had been seized, by force if necessary, all executive decisions would be made by a small, elitist, central committee 'in the name of the proletariat'. Such a party would have made scant headway had it not been for the harsh discipline and ruthless organisation instilled by Lenin, who was at heart as much an autocrat as any Czar.

On his return to Russia following the March revolution, Lenin had been enthusiastically welcomed, his anti-establishment writings having already made him a hero in exile. He gravitated naturally to the Soviet where he, Trotsky and their Bolshevik comrades began to agitate for extreme measures at once. But not even the Soviet was ready for this and there was a rising groundswell of opinion against him. Repeatedly the questions were asked, where had he been when the fighting to overthrow the old order took place? Who was he to tell the people how to run their revolution? And what precisely were the nature of his links with Imperial Germany? Instead of gaining ground, the Bolsheviks began to lose it.

Perhaps because of this Lenin decided to gamble all on the abortive coup known to Communist historians as the July Days. He had the support of the seamen from the Kronstadt naval base and a substantial element of the capital's industrial workforce, both having been heavily infiltrated by Bolshevik agitators. Once again crowds milled in the streets and there was some wild shooting, but the Provisional Government kept its head and actually received the support of those regiments of the Petrograd garrison which were not completely indifferent. Eventually, heavy rain began to fall and everyone went home, soaked to the skin.

Kerensky now acted against the Bolsheviks. Many, including Trotsky, were imprisoned for a while, and Lenin was forced into hiding. Unfortunately, the process was neither sufficiently thorough nor ruthless nor permanent, and Kerensky seems to have underestimated both Lenin's iron will and his determination to seize power at any price.

It was against this background that Locker Lampson's squadrons had suddenly found themselves fighting for their lives in circumstances which any unit would have regarded as the supreme test.

CHAPTER EIGHT

Wanted - Dead or Alive

'We have only to kick in the door and the whole rotten house will come tumbling down,' was Adolf Hitler's verdict on the state of Soviet Russia and the Red Army shortly before he launched his invasion in 1941; that his prophecy remained unfulfilled was largely the result of his own interference in the conduct of the subsequent campaign.

Similar thoughts were passing through the collective mind of senior German and Austrian officers at *Oberost* in July 1917. The manner in which Kerensky's offensive had failed convinced them that the Russian Army was on the verge of disintegration and that only a very modest effort would be required to bring about total collapse. On 16th July nine Central Powers divisions began exerting pressure against the Russian 11th Army on the Tarnopol sector, and within days the front had been completely broken.

During the evening of 20th July Locker Lampson received an urgent message from Headquarters 41st Corps to the effect that his unit was to be transferred to the command of 11th Army, on whose left flank it would be working.

> It seems that the Austrians had made a mild counter-attack and finding no resistance had pushed on against yielding infantry till the town of Izerna was unexpectedly taken and even Tarnopol threatened. This abrupt success came as a thunderbolt to the Russians, who were superior in arms, numbers and equipment and could never have lost Izerna so easily in normal times. It left them not knowing what to expect, but realising that in advancing thus rapidly the enemy had formed a salient highly vulnerable on his right, they hoped by rushing up troops during the night between Kurpatniki and Izerna to stop the advance. For this purpose our cars were hastily ordered by 11th Army to operate over roadless land ahead of the Russian infantry.
>
> Two hours after receiving the order all our armoured cars with three days' food and ammunition had left their front and reached Kozova ready to take the field at daybreak. The country over which they must

work was undrained and the slightest rain would make it impassable, but morning broke clear and they reached the village of Helenkuf at dawn and reported to the general in command of the Orenburgsky Division. Supports had trooped up during the night and worn-out Cossacks still slumbered round their camp-fires on arrival. The General was very affable to us, very angry with everyone else, and quite ignorant. He had received contradictory orders from the Staff and conflicting reports from the front, and did not know where either he, his infantry or the enemy were. He confided to us that the Corps Staff itself could get no certain news, and the least he asked of our cars was to keep him informed. The depth of the enemy salient was roughly twenty-five miles and he gave us carte blanche along his front, explaining that it was useless for him to suggest our reporting to any subordinate Staff, as their whereabouts was quite doubtful.

I at once divided up this front between the three squadrons of cars and allocated the right flank up the Tarnopol road to Lieutenant-Commander Smiles, spreading the rest out towards Kuropatniki. All cars came into action during these positions during the day. I gave further orders for them to stick to the horsetracks as far as possible, and at all costs to attack enemy infantry and cavalry even if our own infantry retired, and to hold on until the arrival of the enemy artillery made further resistance useless. Prior to this, on my own initiative, I had sent a car from each squadron on reconnaissance and received reports just after my return from the General. The enemy, it appeared, had advanced so swiftly that he had made no adequate effort to dig himself in and was drawing breath in temporary trenches pending a further lightning advance ahead of the artillery. It was just the kind of war armoured cars pray for and we made the most careful dispositions.

The Russian infantry occupied a line of trenches beyond Helenkuf and some hundreds of yards from the Austrians, and Lieutenant-Commander Smiles found a good observation post beside them. The colonel in command of the battalion there could offer no advice. He described the preceding day's flight in the bitterest language and promised no improvement in the future. The Austrians could be clearly seen but had outrun their artillery, which was conspicuous by its absence. Without delay, Smiles decided to send his cars ahead of the Russian trenches to hearten the troops, and the mere spectacle of them moving forward revived the Russians, who started to fire in earnest. Lieutenant Shadwell's car remained unseen in its progress forward and, having reached a dip several hundred yards beyond the Russian line, slowly mounted a rise beyond.

On reaching the top he beheld some Austrian infantry in the act of deploying and took them completely by surprise. They were cut down and as the remnants gathered in the trenches on each side he turned his fire repeatedly upon them. Lieutenant Gawler in his car ran up and striking a branch road ahead of Shadwell, reached some isolated bands of the enemy whom he drove into the woods and pursued, while a Ford armoured car, especially built for this type of work, threaded its way over the bare fields and wiped out two companies. Those who escaped from these encounters took refuge in some farm buildings and retaliated with Maxim fire. At once Smiles ordered the *Ulster* 3-pounder car into action and she ran up far past the Russian lines, got onto the farm buildings after the third shot and demolished or set fire to them all.

It was now 1030 and the enemy began advancing again, but were met by our cars on all sides and killed in hundreds. Many thousands of rounds had now been discharged by the cars and they withdrew for more, leaving the *Ulster* to carry on until they returned. She remained doing good work against groups of enemy infantry and then, in passing over bad ground, shifted a spring and stopped dead some 300 yards deep in No Man's Land. She sent back a message, and Lieutenant Shadwell and the Ford ran out to protect her while she extricated herself.

But in the meanwhile enemy artillery had arrived and was increasing in effect every minute, and much of the fire became concentrated upon the exposed car. Shadwell found great difficulty in keeping between the fire and the men on the *Ulster* who had temporarily repaired her and were now busy trying to start the car again. The engine had got heated and no efforts to wind her up prevailed: she was therefore left to cool. During this time the crew had been ordered to take shelter in the neighbouring ditches but returned after twenty minutes to set her going. Petty Officers Ritchie and Rodway then each tried four times to start her up under heavy fire, but failed. The enemy were now very near but both Petty Officers clambered back into the car and removed all vital parts from the guns before leaving, by which time the Austrians were barely fifty yards away. Petty Officer McKeown was badly wounded in the open. At the same time some copper-nosed bullets or splinters entered Shadwell's car, wounding him and nearly all his crew, and driving pieces of armour plate into their boots. The car was put out of action but all vital gun parts were removed and the crew crawled into a ditch and got back into the Russian trenches. The other cars kept solidly at work, firing continuously and hindering the enemy.

These lonely efforts, however, could not be kept up for long. For six and a half hours the cars had held the enemy in check, and now the Austrian artillery was too near and too accurate to make further work useful. Shells were bursting all round the cars and approaching the Russian trenches. Then the enemy got nearer, and suddenly all down their line rockets flared up and with one long-drawn rising shout of .'hurrah' they charged at a slow trot against the Russians. As one man, the latter flung away their rifles, abandoned their Maxims and ran

...w up in Galicia.

...ne-made' Heavy
...oured with 3-pounder.
...ia 1917.

...aged Model T Ford
...oured after the Galician
...at.

(*Far left*) Lieutenant-Commander Smiles in Galicia. (*Left*) Making repairs to a Ford Armoured car in Austria

The Petrograd garrison parading shortly after the Revolution. One of a series of postcards issued by the Provisional Government

A Russian Austin armoured car during the Revolution

screaming over the fields; some took off their boots to escape the faster. The officers strove in vain to hold them and then died firing ineffectual pistol shots against the Austrians.

Two of our cars were now out of action and their crews nearly all wounded. The other two mowed the advancing enemy down, slowly retreating as they fought, until a frightened company of Russians flung itself onto Lieutenant Gawler's car, hoping to use it for their escape, and by sheer weight broke it down. One of Gawler's crew was picked up by Smiles; the others took to the fields and only rejoined the force four days later after a wonderful escape. Gawler himself took a rifle and vainly for two hours tried to rally the Russians in a trench. Meanwhile a Russian officer with a pistol and some men, seeing the Ford covering the retreat, flung themselves upon its footboards and forced the driver to carry them out of danger. Lieutenant Shadwell reached the second line of Russian trenches as the shout came of the Austrian advance and, although wounded, forced two companies to return and fight until he was too exhausted to go on.

There is reason to believe that at least one car fired over the Russians' heads to prevent itself being swamped in what had become a stampede for safety, and more than a suspicion that, in self-defence, a few rounds were fired a little lower. Petty Officer Round had a grandstand view of the whole action. His car had axle trouble and he had been detailed as spare crew for Smiles' vehicles. On arriving just behind the line he settled himself in a culvert and began filling machine gun belts.

> An hour or so later the Russians left their trenches and fled panic-stricken, followed by a barrage of shrapnel. I waited for our cars to come back. Two passed some distance away, but a Ford Armoured driven by Petty Officer Shaw stopped and I hopped in just in time. Looking towards the trenches, I could see lines of enemy advancing in open order.
>
> Russian horse artillery was being withdrawn at the full gallop and ammunition dumps were going up right and left – one quite close to the Ford, lifting it momentarily off the ground. I remember thinking what a good film scene it would have made!

Locker Lampson's report continues:

> The only car beside the Ford to escape from this engagement was that of Sub-Lieutenant de Coninck, which operated further to the left and fought without rest until noon. The Russian lines where our cars operated were the last on the front to fall; our cars had actually at times advanced one and a half miles beyond the Russian trenches, and the divisional commander assured us that the work of the cars on this occasion gave him six hours' invaluable respite.

As our car losses had been considerable and as the Russian infantry could not be relied on, I decided to send no more cars in support of Smiles but instead despatched Lieutenant-Commander Wells Hood and his squadron to draw off enemy fire towards the left flank and generally to harass the advancing infantry. Wells Hood passed a retreating mob of Russian soldiers on his way up and found the enemy in process of occupying Venisloovka. No Russians were visible in the neighbourhood and no resistance was offered by them except to one point far behind him where a few companies gathered for a moment to repel an attack and then tore off as the first shells lit near them. By pushing boldly forward he engaged the enemy suddenly and with great effect and checked them quite half an hour, when the artillery drove him away.

Lieutenant-Commander Ruston's efforts, meanwhile, had been confined to a less lively sector. Yet Sub-Lieutenant Titterington was able to inflict great loss on the enemy at Veboodov, getting at one time a mile ahead into No Man's Land: the Russians later crowded onto his car and hindered all further work. All the cars which issued from the engagement were splashed from bullets and splinters, with punctured tyres and breakages, but otherwise unhurt.

I was asked to report at Helenkuf again about five o'clock, and was told that the Cossack division had gone and that I should find a cavalry division in its place. On arrival I found both had long since left and was then told to report to the 11th Division, which I did. I asked if I might at once take up some cars against the enemy while it was light, but the general in command was quite unnerved and begged me to return to Kozova, whither he immediately intended to retire.

There had been a report at Kozova in the morning of a breach in our trenches not far from the town and I had ordered the evacuation of our stores. On my return I found that this work had gone on feverishly and that the last lorry had left, abandoning only two very heavy trench mortars, which we sunk at a marked spot in the river, and some mortar ammunition which had been handed over to the Russians to use or destroy. Two armoured cars, badly damaged, had to be abandoned and an old tank wagon which had been in need of spare parts.

To Locker Lampson's annoyance, the Russians had made a specific request that Sub-Lieutenant Benson's section of two 3-pounder guns should remain in the trenches facing Brzezany. Once this was granted, they had promptly abandoned the line themselves, leaving Benson and his men to destroy the guns and make their own way out.

All else was saved and not an ounce of stores lost. But we had moved only just in time, for during my absence a terrible panic had taken place at Kozova. The retreating Russians had been mistaken for advancing Germans and terror had spread through the town. Baron Girard and Captain Hand behaved splendidly, quelling the excitement and stemming the rush of vehicles and soldiery : and Lieutenant Crossing took his armoured car and held the bridge against possible enemy cavalry, thus enabling Red Cross carts and other transport to get through unhindered. But the real enemy had advanced near enough by now to hamper our retreat and shrapnel broke over us, even wounding a man beside me outside the headquarters.

The Staff ordered us to leave for a village beyond Podgaitse and we passed out over a litter of loot to the sound of exploding shells. Our road ran past two villages (Kshiva and Telyache) nearer the front than Kozova and we found its surface already full of holes. Enormous craters (from a 16-inch naval gun, as we learned later) pitted the crossroads and blocked our passage; we could not get out. So in the dark we struck across muddy fields to try our luck among tracks innumerable. But the care with which we had reconnoitred all paths in the past stood us in good stead now, and after hours of wandering in rain, mud and darkness we struck the main road again and looking back beheld Kshiva village ablaze and all the sky quite pink. Our advance base was a few miles beyond Podgaitse at the aviation camp and this we reached at 0500 on 22nd July.

In Podgaitse was an English Hospital run by suffragettes, who had taken in our wounded. They had suddenly been told by the Russian authorities that the town was in danger, that the ammunition stores might at any moment explode, and that not a single horse or cart could be spared to get the nurses away. Surgeon Scott, who was helping at the hospital, arranged therefore it and we loaned cars to take the staff to our camp the same day we arrived and from there they were sent, most fortunately, on to Kiev and thence to Petrograd.

I was awakened at 0900 by Colonel Valentine of the Royal Flying Corps, to whom we had lent a car driven by Chief Petty Officer Boot and Chief Petty Officer Checkley.* These ratings and the car had, it appears, met him on the way from Tarnopol, which was in flames, near his aerodrome at Denisof. He had requested their help and night and day they had worked, salvaging thousands of pounds worth of aeroplane gear and five new machines. With the aid of his car Chief Petty Officer Checkley pulled the trucks upon which the aeroplanes were loaded along the railway lines, and then proceeded to the Russian aviation ground some distance away and assisted in the destruc-

---

* Lieutenant-Colonel James Valentine, DSO, had been a well known figure at pre-war flying events, and had been in Russia for almost a year, commanding a unit which trained Russian pilots to fly British machines. He too was awarded the St George's Cross by Kornilov, but died at Kiev shortly after the incident described above as a result of a heart attack brought on by the stresses of the retreat.

tion of sixteen machines which would otherwise have fallen into the hands of the Germans. These ratings were the last to leave and escaped finally over hurdles placed across the trenches and with the aid of an aeroplane compass. They eventually reached a town near Proskurov and fell asleep from exhaustion in their car. They were awakened at 2.45 a.m. by a staff officer, taken to the Headquarters, and each presented with a St George's Cross by General Kornilov himself.

Colonel Valentine stated that the position was very critical and that even Proskurov would fall. The French aviators in our camp then very kindly sent an aeroplane out, which reported that the enemy was already in occupation of Kozova and nearing Podgaitse. Nevertheless, I sent Lieutenant-Commander Smiles through Podgaitse to try and fire an ammunition dump near Kozova, and I despatched Lieutenant-Commander Ruston and four cars to operate beyond Podgaitse and Telyache to hinder the enemy.

About mid-day we received orders from the Army Headquarters at Buczacz for all our cars to hasten back there as the enemy had reached Tarnopol and his advanced troops menaced the road to that town and Buczacz. I ordered the camp therefore to be cleared and the lorries to be loaded. At 3 p.m. a cyclist rushed into camp with news from a Russian soldier that the German cavalry was only five versts off and that the entire population of Podgaitse was flying towards us. I ran out of my tent, ordered the 3-pounders into position, and sent armoured cars up the road to intercept the cavalry, keeping one to reconnoitre the valley on our flank.

Podgaitse was some nine miles from our camp, and towards it the road ran for half a mile through the open plain and as the ground swelled into a rise, so the road rose and disappeared over the near horizon. The road lay bare except for the cars I had ordered along it, and the plain also, and then quite suddenly not only the road but also the line of the horizon became black, black and moving with cars, carts, horses and people flying for their lives. It is impossible to reproduce our feelings of despair at this spectacle of disorder. But my aim was to save our transport, not so much from the German cavalry, which could easily be met by our cars, as from the maddened soldiery in retreat who would break them down to escape. Rather than complete the loading, I ordered the camp to be instantly cleared of all but active service units and ordered the transport to Buczacz, there to unload and then, if possible, return. The lorries managed to swing out into the road, being loaded even as they moved, and were all on their way before the human tide reached us.

The noise of its approach filled the air – voices, wheels, horses. Very few women seemed to be escaping, and the carts and cars were crammed with soldiers. Hundreds of soldiers went afoot, their clothes torn, their eyes wild and absolutely mad with fright. In their agony to get away, the occupants of the carts kept throwing out valuables, against which the vehicles behind would stick and then traffic would be blocked until an enterprising cart tried to jump the ditch into the fields. Some succeeded, others fell headlong. Whereupon other carts turned and drove over the upturned cart and kicking horses, using them as a bridge. On the whole, motor cars showed the least mercy and charged relentlessly along.

The sight was too much for Baron Girard. Something deep inside him snapped and, seething with anger, he strode out into the road.

He threw himself upon the horse of the first cart and overturned both to block the way, striking the two soldiers in the cart repeatedly over the head. A huge lorry behind in which stood at least 35 soldiers all armed, was thus abruptly stopped. Without pause Girard rushed at the driver and tore him unresisting from his seat, then with his stick he attacked the soldiers in the back. He struck the first in the mouth and hit another so hard over the ear that I could see it bleeding as he fell backwards off the vehicle. At once a counter-panic set in, and these men whose one object a few moments since had been to get on, now had but one desire – to get back. It was a question of which soldier could leave the lorry quickest to escape Girard, and in three minutes the vehicle was empty.

Seeing the Baron's success, Lieutenant Reppmann and a couple of other Russian officers drew their revolvers and threatened to shoot any man who dared drive on. Immediately a few soldiers and Cossacks who arrived took Girard's part and for hours he and his helpers sent back horses, soldiers and cars, firing revolvers and rifles to back their orders. Soon not a soldier attempted to get past and not one dared to defend himself. It was as if the ancient regime had returned, as if the iron discipline of the old army had never decayed. The soldiers stood stiffly to attention as of yore while these officers beat them in the face, tore their beards and kicked them for cowards; others prayed for mercy on their knees, making the sign of the Cross. Baron Girard and his henchmen were a mere handful holding in check thousands of revolutionary soldiers, all armed, any ten of whom could have killed them: yet not a finger was raised.

I would not allow my officers to interfere beyond blocking the road and fording the flood of traffic to turn back. The reports our cyclists brought back from the armoured cars were reassuring. No Germans had reached Podgaitse and our cars were some miles the other side of the town and had seen nothing.

Ruston's cars had reached Podgaitse and, while pausing to refill their radiators in the market square, had witnessed the birth of the panic. An account published the following year in *Blackwood's Magazine* and probably written by Ruston himself, describes the ensuing chaos in the town.

Suddenly, with screams and cries of *'Nemetski cavalari!'* (German cavalry), horses with carts driven by frenzied drivers galloped into the town. Anticipating trouble, we at once endeavoured to get our cars across the road to form a barrier, but we were not quite quick enough. In vain did we plead with them, expostulate with them, curse them and even threaten them. We stood in the streets and pointed revolvers at the mob and told the terror-stricken *Tovarichi* that it was only the work of German agents. S'monoclem, who was an excellent Russian linguist, was in fine form; but even his flow of patriotic eloquence failed to move the Russians.* It was perfectly useless. One and all had seen the German lancers driving the fleeing Russian infantry before them. Wonderful imaginations they were gifted with.

To give a touch of realism to the scene, a travelling cookhouse, going at full gallop, collided with a loaded ammunition limber and an explosion ensued. 'They're shelling us!' wailed the mob, by this time hopelessly blocked in the narrow streets. I am attempting the impossible when I try to describe it. In less than ten minutes from the commencement the whole town was packed tight with transport coming from all directions and trying to go in one way – away from the front. Horses and carts overturned in heaps, horses with legs broken and with hoofs torn off, writhing in their dying agony – a howling, frenzied mob; such was the sight. To lighten their carts and so facilitate retreat, drivers emptied their loads anywhere. Sacks of sugar, flour, bales of provender, officers' kits, cases of hand grenades, field-gun ammunition, spare wheels, and even overcoats and rifles, were all thrown into the streets. Many drivers even cut their traces and, mounting their horses, left their carts behind. At the windows were the grinning faces of the (Austrian) civil population. To them it was a huge joke, but to us . . . My fingers itched to empty my Webley automatic into them.

Thinking that perhaps it was as well to find out if there really was anything in it, we went into an empty house, got into the garret, smashed a hole in the roof, and had a look round through our field-glasses. Everything was quiet; even peaceful. There in the valley, three miles distant, we could see cattle grazing peacefully. We returned to our cars and tried to persuade the crowd that they had been mistaken, but they didn't believe us. We spent the next hour organising the traffic so that they could get away. A Cossack officer helped us, using his *knout* (a lead-tipped whip) very freely. He was the only Russian officer we saw. We heard later that this panic spread the entire length of the road through Buczacz, Chetkov to Gusiatyn on the frontier, and

---

* By now, most of the unit's British officers had acquired Russian nicknames. S'monoclem – the man with the monocle – was Lieutenant Hulls.

terrible scenes were witnessed. It was all a put-up job by the Germans, but it worked very well. In this stunt we had a transport car so badly damaged that it was not worth removing. We set fire to it, leaving nothing for the Hun except our cards with an invitation to come along, as we were anxious to renew his acquaintance; and in due course he accepted our invitation.

It took Ruston's squadron four hours to fight their way through the confusion and reach the forward trenches, where they exchanged shots with the enemy's scouts. The riotous departure of the transport had left those Russians who remained without rations or reserve ammunition, and a withdrawal to the town was made after dark, the cars returning to the aviation camp at about 2100 hours.

Meanwhile, Locker Lampson had learned that the enemy was also advancing south from Tarnopol with the intention of cutting the Buczacz–Brzezany road, which would have the effect of isolating large numbers of Russian troops to the west. Accordingly, Ruston and his men were roused during the early hours of 23rd July and told to move as quickly as possible into an area where this new thrust could be countered. The road was clogged with retreating artillery and transport as well as being thronged with infantry who believed that the war was virtually over and yelled derisively at the cars as they passed. Many had provided themselves with the alibi of a phoney wound, but the sheer number of bandaged left hands tended to emphasise a singular lack of imagination among these 'invalids'. The surface was, however, well above average, and by 0800 hours the cars were driving up to the headquarters of the 34th Corps in the hamlet of Kamiloovka.

> The General fortunately spoke perfect English [wrote Ruston] and at once admitted the sad state of affairs and his lack of information, which he hoped we should be able to correct. He also ordered us to shoot down any troops we met retreating; but when it was explained to him that this was impossible for us, he withdrew the order, though rather reluctantly.
>
> We left the village and reached Darakoov, about six *versts* distant, where we split forces, some cars going straight along the *chaussée* road towards Tarnopol and others turning to the left and striking across country. My car was among the latter, and our objective was first a small hamlet where a divisional headquarters had been. On the way we got bogged in the soft earth, and our car refused to pull herself out owing to the epicyclic gears slipping, so it was a case of 'Take her up another notch', a catch phrase of ours. While this was being done

shells began to fall in our vicinity, and we could not make out from which direction they were coming. We reached the hamlet, which was deserted and being shelled, and went four miles the other side of it. We went along country lanes and into villages reported to have long been in the enemy's hands and found neither friend nor foe there, so about 11 o'clock we returned to Darakoov to compare notes with the other cars. Their experiences had been just the same. They had been down the road for ten miles and had seen nothing except a squadron of Cossacks, but they too had been shelled.

We sent in the results of our reconnaissance to the General, who seemed more than surprised, and again we set off, this time to find and engage the enemy. We took the same routes as before, and the cross-country cars were again shelled. When we reached the small hamlet – Pantiloovka – we found that shell after shell was being pumped into it, and to our amazement discovered that it was the Russian artillery. A message was sent in to the General, who inquired into the matter and had things righted – with apologies to us.

The patrol continued without incident until approximately 1400 hours when Ruston, entering Pantiloovka for the third time, found the enemy trying to work their way into the hamlet from the north-east.

We got them entirely by surprise at a range of 200 yards and drove them out, killing a large number. Our enemy this time were Germans, and it gave us more satisfaction to get up against them.

Apparently they had had enough, for though we waited for another venture they did not come again. A motor-cyclist came tearing up to order us all onto the *chaussée* road, as the enemy was advancing beyond Darakoov. We dashed back, and again were able to do great execution, getting excellent targets. Though the enemy was in open order, we were able to arrest the frontal attack absolutely; but as no Russian infantry was within five *versts* and the enemy had managed to advance further south over bad ground, we were obliged to withdraw slightly for fear of having the *chaussée* road cut behind us. We took up a position to the south of the village, where a hill gave us good observation, and from there we kept the Hun at bay for many hours. We allowed them to reach the village, and then popped up from behind houses and other cover, and drove them off. These tactics were successful, and we killed quite a number. S'monoclem noticed a courtyard full as he passed through the street. He stopped at once and reversed, and met them all in the gateway at point-blank range, doing great execution. Later he got a bullet through the arm, but was able to carry on.

Enemy reinforcements arrived and got a footing in the south-western edge of the village with machine-guns, which they mounted in houses. We sent a message to the corps commander stating that we could hold on, and with infantry reinforcements could recapture the lost portion of the village. The General replied that he had no infantry on whom he could depend, but urged us to hold on. About 16.30 hours the Germans endeavoured to advance from Darakoov to Kamiloovka, but having advanced so far ahead of their artillery, we were easily able to hold them, and though many attempts were made, they were all repulsed with heavy loss.

One solitary field-gun was brought up to clear the enemy machine-guns from their new positions, and it was taken so close under cover of our cars that we actually witnessed the rather unusual sight of a duel between enemy machine-gunners and Russian artillerists. The houses were destroyed, and what occupants escaped came under the fire of our machine guns.

About 1800 hours the position remained as it had been two hours previously – the enemy in part possession of the village, but unable to occupy the whole. An hour later a Russian battalion took up a position about 1500 yards from the enemy, and our cars remained between them and the enemy for the night.

Locker Lampson now decided to concentrate all the cars under Ruston. There were not many available, since the vehicle casualties on 21st July, breakdowns and requests from the Russian artillery for escorts to the rear had steadily eroded the unit's strength. However, during the night Smiles arrived with one Heavy and at least one No 2 Squadron car, the Rolls Royce, also reached Darakoov.

Ruston and his men had been in more or less continuous action for 72 hours and were worn out, the nervous tensions of a night spent between the lines providing scant opportunity for rest. At 0400 hours on the 24th Ruston and Locker Lampson reported to Corps headquarters, which had moved back to Lyaskootse.

> The Corps Commander told us that of his four divisions two refused to move. He begged us to do all we could to hinder the advance, though we knew sooner or later the enemy artillery would drive us back. Then he wept, a most moving sight; he was a fine soldier and a nice man.
>
> On arriving back at the cars we found everything had been quiet, but very shortly after the enemy began to advance in waves through the standing corn. In the distance we could distinctly see mounted Staff officers spying out the land and making their plans for a further advance. As soon as the enemy advance commenced the Russian troops on the right of the road left their hastily dug trenches and ran off. We moved the Heavy up close to the village where it pounded away at the newly chosen machine-gun positions, while the light cars ran

into the village itself, getting behind the advancing Huns. The advance was stopped, but in this scrap several men were wounded, necessitating fresh dispositions of crews. The Huns decided we were a nuisance to them, so they dropped their ideas of an advance and began shelling the road very heavily and fairly accurately.

Observing this development from a vantage point in Kamiloovka, Locker Lampson decided that the cars were too bunched up for their own safety and, no doubt cursing the Russian decision to disband his wireless section the previous year, set out on foot to join them. Half a mile along the road a shell screamed into the road surface, spattering him with mud but failing to explode. He finished the journey in a reserve armoured car.

A hard, confused battle followed lasting several hours, the only certain factor in which was that large numbers of the enemy were by-passing Darakoov and Kamiloovka, and were beginning to exert increasing pressure on the flanks and rear. Two further frontal attacks were repulsed. The Russian infantry on the left of the road, having fought well for a while, suddenly bolted on finding themselves under artillery fire from the flanks; the German gunners at once switched from high explosive to shrapnel, cutting them down in swathes. Sub-Lieutenant Southam, nicknamed the *Slon* (Elephant), worked his way across country to catch a transport column which he dispersed with heavy loss – during the day, his car fired no less than 30,000 rounds. Sub-Lieutenant Woods, also apparently operating on the flank, observed a solitary wounded Austrian walking back across a rise ahead, and moved forward to capture him. On crossing the crest, however, he was confronted by an entire battalion, resting a mere fifty yards away. He opened up at once, killing and wounding large numbers while the rest took to their heels. Smiles, meanwhile, had been battering away at positions in Darakoov, while Sub-Lieutenant Wallace cruised up and down the main street, hunting fugitives and blazing away through windows.

Kamiloovka now came under artillery fire and it was all too clear that the cars would have to withdraw soon if they were to avoid being cut off. Locker Lampson took over effective command, while Ruston went back by motor-cycle to inform the corps commander of the situation, since the despatch riders had all been wounded. On the way he ran into a group of deserters who forced him off the machine, and then smashed it while fighting among themselves for its possession. With difficulty, he managed to reach the headquarters on foot.

In the meantime, Locker Lampson had been conducting the cars' withdrawal through Kamiloovka, with Smiles bringing up the rear in his Heavy.

It was a big village of thatched buildings. The main *chaussée* road divided the village in halves and a strong wind was blowing from the left half of the village across the *chaussée* road towards the right half, beyond which the enemy were advancing. A colonel in command was wandering about and I asked leave to pretend to evacuate the village. For this purpose I wanted to set fire to the left-hand side of the village and ostentatiously send all troops out of it. The strong wind would drive the smoke in dense clouds across the road and I could hide our cars easily in it and actually on the *chaussée*. The enemy would advance against the smoking village believing it to be empty and without shelling it, and would penetrate the right half, quite unhampered, and then reach the *chaussée* before seeing us. We could then dash out of the smoke and wipe them out. But the Russians would not permit this and so we had to watch the enemy get nearer without being able to meet him over the wet fields of his advance. There were some Russian armoured cars and I suggested a plan of cooperation with them, but they had orders to patrol the road nearer Buczacz and went back out of the village. So we decided to go up again against the enemy along the main road.

Here the fighting was very hard and the enemy artillery already stronger and very accurate. A shell set light to the Rolls Royce armoured car and under heavy fire the crew had to get out and put it out. With incredible difficulty they saved both themselves and the car, every tyre of which was destroyed.* Another shell struck Sub-Lieutenant Wallace's car direct, wounding him and all his crew badly, but so excellent was the armour that no one was killed and Petty Officer W. D. Swan managed to drive them all out safely although he fainted twice from his wounds.

The enemy were shelling the road far behind our cars and both flanks had been cleared of Russian infantry. The latter had received an order to retire and the front remained unprotected except for our cars, which kept at work, remaining in the village half an hour after the Russians had gone. The Russians retired across country to Chertkov, while our cars withdrew down the road. Some way outside the village Lieutenant-Commander Smiles met an officer who told him that his regiment had had great losses on the left; he had then tried to reform the regiment on the bank of the road behind our cars, threatening the troops with his revolver. Smiles held the armoured cars on the road to help, and then gave the Russians a start of 500 yards

---

* According to Ruston's account, the turret crew came out clinging to the outside of the vehicle.

before retiring. But a shell broke his petrol pipe and forced him to hurry, while a couple more shells struck Sub-Lieutenant Southam's car, blowing the engine clean out without even wounding a man. We lost this car and two bicycles during the day, but saved all guns and vital parts.

Three *versts* along the road our cars met the Russian rearguard, about half a company of infantry and some cavalry, evidently sent with great kindness to our assistance. These turned back on being informed by Smiles that the road was clear of Russian troops. Another half *verst* further back we found two Russian armoured cars patrolling the road.

I returned to camp at Buczacz to find the roads stagnant with traffic and to learn that a panic, even more serious than the previous ones, had taken place. I had an hour's sleep and motored on to Chertkov where I selected a camp for our base in the evening. Once there, however, I could not stop but had to see the Staff which had left Buczacz suddenly in the night and retired right back to Gusiatyn. The drivers were so tired that I could only use a car just in from Main Base, and in this I reached Gusiatyn very late. The Army Staff were worn out and thought that even Chertkov was a dangerous base. I returned there at once, woke the camp and brought it on some thirty miles to Gusiatyn, which we reached at 0900.

Throughout these days our transport under Lieutenant Hanna and Sub-Lieutenant Lefroy did wonders feeding and munitioning the troops in the field and evacuating base after base at the double. They worked every day and night of the retreat and brought up all the 968 tons of stores we had moved up : and not for one moment all this time was a gun in want of ammunition or a man in need of food.

Ruston and his crews reached Chertkov at 2200 hours and camped at the roadside, sleeping the deep sleep of exhaustion without being disturbed by the incessant flow of traffic heading for the rear. The next morning, 25th July, they were told to report to the 22nd Corps as a matter of urgency, the enemy having crossed the river Sereth upon which the Russians had hoped to make a stand. The cars set off at once, forcing their way through the congestion with klaxons blowing. It was some measure of the confusion existing even at command level that they were told on arrival that they were not required; the 22nd Corps was already being supported by the Belgian armoured car squadron, which was performing sterling work. The British took advantage of the unexpected respite to settle down for the night at Kopyczincze.

The Russian collapse had not been confined to the Galician front. The Provisional Government, and even the Petrograd Soviet, were so seriously alarmed that they acceded to Kornilov's plea that the officers' authority should be restored and with it the death penalty. In theory, this could only be awarded by a court martial consisting of three officers and three soldiers chosen by lot, but the time for such niceties had long passed and local military authorities were already resorting to draconian measures to restore order. Long railway trains, flanked by Cossack battle police, were drawn across the level crossings and the large numbers of bandaged left hands individually inspected, following which those men who had provided themselves with a precautionary scratch were marched back to the lines under escort; others with less forethought received summary justice.

At Gusiatyn, now swarming with 40,000 armed deserters, nemesis appeared in the shape of the notorious Wild Division. This semi-savage, half-disciplined formation was recruited from Caucasian Moslem Cossacks who feared that their ancient privileges conferred by the Czar would be swept away by the Revolution, to which they were violently opposed. They enjoyed killing for its own sake and were regarded slightly askance by other Cossacks.

Locker Lampson had steadfastly refused to allow his unit to become involved in Russian disciplinary proceedings, but he did provide the Wild Division with a dozen Lewis guns, 50,000 rounds of ammunition and some instructors. The Cossacks learned quickly and that night galloped through the town firing the heavy weapons from the saddle – it proved to be an extremely effective but highly dangerous way of clearing the streets.

The Wild Division meant business. A group of political activists who held a meeting were shot down in cold blood. A party of 300 deserters was stopped on the road and threatened with decimation unless they disclosed the identity of the agitator who had led them away from the front. This they did, and when the man confessed his guilt he was promptly shot dead. His body was nailed to a tree as an example, together with a large warning notice in Russian and German. Both incidents were witnessed, with mounting disgust, by British personnel. Elsewhere, a Guards regiment which had murdered its colonel and battalion commanders was surrounded and forced to surrender after a pitched battle.

These measures took some time to become apparent at the front. During the morning of the 26th Ruston and his men received a visit from their old friend the commander of the 34th Corps, who refused to accept that they now formed part of another corps, and at once despatched them on a mission.

Evidently during the night the enemy had effected many crossings of the Sereth and was advancing down the road from Tarnopol to Chertkov. This was also a magnificent road, but from our point of view the country was none too good. Huge forests approached the road from either side, and while doubtless they had their good points, it would have been an easy matter for the enemy to have felled trees behind us.

We turned off the road to the left and following the tracks entered the village of Kobelovloki, taking German cavalry by surprise. The enemy's advance was becoming more cautious, and this was the first occasion we had encountered cavalry. We cleared the village and going beyond it drove off several other cavalry patrols with severe losses to them.

We were then recalled and despatched to another spot further down, where help was badly needed. Unfortunately, it was necessary to cross a small stream and during the retreat the light bridge had been badly broken. Though we worked hard to repair it we could do nothing and had to retire to Kopyczincze.

It was about 2100 hours when we reported to the General, who thanked us warmly for our work. He had received instructions from Army to hand us over to the corps on his left (i.e. the 22nd), so this time we had to say good-bye for good.

On going back through the village we found looting going on everywhere. The infantry being in full flight, meant to take away all they could and ransacked house after house, taking all. They began to file out with carpets, articles of clothing, ornaments and so on. Some of these they did not like, so they calmly threw them in the street. We could stand it no longer and Ted was first in.* Seizing man after man he threw them out, whilst S'monoclem smote them hard with a huge ash stick he was in the habit of carrying. We all rushed over to join in and for a time things looked ugly. Many of the Russian soldiers were stunnned and cut about the head, but we didn't care. The situation was saved by S'monoclem, who in a wonderful speech appealed to the soldiers to behave as Russians. This had the desired effect, and the looting ceased.

Again we flitted by moonlight, this time bound for Gusiatyn, the frontier town. We halted by the roadside about 2300 hours and tried to sleep, but it was much too cold. I spent the whole night walking about, my teeth rattling like castanets. Quite early next morning we reached Gusiatyn.

The condition of the cars was now appalling but the repair crews were working round the clock and by the afternoon of the 27th Smiles was able to report to the 2nd Cavalry Division with three vehicles – a Pierce Arrow Heavy, a Ford, and a Fiat lorry fitted with

* Probably Sub-Lieutenant Ted Titterington.

...e sick bay going through ...e Caucasian mountains ...ar Tabriz. A photograph ...m Petty Officer Baker's ...um.

...e end of the ...ck – Locker Lampson ...d others reconnoitring on ... Mush Plain.

...ntenance in ...scaucasia. Note the old ...Squadron plate.

(*Top*) Russian aircraft brought down this German aircraft near Braila. (*Left*) Model T Ford Armoured, designed by Chief Petty Officer Gutteridge. (*Right*) 3-pounder gun emplacement near Galatz. Rumania 1917.

Lieutenant Ingle's car after recovery from No Man's Land.

the armour from a wrecked Ford. With these he went out to Glustenka and fought a series of rearguard actions against German cavalry and artillery until dusk.

The following day Smiles again covered the rearguard at Suchadol, this time with a Lanchester and a Ford, and these two vehicles were the last to leave Austrian territory. The bridge over the river Zbrucz, marking the frontier, was blown immediately after they had driven across into Russian Gusiatyn, where their safe arrival was cheered by the Russians.

The new forward base was at Kootkovtse, ten miles east of Gusiatyn on the Proskurov road, and close to the headquarters of the 22nd Corps. During the 29th work continued on the cars and by evening the unit's vehicle state was much happier. The next morning Ruston's squadron was called forward again, reaching the front through Alhovtse.

> The enemy had crossed the river and was trying to eject the Russians from their trenches. The Russians, who were fighting on their own territory, were putting up a better show and hoped to be able to hold on. The crossing of the river was undertaken by a division of Turks and a division of Austrians, both of whom had been filled up with vodka beforehand, as we learned from prisoners. They fought like fiends but suffered very heavy losses. The cars were in action many times during the day, Wallie doing particularly good work in the town of Gusiatyn. Towards evening the artillery began to come up and things got decidedly warm.

Wells Hood's squadron was now also back in business and was continuously engaged throughout the day. On one occasion he was so close to the enemy that he could hear the thud of his bullets striking and his victims' gasp for breath; on another, both his car and that of Lieutenant Crossing were subjected to a violent close-quarter grenade attack in a wood. Sub-Lieutenant Benson fully justified his reputation for good gunnery when his Heavy engaged a machine gun post in a church belfry at 2,000 yards; after fifteen minutes' firing the belfry was completely wrecked. The *pièce de résistance* was, however, reserved for the evening. An enemy aircraft crossed the lines, shooting up the cars quite accurately from a height of 800 feet. Seizing a Lewis gun, Petty Officer Rogers replied and with his fourth magazine evidently hit the pilot, for the machine failed to pull out of its attack dive and plunged straight into the ground; quite possibly, this was the first occasion in history when an aircraft was brought down by fire from a fighting vehicle.

On the 31st Ruston was in action again.

With the exception of the few battalions which the enemy had managed to get across the river, both sides were entrenched – the one in Austrian Gusiatyn and the other in Russian Gusiatyn, with a distance of about 1,200 yards between them. During the night the enemy had got up a good deal of artillery, including 4-inch and 6-inch howitzers, whilst the Russians had nothing but field-guns, having sent their heavy guns further back. Shortly after 1000 hours the enemy attempted to attack the Russian trenches, whilst under cover of the guns supports crossed the river.

Our cars were rushed in, and at once a heavy barrage was put across the road behind the Russian trenches. One car was soon outed but the others got through, though they were only just able to discern the enemy through the dust and smoke. A steady fire was maintained on the enemy, who eventually withdrew with severe losses, though the supports had been able to cross the river in the meantime.

The remainder of the day was intensely hot and very quiet, and as we sat on the road little disturbed us. I remember how upset one dear old lady was because we cut some branches off her trees to shield our cars the better from aerial observation. We were polite but firm, and took more branches. About noon the enemy took a dislike to the church in the Russian village, and amused himself with a little target practice. Out of six shots fired – big stuff they were too — four were direct hits.

At 1800 hours it was decided to drive the Germans across the river by means of a counter-attack, in which our cars and an armoured train were to participate. An hour's artillery preparation was to precede the attack, and the cars were to leave the village at 1955 to give encouragement to the infantry going over the top five minutes later. The bombardment commenced, but Fritz answered not a word.

The minutes passed and at 1950 we started up our engines and emptied our cars of all impedimenta, for this was the real thing again. Right on time we dashed off for the front line, but no sooner had we shown our noses over the hill than a terrific fire was put on the road and the Russian trenches. The troops in the trenches – a Siberian regiment – led by their gallant colonel, went over the top and advanced under this fire, and in the face of a murderous machine gun fire, with magnificent courage. The *Slon* got through the barrage, though how he did it he doesn't remember, and made for the enemy trenches. He pumped lead into them for some minutes till a piece of shell blew the end off his machine-gun, and then retired. His car had four shell-holes in it when he returned. The armoured train had done good work, but the artillery was too feeble, and the attack failed. The losses on the Russian side had been awful. Early next morning the enemy was

The Armoured Car Mess: The *Times* Petrograd correspondent (1), Captain Hand, MC (2), Lieutenant Commander Wells-Hood (3), Mr Mewes of *Daily Mirror* (4), Captain Gayden (5), Commander Belt (6), Lieutenant Hanna (7), Commander O. Locker Lampson (8).

The Kursk squadron leaving Russia on trawlers.

Duncars' officers in Baghdad.

Duncars' operational b at Hamadan.

Bicherakov's Cossack cavalry. North Persia 1

Bicherakov's Cossack Infantry.

driven across the river, and both sides commenced to entrench and sit tight.

So ended the Great Retreat, one of the most shameful episodes in Russian military history. Incredible as it may seem in view of its continuous involvement, the British unit's casualties amounted to a mere twelve men wounded, of whom only one is described as having serious injuries. However, two out of every three cars had been written off by enemy action or other causes, although the equipment position eased slightly in August with the arrival of the eight armoured Fiats promised by the Russians.

The unit had for ten days covered a yawning 25-mile gap in the Russian line and by its skilful deployment had repeatedly balked the Austro-German advance and so bought priceless time for the harassed Russian command. Prisoners stated that the cars seemed to be present whichever way they advanced, and that there was a general belief that the unit was three to four times its actual size. Further interrogations suggested that some 600 casualties had been inflicted during the fighting at Darakoov, and probably not less than 2,000 for the entire retreat. There was no doubt that the Germans regarded the British as the only serious opposition they were likely to meet.* The entire range of armoured car tactics had been employed and although communications had been restricted to hand signals and messages passed by despatch rider, tactical control had never broken down.

At the Admiralty Locker Lampson's report was read with intense interest, but a suggestion that it should be released for public consumption through the Department of Information was turned down flat on the grounds that such an account 'would almost amount to a breach of faith if this record of disgrace of one of our Allies was given to the world'. Locker Lampson need not have worried that the hard earned publicity he had so diligently sought was thus forfeit. Robert Wilton, the *Times*'s Petrograd correspondent, was a regular visitor, while the *Daily Mirror*'s correspondent, a popular man named Mewes, stayed with the unit throughout its long ordeal, and their reports succeeded in making a national figure of him even after the

* From this grew a wild rumour that the British were to be brought in 'dead or alive', and that funds were being offered for their capture. Writing for *Lloyd's Magazine* the following year, Locker Lampson claimed that the Kaiser had personally put a price of 20,000 Marks on his head; we have discovered no evidence to support this, although the effect on circulation must have been impressive!

censor had done his work.

Kornilov wrote to him as soon as the front had stabilised.

> I consider it a sacred duty to convey to you and to your officers, non-commissioned officers and men my sincere and heartfelt thanks for their gallantry and for the aid they have rendered in repulsing the attacks of our relentless foe.
>
> I send you herewith 24 Crosses of St George which you are to award at your discretion; besides this I ask you to be good enough to recommend at your earliest convenience those others of your gallant fellows whom you consider deserving of the St George. At the same time please send me a list of those of your officers who, in your opinion, are deserving of honours, indicating the particular services which they have rendered.
>
> It is a source of gratification to me to have this opportunity of rewarding such brave officers and men, and I beg you, dear Sir, to accept my heartfelt thanks and respects.
>
> L. KORNILOV, General.

Wells Hood had already received the St George from the commander of the 22nd Corps for his squadron's action on 30th July, and Locker Lampson was subsequently awarded the Order of St Anne, but no record exists of further Russian awards to the unit's personnel, although it is likely that some were made.

It was October before any British decorations were approved, and these related only to the actions fought at Brzezany at the beginning of July. Lieutenant-Commander Belt received the Distinguished Service Order, and Lieutenants Samuel Hanna and George Turner the Distinguished Service Cross; the Distinguished Service Medal was awarded to Chief Petty Officer Boutall and Petty Officers Harrison, Gardner, McEwan, Algate and Gregson.

The list confirms Locker Lampson's admitted reluctance in the matter of his officers' decorations. Belt and Hanna received their awards for outstanding service during the whole period that the unit had been in Russia; Turner for his exemplary courage in the trenches. Again, in his long and detailed report on the Great Retreat, written on 16th August, Locker Lampson concludes with 'I would respectfully suggest postponing to a later despatch recommendations of officers and men who have done well.' The reasons for such a suggestion remain obscure; nor have we been able to discover either the recommendations themselves or a list of awards, although both may well exist.

In the meantime, everyone had a great deal more to worry about than medals. Poor tormented Russia was a volcano which had erupted once and had continued to pour out the black clouds of unrest ever since. The British, all but friendless, were sitting on the edge and if a second eruption occurred, as many predicted it would, they had no wish to be caught in the explosion; in fact, forces were already at work which would make that explosion inevitable.

CHAPTER NINE

Through a Glass Darkly

The cars were called forward once or twice during the next week as a precautionary measure, but no serious engagement developed. Locker Lampson was, however, far from being satisfied that the new front would hold, and considered that his main base at Proskurov would undoubtedly fall if the Austro-German armies continued their advance.

> I made arrangements to evacuate the hundreds of tons of stores which we had collected at Proskurov for the next year. The difficulties in our way cannot be detailed. The railways were blocked, the officials tired out and the demands on both were daily growing, yet we managed in a week to send off 500 tons of material right back to Kursk, and another 700 tons to a new base which I decided to start not at Kiev itself, which may fall, but beyond it and over the river at Brovari. Simultaneously I despatched by train and car as many wounded as could move and in view of the shocking state of Russian politics I ordered them straight to England via Kiev and Archangel. We were then left with a balance of stores with which our cars could negotiate.

Whilst the unit was in no immediate danger, Locker Lampson had already glimpsed the approaching spectre of civil war, and his impressions of Kornilov had done nothing to allay his fears.

> He is already spoken of as the coming Dictator. He is a small, wiry man with a big head, and of Tartar origin. His father, though a simple Cossack, gave him a good military education and quite early Kornilov determined to get on. He volunteered for duty in Turkestan, where the fighting affords him leisure for study, and there he taught himself French and English. Disguised as a native he subsequently ran great risks photographing in Afghanistan. He has been wounded as a *General* four times in the war, and the story of the rearguard actions he fought until his last man had gone and he himself was wounded and captured, is modern Russia's epic; while his subsequent escape is the dream and envy of every boy. He broke from his Austrian prison and in disguise

wandered for a month in the Carpathians, until he reached the Rumanian border – a wreck with no shoes or skin to his feet – just ten days after that country entered the war and could therefore welcome him in.

He is a resolute and honest man without fear and impresses one by his directness, simplicity and calm. Before accepting his post of *Generalissimo*, he laid down certain conditions which were accepted by the Government. He is now the outstanding figure in this country and lacks nothing to succeed except perhaps a knowledge of Western life and sympathy with democratic ideals. As a Tartar, a Cossack and a soldier he inclines to solve all problems with the sword and believes with Cromwell that 'stone-dead hath no fellow'. His strength lies in his age – he is only 47 – his solid Cossack backing, his force of character and the legend of his name.

He tells us that the war has now entered its second stage and that we must look for two more years of strife. He thinks that Germany aims at taking Bessarabia, Odessa and possibly even the Donetz Basin with its minerals and coal. This has since been borne out by some plans found upon a German officer just captured. The plans indicate the presence of a full corps of Prussian Guards upon this front. The Prussian officer, when asked why Germany did not make for Kiev, explained that the capture of Bessarabia and Odessa automatically lost Kiev to the Russians, who under these circumstances could neither victual nor supply it.

All this may, of course, be falsehood but the fact remains, as Kornilov himself insists, the enemy might march to Odessa with the troops they already have, in view of the present state of Russia's armies. Moreover, may not this be just what monarchists like Kornilov want? In a sense, the worse the present disaster the more his hands will be strengthened. For as matters now stand, the loss of Austrian territory has not been very badly received in the Army outside the area of the loss itself, and it is difficult as yet to saddle the soldiers' committees and spy specialists with the blame and to make Russia as a whole sick of their interference. It requires the loss of some *Russian* territory and perhaps a winter of famine to make the prayer for a Dictator and for order universal and profound.

Kornilov was not prepared to wait that long, and his relationship with Kerensky steadily deteriorated. Each could, and should, have supported the other, but their viewpoints could not be reconciled. The Prime Minister regarded the Commander-in-Chief as a dangerous reactionary who would overthrow the Revolution at the first opportunity, and was looked upon in return as an intellectual weakling who was driving the country to ruin while he temporised with the Left. Both views were extreme but did contain an element of truth.

What Kornilov actually wanted was a restoration of discipline in the Army, on the railways and in industry; an end to the unwarrantable influence of the Petrograd garrison, snug in its billets far from the front; the dispersal of the Soviet; and the hanging of Lenin and his Bolsheviks before they could stage another rising. Heavily involved in short-term politics, Kerensky would have none of it.

By the end of August Kornilov's patience had run out and he decided to mount a coup of his own. Using the Wild Division and the 3rd Cavalry Corps as an advance guard, he intended marching on the capital, where his supporters would declare in his favour. Unfortunately, the whole thing was an open secret and the capture of the Baltic city of Riga by the Germans on 3rd September gave Kerensky the chance to entrap his opponent into believing that his demands were now acceptable, and then denouncing him as a traitor.

Thousands once more poured out onto the streets of Petrograd, anxious to defend what they saw as their freedom. Significantly, they were organised by the Soviet and not the Government, and arms were handed out to all who wanted them. Many of the recipients were Bolsheviks, who were steadily recovering the ground they had lost during the July Days; Lenin, still in hiding, had declared that the Party would on no account fight for Kerensky, but that it would willingly fight against Kornilov.

His hand forced, Kornilov began his march on the capital on the night of 8th September; within twenty-four hours it was over. His support from the Army was less than he imagined, the Wild Division suddenly lost its stomach for fighting, and the 3rd Cavalry Corps willingly allowed itself to be talked round by delegates despatched from the Soviet. The coup collapsed, Kornilov was arrested and Kerensky personally assumed the mantle of Commander-in-Chief.* The Bolsheviks were asked to hand in their arms, a request which they ignored.

The suggestion had been made that Locker Lampson was implicated in the affair. He had certainly visited STAVKA at Mogilev, got on well with Kornilov, broadly supported his aims, and perhaps even encouraged him privately, but the idea of his involving his small and now sparsely equipped unit in a full-scale counter-revolution when he had repeatedly refused to let it be used to maintain order at the small frontier town of Gusiatyn is not merely illogical, but

---

* Kornilov managed to escape some months later and went south to join Alexeiev's White Volunteer Army. He was killed during the civil war.

quite out of character. It is, however, worth mentioning that Putilov, the wealthy industrialist, had almost forced his way into the presence of the British Ambassador, Sir George Buchanan, just prior to the coup, demanding that the British cars be used to support Kornilov. Buchanan quite properly regarded the suggestion as outrageous and had Putilov shown out; Locker Lampson was not even aware of the conversation until much later.

What is clear is that he had decided to get as many of his men as possible out of Russia, using home leave as an excuse while the cars were left with a small care and maintenance party during the winter months. Throughout August and early September the unit was steadily back-loaded from Gusiatyn to Brovari and then on to Kursk, where the winter quarters were located. The first draft, 48 strong, left for Archangel on 22nd August, and the main body followed a fortnight later. It passed through Moscow when the agitation arising from the Kornilov affair was at its height, and the men were confined to the station for their own safety. In sharp contrast with their arrival, they were now universally regarded with suspicion if not dislike. On one of the trains going north the engine crew had to be bribed repeatedly with tobacco and bully beef every few miles, and eventually refused to move at all; to their annoyance their locomotive was taken over by two petty officers with railway experience and brought safely into Archangel. On Petty Officer Spencer's train one of the coaches caught fire and the occupants were forced onto the roofs of the adjoining vehicles. All other methods having failed, several revolver shots were required to draw the driver's attention to the matter; by the time the train had been brought to a standstill and coach uncoupled the fire was out of control and over forty men had lost everything but the uniforms they were wearing.

At Archangel the men lived on board their trains pending the arrival of the next convoy. The exodus of the wealthy, the middle class and the moderate from Russia had already begun and the town was crowded with people who were only too willing to pay well in cash or kind for a passage or assistance in obtaining one. There were opportunities for the enterprising to make considerable profit in such circumstances and several of the unit's personnel left Russia a lot better off than they had entered it, their consciences stilled by the knowledge that authority had been flouted in a humanitarian cause.

When the convoy arrived it included their old friend the *Umona* as well as the Russian liner *Dvinsk*, but most of the men embarked on the 5,000-ton *Stentor*, described as being 'a very decent boat' which served excellent food. The convoy weighed anchor on 16th October and steered a zig-zag course for home, escorted by minesweepers and an auxiliary cruiser. The voyage was uneventful and the *Stentor* docked at Newcastle on 29th October; other vessels carrying the unit's personnel were destined for other East Coast ports and some men even landed within sight of home at Cromer. The advance party had already arrived at Dundee on 17th September.

The majority were granted disembarkation leave, which was extended well beyond the norm as the Admiralty had decided to disband the unit and its future was under discussion. The Admiralty also made good the deficiency in funds which had arisen following the mysterious disappearance of the pay chest at Kursk shortly before departure; it has been hinted that the gold content was used to establish at least one successful business, and many of the less useful high denomination Imperial Rouble banknotes do still exist.

Meanwhile, the Eastern Front had stabilised and the rear party under Lieutenant-Commander R. J. Soames had gone into winter quarters at Kursk. Here its lonely story is seen through a glass darkly against the glowering background of political developments in Russia. Kerensky, having made an implacable enemy of the extreme Left during the July Days, had also alienated the Right by his behaviour towards Kornilov, and was now all but friendless. The Bolsheviks, now armed, became more active than ever in the affairs of the Soviet and once more set about planning the downfall of the Provisional Government.

This was accomplished with ridiculous ease on the night of 6th/7th November. While agitators ensured the neutrality of the Petrograd garrison, the Bolsheviks were steadily taking over key points in the city, supported by sympathisers from the decaying Baltic Fleet at Kronstadt. The coup was completed with the arrest of several Government ministers inside the Winter Palace. Many were unaware that anything had happened until proclamations were made in the streets the following day to the effect that the Soviet was now the supreme authority. Far from being the epic struggle of Communist myth, the coup was a rather shabby little *opera bouffe*; while the mob was allegedly storming the grand facade of the Winter Palace, some American visitors were having their coats politely taken by the staff at an unguarded side entrance. Kerensky had had some warning of the rising and had left Petrograd in a fruitless attempt to raise support for the Government among the troops of the northern front; betrayed, he escaped from Russia disguised as a seaman.

Events now began to move at a bewildering pace. The price Germany had demanded for the substantial investment made in Lenin and his Bolsheviks was the withdrawal of Russia from the war, and this debt Lenin now set about paying. An absurdly junior Bolshevik officer, Ensign Krylenko, was appointed Commander-in-Chief on 23rd November, and set out for Mogilev accompanied by a bodyguard of fifty Red sailors. Their first act on arrival was to lynch Kerensky's former Chief of Staff, General Dukhonin, who was simply a loyal Russian officer doing his duty. Krylenko then sent a parley across the lines to request an armistice, which was granted, and the warring parties met to discuss peace terms at Brest-Litovsk. What remained of the old Army promptly left the trenches and walked home.

The course of the negotiations themselves is another story, but it is worth noting the outcome. The Bolsheviks seemed to think that they could behave at the conference as they did in the Soviet, and that they were bargaining from a position of strength. To the Central Powers' delegation, however, they were merely men who had served their purpose, who actually controlled only a fraction of European Russia, and who were clinging to power by their fingernails. By the end of February Bolshevik intransigence had exhausted the negotiators' patience and on 2nd March the Austro-German armies marched on into Russia. The new Red Army was incapable of offering resistance and a fortnight later the Bolsheviks capitulated, signing away one third of the total Russian population, the same proportion of the country's crop-bearing farmland, one quarter of her entire territory, half her industry and 27% of her income.

Elections for the Constituent Assembly had begun on 25th November, and Lenin promised to abide by the result. In the event, the Bolsheviks polled less than one quarter of the total vote, but when the Assembly actually convened on the 18th January the delegates were swamped by Lenin's armed bully-boys who jeered and scoffed throughout the day and eventually closed down the session. The following day the Soviet passed a resolution disbanding the Assembly and civil war became inevitable.

Bolshevik government at the local level merely mirrored that at the national, and Soames had given his squadron, which was approximately 100 strong, strict orders against becoming involved in any discussion concerning Russia's internal affairs. As few men as possible left the barracks on duty and those that did carried counter-signed passes in Russian. Even so, some contact with the increasingly sullen authorities was inevitable.

During the night of 22nd December a Ukrainian colonel and his family of eight arrived at the barracks seeking sanctuary. The local Bolsheviks had broken into his home, ripped off his epaulettes, confiscated his revolver and sword, wrecked his furniture and stolen his valuables, and finally flung the family into the street. In anticipation of trouble the squadron stood to but nothing happened, for the Kursk Soviet had other plans for the British.

At first light on Christmas Day a man approached the main gate sentry and engaged him in conversation; simultaneously, two others with loaded revolvers crept up from behind and overpowered him. The officers' quarters were then surrounded and Soames was told to hand over the cars, guns and all military stores. Soames quickly realised that he was dealing with fairly junior members of the Party hierarchy and told them that he was only prepared to discuss the matter with the Commissar himself. He then spoke by telephone to Admiral Stanley, his immediate superior in Petrograd and was told to concede as little as possible and to avoid bloodshed at all costs.

By the time the Commissar arrived the men were up and their mood was extremely ugly. If the Bolsheviks imagined that relationships between officers and men in the British service were similar to those in the Russian they were sadly disappointed. It was bitterly resented that the officers were being held at gunpoint, as was the fact that the despised Bolos had chosen Christmas Day to invade the camp – the Russian Christmas did not take place until 7th January in the Western calander – and the raid had obviously been planned to take place when the British were at their most vulnerable.

Further, the men had the Maxims in their billets, as well as their small arms, and plenty of ammunition. With difficulty Soames prevented an attack on those Bolsheviks who had already penetrated as far as the vehicle park. Somewhat taken aback, the Commissar resorted to bluff; there were, he said, 5,000 Red Guards surrounding the camp, which would be taken by storm if his demands were not met. Soames replied to the effect that he and his men were flattered by such attention; that the Bolsheviks were welcome to the cars which, he said, were useless and merely at the base for repair, but that he intended retaining most of the transport vehicles for the squadron's own use; and that, in the meantime, as Christmas had a special significance for the British, the Commissar and his hairy followers would get out of the barracks if they wished to avoid a bloodbath. Grateful for the lifeline, the Commissar left, posting a couple of sentries at the gate for the sake of face. The crews then set to, rendering the cars and guns useless by the removal or smashing of vital working parts.

From the wistful expressions of the Commissar's sentries it was soon apparent that being a Bolshevik soldier wasn't much fun.

> They were very badly fed by their own Committee and orders were given that they were to receive food at the Armoured Car food house at certain times. The result of this action and the general way in which our officers treated the Bolshevik Guards was that they always saluted the British officers and a large number of them expressed a wish to join the force. The concerts held on Christmas and New Year evenings very much surprised the guards and were greatly appreciated by them*

In consequence, the sentries actually assisted those who wished to leave camp and go into Kursk for the night – against Soames' advice – and several RNAS men actually spent the Russian Christmas with local familes.

On 8th January a party from the Moscow Soviet arrived demanding armoured cars and guns. Soames suggested that they discuss the matter with their Kursk counterparts. An evidently acrimonious meeting was held, followed by some brotherly street fighting and a certain amount of comradely machine-gunning from the one car the Bolsheviks had been able to piece together. During the subsequent drunken reconciliation there was maudlin agreement that the British were responsible for the whole thing, fuelled by Kursk fraternity's slowly dawning perception that they had been sold a pup.

The following day

> an incident occurred which might have caused considerable trouble as, in accordance with the usual practice, at 9 a.m. the electric lighting set belonging to the Armoured Car Squadron was stopped as usual. The Bolsheviks, not understanding this rule, immediately threatened to shoot the man in charge, but their action was stopped by the arrival of Lieutenant-Commander Soames. Considerable discussion took place and the Bolsheviks were most aggressive in their accusations as regards the unsatisfactory state of the cars, etc, and were eventually persuaded that the British squadron was in Russia to fight the Germans and would also be strictly neutral as regards any local fighting between political parties.†

---

* Letter from Major-General F. C. Poole, British Military Equipment Section in Russia, to Lord Milner's Committee. Several of Poole's officer and NCO instructors were living with the squadron at the time.

† Ibid.

Soames was later to receive a personal letter of commendation from the Admiralty for the astute manner in which he had handled a potentially explosive situation, but the fact remained that with the loss of the armoured cars the need for the squadron's presence in Russia had come to an end. Admiral Stanley and General Poole agreed that their personnel at the Kursk base should be evacuated as soon as possible. Soames was warned in advance that a special train would be provided, and had his command ready to move when it arrived at Kursk on 12th January. The local Soviet, almost certainly on instructions from Petrograd, gave every assistance and even despatched an official to travel with the squadron and deal with any political difficulties encountered en route to Murmansk, the new rail link to which was now open. Some details of the journey are recorded in the diary of Petty Officer T. Read:

> *Jan 12th*: Got a special train all to ourselves, but have a hard job keeping the Russians off at every station. A hard job to get water.
>
> *Jan 13th*: Arrived at Moscow 3 p.m., left at 10 p.m. Our train was fired on about three miles out of Moscow, two bullets striking, but no damage: also a log of wood crashed through the windows.
>
> *Jan 14th*: Our train is making pretty good time, stopping at very few stations. It is now terribly cold and our worst job is getting water. 62 degrees of frost, 30 degrees below zero.
>
> *Jan 15th*: Could not keep warm, awake nearly all night. This morning we were told that the paraffin was short – only one primus-full for each carriage per day for cooking. The men are continually making a mistake and catching hold of the carriage handles without gloves and skinning their hands.
>
> *Jan 16th*: We ran into a snowdrift last night and were snowed up until noon about three miles before we got to Petrograd, where we arrived at 5 p.m. We are in the station about two hours and have orders not to leave the train. There seems to be more trouble brewing, as one of our interpreters on going into the town says that some of the streets are barricaded. Our train moved about three miles out of the station onto a siding.*
>
> *Jan 17th*: Still on siding. Our officers and interpreters went into town this morning. We have orders to make ready for 40 men of the British Mission in Russia to come on our train. Our Russian interpreters are not allowed to leave for England.
>
> *Jan 18th*: Still on siding. A few Russian officers come on board with the intention of coming with us. Pleasant surprise today – mail arrived at dinner time.

---

* In the troubled aftermath of the Constituent Assembly debacle, General Poole felt that the appearance on the streets of armed British personnel could easily provoke misunderstanding and even lead to loss of life.

Jan 19th: Still on siding. A little street fighting going on. Some more artillery officers came on board today, also an escaped prisoner from Germany, a Frenchman from Alsace-Lorraine. One of our men went to exchange food for paraffin and was arrested by a party of Russians and brought back under escort.

Jan 20th: Still on siding and getting fed up. If we stay much longer our rations will run out. Machine gun heard about 8 p.m. not far from our carriage; we can hear the bullets hitting not far away.

Jan 21st: We left Petrograd at 10 a.m. Another train is attached behind us with Russians on board. We are thankful to be on the way.

Jan 22nd: Making good progress. Hot water pipe burst in our carriage, flooding the place. We have two sick Rumanians to look after.

Jan 23rd: Making good headway, made two stops of an hour. Strolled up and down the line during the night as we are at a standstill owing to a train ahead running off the rails.

Jan 24th: We are now at a very lonely place. No wolves, but a few bears. A guard was killed by a bear two days ago. Moved off at 3 p.m. and pass the breakdown on the way. Had to carry water from a lake 500 yards away. A lot of snow so we have to go very slowly.

Jan 25th: Train made very slow headway all night. Came to a standstill at a station called Kandalaksha about 200 *versts* from Romanoff.* We are now in the Arctic Circle. Receive orders to put up our decorations before leaving the train. We now have three Rumanian patients. Shall be pleased to get on board ship as it is very awkward looking after patients on the train, there being very little room to work. Arrived at Romanoff about 12.30.

Jan 26th: British Transport Officer came over this morning to see if we had enough food and stores. The *Glory* and other craft lay half a mile off the town. At present there is no ship to take us so we look like staying here for a while. CPO comes round at night to see who are good sailors and who are bad. Cannot understand rumours about trawlers.

The reason for the solicitous enquiries regarding sea-sickness and the rumours about trawlers soon became apparent, and are explained by an encoded signal despatched to the Admiralty from Murmansk just before midnight on 31st January.

ON TELEGRAPHIC INSTRUCTIONS FROM TROTSKI .(sic) ALL BRITISH ARMOURED CAR SECTION AND RUMANIANS WHO ARRIVED HERE A FEW DAYS AGO FROM PETROGRAD WHO WERE NOT FURNISHED WITH PASSPORTS SIGNED BY TROTSKI HIMSELF WERE TO BE SENT BACK UNDER GUARD TO PETROGRAD. FURTHER, ANY REFUGEES, BRITISH OR RUMANIAN, WHO ARE AT PRESENT ON THE WAY TO MURMANSK WERE TO BE STOPPED

---

* Romanoff was the pre-Revolutionary name of the village on which Murmansk was founded.

AND FAILING PRODUCTION OF PASSPORTS AS DESCRIBED WERE TO BE SIMILARLY SENT BACK UNDER GUARD TO PETROGRAD.

SIXTY ONE MEMBERS OF BRITISH ARMOURED CAR SECTION, BRITISH MILITARY SUPPLY AND PNTO STAFF SAILED FOR UNITED KINGDOM YESTERDAY JANUARY 30th IN HMS 'TITHONUS'. THE BALANCE, VIZ. 56 BRITISH AND 28 RUMANIANS WERE BY ORDER OF ADMIRAL KEMP TODAY JANUARY 31st REMOVED FROM TRAIN (IN WHICH THEY WERE WAITING PENDING ARRIVAL OF SHIP TO CARRY THEM TO UNITED KINGDOM) TO HMS 'GLORY' WHERE THEY NOW ARE.

I HAVE COMMUNICATED THIS NEWS TO EMBASSY AT PETROGRAD.

Trotsky, responsible for Foreign Affairs, was having to play a very difficult and devious game, and was playing it with native Russian skill and not a little humour. Although under no illusions as to the official British attitude to the Bolshevik government, he nonetheless wished to remain on good terms with Great Britain pending conclusion of the peace treaty with the Central Powers. The negotiations at Brest Litovsk were going badly and the Germans, fully informed as to everything that was taking place in Russia, were entitled to demand that the Russians curtail the movements of former Allied troops in the country.

Having already secretly approved the release of the British squadron, Trotsky now had to demonstrate to the Central Powers' negotiators that he was doing his best to comply with the terms of the armistice, but despatched his recall instructions only after he imagined that the British authorities at Murmansk had had time to embark the party. There seems little doubt that the British contingency plan to supplement the available shipping space with minesweeping trawlers was made with foreknowledge, and it is tempting to suspect the involvement of the legendary Bruce Lockhart, officially acting Consul-General in Moscow, in reality an extremely able intelligence agent who was well acquainted with the leading Bolsheviks.

Having already absorbed all available space on the armed merchant cruiser *Tithonus*, Admiral Kemp gave the local Soviet no time to act on Trotsky's signal. An armed Royal Marine landing party escorted the remainder of the squadron on board the *Glory*, where they felt secure and welcome for the first time in many months. 'They made a great fuss of us and we spent a jolly time,' wrote Petty Officer Read.

They dished us out with hammocks and put us in with the Petty Officers. Had supper at 8 p.m., piped down at 10 p.m. Slept fine. Warmest I have felt for weeks.

The *Glory*, referred to as 'the cruiser' by the squadron, was actually a pre-Dreadnought battleship launched in 1901. For all that, her main armament of four 12-inch guns was quite capable of blowing Murmansk to matchwood and she was regarded with respect by the town's Bolshevik element. She had been on the North Russian Station since 1916 and would remain a while longer, safeguarding British interests in the area. On 1st February her passengers transferred to the waiting trawlers in small groups and the following day a second signal was despatched from Murmansk to the Admiralty.

EIGHT MINESWEEPING TRAWLERS SIR JAMES RECKITT, OLIVER PICKIN, JAMES HUNNIFORD, IDEMA, RESMILO, URKA, CHARLES CHAPPELL, DANIEL HENLEY UNDER COMMAND OF LIEUTENANT RYAN RNR OF SIR JAMES RECKITT LEFT HERE FOR LERWICK 0800 GMT 2nd FEBRUARY 40 RATINGS OF ARMOURED CAR SQUADRON, 15 RUMANIAN OFFICERS AND 13 RUMANIAN NCOS.

The trawlers, travelling in two lines of four, hit heavy weather almost at once and their motion proved to be even worse than had been predicted. Most of the passengers were violently sick for the first few days and then settled down, taking part in the ships' routine to pass the time. Read for example, travelling on the *Urka*, set a complicated bone fracture, took a turn on the pumps, helped the stokers, worked in the galley, and stood submarine watches. At 0300 on 5th February contact was lost with the *Idena* and Ryan ordered three of the trawlers to turn back and search for her while the rest went on. The *Idena* had sprung a leak and sunk, but her passengers and crew were picked up next day by the *Charles Chappell*. Lerwick was reached on 9th February, by which time the RNAS personnel had acquired a very high regard for the trawlermen.

The sole remaining members of the unit left in Russia were the small staff of the Petrograd office, and of them Reuter's correspondent was already forwarding a despatch even as Ryan was leading his flotilla out of Kola Inlet.

Petrograd, 2nd Feb : Red Guards appeared at the quarters of Commander Dye and Lieutenant C. J. Smith, of the British Armoured Car Detachment, at 3 o'clock this morning and presented a warrant for the arrest of Commander Dye on a charge of being the owner of two bombs which were found in a room in the Hotel Astoria after their departure. The warrant was signed by the commission for combating the counter-revolution.

After his belongings had been searched, Commander Dye, whom

Lieutenant Smith accompanied, was driven under arrest to the former Prefecture of Police, where he was to be brought before the commission. Several hours were spent over the examination. The officers were eventually enabled to communicate with the Embassy, and after assurances had been given by Colonel Thornhill, the Assistant Military Attaché, they were released.

The officers and men of the Armoured Car Detachment had been asked to leave the Hotel Astoria at short notice, and one of the men while packing overlooked two unloaded grenades, souvenirs of the fighting in which they had participated – Reuter

The report was not quite accurate. Dye was certainly released, but Smith remained in custody for several days and was closely questioned about the immobilisation of the cars at Kursk, at which he had been present. At length, being unable to make their charges stick, the Bolsheviks released him.

At the Dover Street headquarters in London, Locker Lampson was extremely concerned, not merely for his Petrograd staff, but also for the safety of the three Russian liaison officers who had served the unit so well, and a signal was drafted to the Naval Attaché in Petrograd.

LOCKER LAMPSON HAS ASKED THAT DYE SHOULD BE INSTRUCTED TO STAY AS LONG AS HE THINKS FIT – STOP – HE ALSO WANTS TO KNOW WHERE SMITH IS AND EXPRESSES HOPE THAT GIRARD REPPMANN AND ORLOFFSKY WILL RETURN TO ENGLAND FOR DUTY WITH THE FORCE – STOP – YOU SHOULD GIVE THIS MESSAGE TO GENERAL POOLE AND ADD THAT IT IS LEFT TO HIS DISCRETION WHAT INSTRUCTIONS SHOULD BE GIVEN TO DYE.

The signal contained a yawning breach of security concerning the future employment of the unit, and its despatch was not approved. Nor was a second draft including the word 'rescue', which was deemed to be tactless in that His Majesty's Government was still some way from commencing hostilities against the Bolsheviks. However, a third signal, sent on 14th February, simply asked if it could 'be assumed that steps are being taken by General Poole to evacuate the remainder of the British Naval Armoured Car personnel as soon as practicable' was answered shortly in the affirmative ten days later, and the last officers and men arrived in the United Kingdom shortly after.

The liaison officers did not accompany them and their ultimate fate is unknown, although a final reference to Reppmann is contained

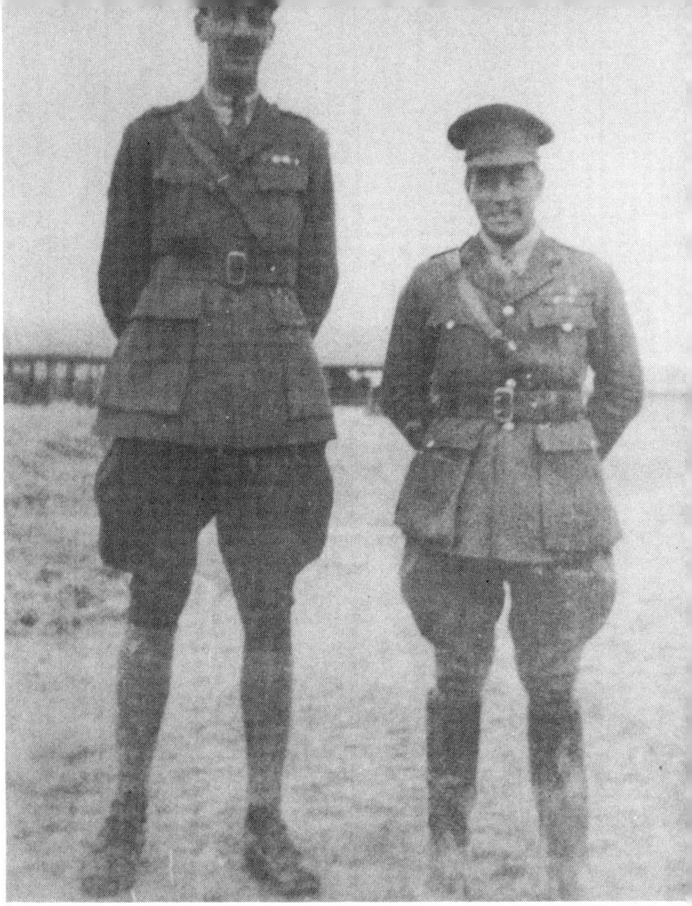

(*Right*) Colonel Crawford (left) and Major Wells-Hood (right). Dunsterforce 1918.

(*Below*) An Austin Armoured Car bogged down in a ford in North Persia.

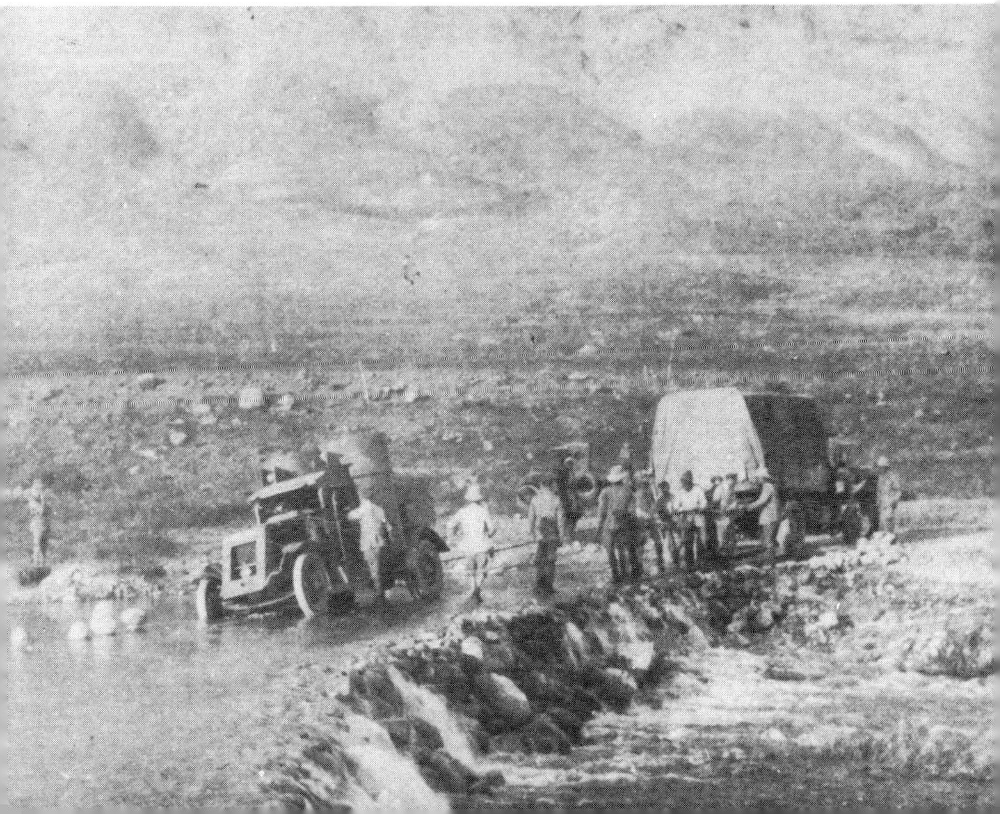

Assisting an Armoured out of a *khud*. North P 1918.

Wheel changing, a freq occurrence on the Enz road.

Austin Armoured Car a Mud Volcano, Baku 19

Through a Glass Darkly

in a cryptic exchange of messages between the Naval Attaché's office and the Admiralty. On 15th May the former telegraphed:

> REPPMANN HAS ANTAGONISED LOCKHART BY MAKING FALSE STATEMENTS TO CONSUL-GENERAL AND VARIOUS COMMISSARS. L WHO HAS GREAT INFLUENCE WITH TROTSKY ETC THREATENS TO FORBID OUR SEEING COMMISSARS AND EVEN TELEGRAPHED LONDON DEMANDING OUR RECALL WHICH I DO NOT CONSIDER ADVISABLE. FEAR OPEN BREAK WITH REPPMANN WOULD LEAD TO HIS ACTING AGAINST OUR INTERESTS THEREFORE SUGGEST YOU CALL REPPMANN TO ENGLAND FOR EVIDENCE RE KURSK AFFAIR. AM ENDEAVOURING TO KEEP IN WITH L AS RECALL OF ARMOURED CARS DEPENDS LARGELY UPON HIM.

Locker Lampson replied briefly to the effect that the sender must settle the Reppmann difficulty himself in Moscow. The only inferences that can be drawn from the exchange are that the former Tobolsk Militia officer was still performing liaison duties with the Naval Attaché's office, that he was playing some tortuous role upon which his survival may have depended, and that this was prejudicing negotiations for the recovery of the cars which had been illegally seized by the Kursk Soviet. The cars were never returned and to the end of his days Locker Lampson maintained that the Soviet Government owed him £30,000 for them.

Meanwhile, in the months prior to the Reppmann affair, Locker Lampson's unit had been re-formed and re-equipped and sent to the Middle Eastern theatre of war, although its next major actions were, ironically, to be fought in Russia.

CHAPTER TEN

Back to Russia

With the exception of regular naval officers and warrant officers, the majority of the personnel on leave received recall papers in January 1918, advising them that the unit had passed from Admiralty to Army control and was to form the basis of a brigade of the Motor Machine-Gun Corps. The former Petty Officers reported to a camp at Grantham, were formally sworn as soldiers, remained privates for the rest of the day, and were then promoted sergeants, staff-sergeants or warrant officers according to their experience and their officers' recommendations, thus avoiding financial hardship which might have resulted from the change of service.

Commissioned ranks in the Royal Navy and the Army not being precisely equivalent, most officers benefited from the transfer, for their ranks were rounded up. Smiles took over as second-in-command with the rank of lieutenant-colonel, since Belt was considered too old for a further tour of active service; Wells Hood, Ruston and Scott, the Staff Surgeon, became majors while the senior lieutenants were promoted to captain. A handful of suitable warrant officers, including George Bromley, were commissioned as second lieutenants.

Under Smiles's command, the brigade sailed from Southampton to Cherbourg on 28th January, then travelled by train across France and Italy to Taranto where it boarded the troopship *Malwa*, reaching Alexandria on 15th February. It was then transferred by train to Port Suez, where it embarked on the steamer *Nile* for the sweltering voyage down the Red Sea and across the Indian Ocean to the Persian Gulf. The Tigris was entered on 1st March and the following day the men disembarked at Basra, going into camp in mud huts just outside.*

The journey round the world and their destination were accepted philosophically; like untold thousands of British soldiers before and since, they 'were there because they were there', and there was no point in trying to disentangle the thought processes of authority. In

---

* The Kursk squadron's personnel rejoined in May.

fact, the task which they were to be called upon to undertake was even more bizarre than anything in which they had previously been involved.

The collapse of the Russo-Turkish front had been viewed with serious alarm by the British government. Yudenich's army had been the last to be infected by Bolshevik agitators, but eventually it had succumbed and disintegrated. This left the Turks free, if they wished, to march into Persia, aided by the distinct possibility of an armed rising against the British presence, thus placing the Empire's oil supply at risk. Again, under the Treaty of Brest Litovsk, Russia had ceded three Trans-Caucasian provinces to Turkey, and it was entirely reasonable to assume that the Turks would exceed the strict provisions of the treaty and seize the Caspian oil centre of Baku as well. It was, therefore, almost as important for the British to prevent the Central Powers gaining access to the Baku oil as it was to safeguard their own interests in the Gulf, and the Imperial General Staff had instructed the local commander, Lieutenant-General Sir W. R. Marshall, to mount an expedition into the Caspian area with the intention of thwarting Turkish ambitions, using comparatively small British forces but raising local levies along the way.

This was far easier said than done, for the whole Russo/Turkish/Persian border zone was in uproar. The Turks had shown an early preference for the Baku option, but their progress was being impeded by the Russian population of the ceded provinces, who had no intention of being ruled from Constantinople and who were putting up a fierce but hopeless resistance. This, however, states the position at its simplest, for the traditional blood feuds between Russian and Turk, Christian and Moslem, Kurd and Armenian, were now overlaid by the civil war factions of Red and White and compounded by private armies which were little more than well-armed bandits. In this melting pot the only certainty was the unexpected and alliances and loyalties were apt to change with bewildering frequency.

The mission, described by one romantically inclined journalist as 'Quixotic', and by the more practical Marshall as 'madness', was to be led by an Indian Army officer, Major-General Lionel Dunsterville, a man whose powers of persuasion were accompanied by considerable charm but whose principal asset was his remarkable gift for languages – he was, in fact, fluent in French, German, Russian, Persian, Urdu, Punjabi, Pushtu and Chinese. As a matter of general interest, during his schooldays he had shared a study with Rudyard Kipling and was the original Stalky of the latter's *Stalky & Co.*

Dunsterville was perfectly aware that he had been handed the dirty end of the stick. Nonetheless, accompanied by a small contingent, he had in February made the difficult journey from Baghdad to the port of Enzeli which, like Baku, was in Bolshevik hands. The Russians knew all about his purpose and a message from the Baku Soviet was awaiting him, curtly rejecting his offer of technical assistance and other aid. Lacking the means to execute his task, he had perforce to withdraw and await the concentration of the troops which had been placed at his disposal and which would be known collectively as Dunsterforce.

Among those detailed was the armoured car brigade, the operational designation of which would be Duncars. At Basra the brigade had been forced to kill time while its cars were being shipped out, doing a great deal of weapon training and route marching but also forming a harriers' club and playing football. Its official fighting vehicle establishment was 40 armoured cars, organised in five eight-car squadrons, each consisting of four two-car sections. However, when the cars – twin-turreted Austins of a superior design to those formerly supplied to the Imperial Russian Army – arrived at the end of April, there were only sufficient to equip A, B and E Squadrons; C and D Squadrons were therefore re-organised as 8-gun motor machine-gun squadrons with Ford and Peerless transport.

The missing sixteen cars had a most interesting active service history. In March they had been rushed to France to combat Ludendorff's dramatically successful spring offensive, and were used to equip the 17th Battalion Tank Corps. During the Battle of Amiens in August they were towed across the trench lines by tanks and carried out a classic exploitation, capturing a German corps headquarters virtually intact. Flying the Tank Corps flag, one of these cars was the first British vehicle to cross the Rhine following the Armistice; the same flag was flown from a Buffalo of 4 RTR during the 1945 Rhine crossings.

Meanwhile, Duncars checked over their vehicles and proceeded upriver by barge, passing the little flat-walled town of Kut and its long abandoned trenches, and then the strange ruins of Ctesiphon. Baghdad, captured by General Maude in March 1917, was reached on 5th May and the brigade went into camp at Hinadia nearby. Here it was announced that Locker Lampson would not be coming out to join them, as ill health and other matters prevented him from leaving England. He was genuinely sorry about this and his very sincere regard for the men was shown when, over the next few weeks, he wrote personally to everyone who had served with him in Russia thanking them for their services; further, entirely at his own expense, he presented each of them with a 15s savings certificate, to be held in trust for their return.

He would have been an immensely difficult commander to follow and one has more than a little sympathy with his successor, a Colonel Crawford. Unfortunately Crawford, a former Indian cavalry officer, got off on the wrong foot. He knew nothing of his new command's history and seems to have made no effort to find out. Thus, when he addressed the brigade for the first time he displayed a startling lack of tact. In brief, he said that no one had heard of them; and since they were going up into the back of beyond no one was likely to, unless they did well; which was what he demanded of them. To his chagrin, he was advised that the majority of the men had, in fact, been involved in operations in Trans-Caucasia and north Persia only two years previously. His remarks were remembered and the men remained Locker Lampson's.*

This was a great pity, for Crawford was a capable officer with a thorough knowledge of logistics whose planning enabled the brigade to function smoothly in trying conditions. Dunsterville planned to advance on Enzeli along the route Baghdad–Kermanshah–Hamadan–Kasvin–Resht, and had been advised by his staff that the armoured cars and their heavy Peerless support lorries would not be able to negotiate the several high mountain passes which had to be crossed. Crawford, supported by his officers, did not agree, although it was conceded that the obstacles were formidable. The basic problem was essentially similar to that which had faced Locker Lampson when planning the Mush operation in 1916. Over 400 miles of difficult and almost certainly hostile country separated Baghdad from Enzeli, and this meant that only one armoured car squadron and some motor machine-gun sections could be supported operationally in Trans-Caspia. The remainder of the brigade would be engaged in maintaining the line of communications and in manning the three fuel and spare-part dumps which would be established along the way.

Ruston's A Squadron was detailed as the spearhead, but events now began to move so quickly that one of its members, Sergeant George Martin, confided to his diary that 'we are now an important secret mission'. The proximate cause of this entirely accurate entry was

* On the fly-leaf of my copy of *The Adventures of Dunsterforce*, published in 1920, the previous owner has written in a firm hand *Alex. W. Aird. late Sgt Comd Locker Lampson's Armoured Car Brigade, Dunster Force.* B. P.

that the last Russian commander on Persian soil, Colonel Bicherakov, was evacuating his Cossack brigade from Hamadan and was himself marching towards Enzeli. Bicherakov, a strong character to whom his men had sworn their personal loyalty, had a deep loathing of Bolshevism and his burning ambition was to join the White armies fighting inside Russia.

All had gone well until, halfway between Kasvin and Resht, further progress was barred by some 5,000 Jangalis who had entrenched themselves on a ridge which commanded the vital bridge at Menjil.* The Jangali commander was one Mirza Kuchik Khan, a local idealist who was playing the role of Turkish irregular with a German officer named von Passchen to advise him. Bicherakov was advised by von Passchen that Kuchik Khan would permit the Russians to pass through to Enzeli in small parties, but as far as the British were concerned the road would remain closed. The arrangement did not suit the Cossack colonel, who informed Dunsterville of the situation, and the latter set his command in motion along the road from Baghdad.

First to leave was George Martin's section of two armoured cars, and their route was followed by the remainder of Dunsterforce. The first obstacle was the Pai Tak Pass, 2,000 feet high, halfway up which was the triumphal arch erected by Alexander to commemmorate his capture of the Persian King Darius. The cars laboured to the summit, but their efforts were as nothing in comparison to what followed. Before Kermanshah was reached came two further passes, the Khurkur (6,000 feet) and the Kuh-e-Safid (4,000 feet). Beyond Kermanshah lay a notable landmark at Bisotun, a huge panel carved into the rockface depicting Darius dealing with subject kings; unaware of its history but observing a stream emerging from a fissure in the cliff below, the men named it Moses' Rock. Then came the Kuh-e-Alvand Pass (9,000 feet) and the most difficult pass of all, the Asadabad (8,000 feet), before the road dropped sharply down to Hamadan, known in ancient times as Ecbatana.

The journey was an epic which made even the Mush operations seem easy. The cars coped with precipitous gradients, squeezed their way through defiles barely their own width, negotiated countless fords which had never been intended for mechanical transport, and traversed narrow mountain ledges bordered by sheer drops of several thousand feet. They operated in temperatures which varied from the

* The Jangalis were not a tribe but simply the inhabitants of Gilan Province. Parts of this were covered in forest and jungle and for this reason Kuchik Khan's followers are referred to in other accounts as the Junglis.

baking heat of the Tigris valley to the frost, snow and thin air of the high passes, in which their crews found the cold so intense that they were unable to sleep.

There was, too, a technical problem. The Austins should have had two sets of tyres, one pneumatic for road use behind the lines, and the other for use in action. Unfortunately, the pneumatic sets were still in transit from the United Kingdom and the journey was made on the combat sets, which were made from a substance called Rubberine. This had been designed for use in temperate climates, and broke up rapidly when exposed to hard usage in contrasting extremes of temperature. Further, as each tyre weighed 200-lbs, the labour involved in changing a complete set was considerable. Before a supply of pneumatic tyres became available Duncars had in one month used 75 per cent of an anticipated year's supply of Rubberines, and even then the position was complicated by the ten day round trip between the brigade's base at Hamadan and the rail-head at Baghdad. It was, as Martin laconically put it, 'some drive!'

Martin's section reached Hamadan, presently in the grip of such famine that cases of cannibalism had been reported, on 6th June. From this point the road became somewhat easier and after a few days' rest the cars proceeded to Kasvin, where they were made battleworthy. They then went up to join Bicherakov, with whom C Squadron 14th Hussars and two Martinsyde Scout aircraft of No 72 Squadron RAF were already working.

The Jangalis were still blocking the Enzeli road, but Bicherakov had noticed that their position was dominated by an outlying spur of the Elburz mountains. This spur had been overlooked by von Passchen and on it the Russian posted his Cossack mountain battery. The so-called Battle of Menjil Bridge began at dawn on 16th June with the two aircraft buzzing Kuchik Khan's trenches. The occupants stood up to pop off their rifles at them, and the Russian howitzers promptly sent over several shells which burst among them. Shaken by experience, the Jangalis bolted as soon as the Russian infantry deployed to attack. The cavalry, British and Russian, then swept round the enemy's right flank while the two armoured cars raced along the road to secure the bridge itself, doing substantial execution and cutting off many of the fugitives. After Galicia it seemed a very low key affair and Martin's diary comment was confined to, 'A bit of a scrap up the road. We drove them back and captured a bridge which they have been holding.'

The road to Resht and Enzeli was now open and Bicherakov's brigade advanced along it, holding key points until they could be handed over to Dunsterforce's advance guard. This consisted of a flying column made up of detachments from 1/4th Battalion The Hampshire Regiment and 1/2nd Gurka Rifles and two guns of No 8 Battery Royal Field Artillery, escorted by Duncars' leading squadron. Over 500 Model T Fords were used to transport the force, and although the infantry had dismounted to march up the worst passes, only half these vehicles remained serviceable at the end of the journey.

Bicherakov now began to play a devious game which it is necessary to follow. To get his men into Russia he was prepared to use any means, including deception, and as he approached Enzeli he announced his total conversation to Bolshevism, offering to take command of operations against the Turks, who were moving on Baku along the railway line from Tiflis. Both his conversion and his offer were accepted with enthusiasm by the Baku Soviet, who arranged for ships to transport him. Dunsterville approved of this development since it was in accord with the terms of his own brief, and Ruston's squadron was ordered to provide a second armoured car section for service with the Cossacks. The adventures of this tiny unit, commanded by Captain Crossing and known as No 2 Battery 'A' Squadron Duncars, are unique in that for a while it actually fought for the Belsheviks, almost certainly the only British troops to do so during the period of Intervention.

On 4th July Bicherakov sailed from Enzeli with No 2 Battery and its supporting transport, arriving at the small harbour of Alyat, fifty miles south of Baku, that night. Contact with the enemy was made on 9th July and for the next ten days the cars were in action covering the Russian withdrawal, finding good targets among the Turks' advanced cavalry screen. Neither side impressed the crews greatly. On the one hand the Turkish Caucasus-Islam Army, composed of one half regular troops and the remainder Kurdish and other Moslem levies, was a ragtag organisation but had the advantage of numbers; on the other, the Bolshevik infantry, described by Martin as 'a rough lot', were rubbish, although the Cossacks fought well. On one occasion the second car in Martin's section became bogged and was almost overrun by the Turks when the desperate application of main force heaved it free from the mud. Finally, Bicherakov's force having been outflanked, the cars were rail-lifted back to the outskirts of Baku.

On 26th July, with the Turks closing it, Lieutenant Hulls took out a reconnaissance patrol consisting of one armoured car and two lorries. Their route took them across a bridge which spanned a defile around which there was no alternative way. The Bolshevik bridge-guard commander promised to hold the bridge until the patrol returned, but deserted his post as soon as the Turks appeared. None of the patrol was seen alive again, and it seems certain that they were ambushed at the bridge, perhaps mistaking the Turks for Bolsheviks. The following day Martin was on patrol in the area and observed two stripped bodies lying beyond the defile; of the vehicles there was no sign.

Bicherakov had no intention of becoming caught up in a siege and, as the Baku Bolsheviks had served their purpose, he broke with them. They were in no position to argue when he commandeered a train and steamed off for the north on 31st July, taking No 2 Battery with him. By fits and starts the train moved up the Caspian coast, passing village after village in ruins as a result of the civil war. On 16th August it reached Derbent, which Martin remembered from a halt there two years previously.

The Cossacks now broke out their true colours and opened hostilities against the local Bolsheviks, pushing them back up the line to Petrovsk. The armoured cars were not involved, Bicherakov evidently having received instructions that they could be employed solely against the Turks, but entered the town when it surrendered on 3rd September. Here, with the exception of one car which was beyond local repair and which was shipped back to Persia, they remained for the next eight weeks, assisting in the defence of Derbent against the continued Turkish advance. In an action on 16th October Crossing was wounded and four men were killed, bringing the total casualties incurred to what was, in view of the unit's size, an unacceptable level. By this time, too, many were suffering from malaria, and the battery was not sorry when orders were received on the 25th to board the transport for Enzeli, taking its remaining vehicles with it.

Since No 2 Battery had been detached for duty with the Russians, Dunsterforce's whole situation had changed dramatically. Following his defeat at Menjil Bridge, Kuckik Khan had lost face with his followers. He had, he claimed, never intended to fight the Russians, for whom he had the highest regard; the British, on the other hand, he said, had neither liking nor aptitude for war, and would be easy prey. He should, perhaps, have re-examined his opinions when a Hampshire detachment survived an ambush on 18th June, inflicting considerable loss in return, but instead he planned to capture Resht from Dunsterville.

Had the town been formally defended, it would have required a perimeter of seven miles. There were, however, only 450 Hampshires and Gurkhas available, supported by No 8 Battery RFA's two guns and Nos 2 and 3 Cars of B Squadron, and these established a defensive camp on the outskirts, with a small party detached to defend the British Consulate, inconveniently situated in the centre of the town.

On 20th July 2,500 Jangalis swarmed into Resht, wildly elated by what seemed a bloodless victory. Their early euphoria quickly evaporated when their attacks on the camp were bloodily repulsed, and entirely dissipated when a Gurkha company, spearheaded by an armoured car, fought its way through the narrow alleys to rescue the occupants of the embattled Consulate. During the next two days the British and Gurkha infantry, supported by the cars, systematically cleared the town of the enemy who left behind 100 dead and 50 prisoners, some of whom were Austrian; an unknown number of wounded limped or were carried back into the forest. Kuchik Khan's power and prestige were broken, and although he remained an irritation for a little while longer, he eventually gave himself up and kept to his promise of good behaviour.

Arriving at Enzeli, Dunsterville found the local Soviet a great deal less truculent than on his first visit. He also found that they had been conducting an inflammatory correspondence with Kuchik Khan and promptly had them arrested and sent back to Kasvin. Beyond this, he could only await events in Baku.

These occurred somewhat sooner than expected. Almost as soon as Bicherakov had broken with the Bolsheviks the Baku Soviet, discredited by its failure to stem the Turkish advance, was overthrown and replaced by a body calling itself the Central Caspian Dictatorship. Dunsterville's aid in defending the town was immediately invoked and three vessels, the *President Kruger*, the *Kursk* and the *Abo*, were placed at his disposal.

A small party of Hampshires was sent over at once accompanied by Ruston with four cars (one of which belonged to B Squadron) and some of Duncars' machine-gun teams. The 39th Brigade (7th Battalion The North Staffordshire Regiment, 7th Battalion The Gloucestershire Regiment, 9th Battalion The Royal Warwickshire Regiment and 9th Battalion The Worcestershire Regiment) was already moving up from Baghdad and would be shipped across as soon as its various echelons reached Enzeli.

Ruston later recorded his impressions for *Blackwood's Magazine.*

> The position on our arrival was as follows: the Turks had that very morning succeeded in breaking through and entering the outskirts of

the town, to the general consternation; but the Armenians and Russians, armed with all kinds of weapons, not only drove them to where they came from, but actually pushed them two miles beyond.

For some days we remained in the town, by day doing nothing in particular, by night standing to. Anxious days they were, too. Things were very unsettled and the Bolshevik element did all they could to make things bad for us, so much did they resent the arrival of the British *bourgeoisie*. The culminating point, however, was reached when two Britishers were arrested by a crowd of Bolsheviks for some alleged injustice to their followers. The whole of that evening a fight seemed imminent and the entire populace seemed to go about in a state of armed frenzy. Eventually, wiser counsels prevailed and, as a result of our firm attitude, the Bolsheviks allowed themselves to be disarmed and were told politely, but forcibly, that if they did not clear out of Astrakhan at once we should give them a bad time. They went with much gnashing of teeth from their chief, Petrov, a clever, plausible old scoundrel. Thus, in addition to removing a grave menace in our midst, we secured a large quantity of arms and ammunition, of which we were badly in need for the equipment of the Armenians. Several batteries of field guns were also handed over.

The following day, the town being in a state of absolute tranquillity, the British troops were posted at various parts of the line with the object of strengthening the Armenian troops already there. In the accomplishment of our aims we were quite unsuccessful for, on the arrival of British troops in the line the Armenians, devoid of any sense of duty or discipline and always craven-hearted, said: 'Good. The English have come to drive back the Turk. We can go home.' The result of this attitude was that a front of more than ten miles was manned almost entirely by roughly 800 British. The Armenians were well supplied with machine guns and ammunition, though the former were apparently private property for the most part. So-called soldiers would leave the line without permission and go into town on the spree, actually taking their machine guns with them; and, if remonstrated with by their officers (sic) would merely shrug their shoulders and retort that they could do as they liked with their own property. Women flitted about the line everywhere. Soldiers, sailors and civilians lazed about in the sun, occasionally firing their rifles in the blue in much the same way as one scares birds. The Chief of local Staff was known to the British as the Village Idiot and lived up to his name.

The position held by the local troops was a crescent-shaped ridge, half encircling the town, the southern portion resting on the sea-shore, and the northern point sloping down to a dried-up salt lake of large dimensions. This ridge was roughly five miles from the town. From the salt lake to the coast north of the promontory on which Baku was situated no specific line existed, but odd isolated posts were to be found. Thus, our left flank rested on the sea coast, and our right flank was entirely in the air. The position taken by the local troops from first to last was a useless one, and would never have been selected for one moment by a soldier. But there it was, and we had to do what we could with it. It afforded no field of fire and was entirely dominated by the Turks on the opposite ridge. Between the two positions stretched a valley about 1,700 yards in width, through which ran the main railway line from Tiflis to Rostov. A small station stood in No Man's Land, and from this ran a good *pave* road across the valley, zigzagging up the slopes of the ridge held by the Armenians, passing through Wolf's Gap and thence to Baku.

For some days all was quiet. The Turk lay low, and though we pounded his positions soundly he made no reply. However, we could not fail to notice that stores, etc, were being continually sent to their left flank and the dried salt lake became a maze of roads. These stores were finding their way to Mastagi. Now Mastagi was the garden city of Baku, and from this source was drawn the vegetables, fruit and farm produce so sorely needed. The main water supply of Baku also came from this neighbourhood.

It was therefore decided by the Staff that Mastagi must be taken. Accordingly, two battalions of Armenians, numbering in all about 500 men, 70 Cossacks, two armoured cars and a mobile section of four machine guns with Ford transport were sent up to clear the village, assisted by one battery of 77s.

The attack was intended to be a surprise but, when on August 11th it commenced, we found the Turks ready for us. In spite of the valuable work done by the armoured cars, assisted by the cavalry, the infantry made no headway against the accurate fire poured in on them from cleverly concealed machine-guns. The armoured cars could bear testimony to the accuracy of this fire. Two gunners were hit by bullets entering the gun port, one being killed and the other wounded. In spite of a nasty wound in the nose, John M— was entirely undaunted and went in again and again with the blood lust showing on his face. It was soon apparent that we were merely running our heads against a brick wall in attempting to take Mastagi by a frontal attack. The place was admirably suited for defence, being well-wooded and possessing many stone-walled gardens and out-houses on the outskirts. These were turned into machine-gun nests by the enemy gunners and were very hard to locate. The intervening ground, too, was broken, and contained under-cover for snipers with enterprise. Again, numerous mosques with their minarets afforded excellent observation for the enemy.

Very little occurred for the next fortnight. Inside Baku food prices rose to such an extent that black bread, often containing stones and pieces of wood, sold for the equivalent of 4/2d (21p) per lb while mutton cost 2/6d (12½p) per lb. Almost everything else save poor quality rice was unobtainable. Caviare, however, was in plentiful supply; many of the

Back to Russia

uninitiated regarded it as a kind of jam and were somewhat disappointed by the experience! Colonel Crawford was appointed food controller and succeeded not only in procuring adequate supplies but also in bringing some order to the chaotic distribution arrangements. Reinforcements continued to trickle in from Enzeli, but never in sufficient numbers to make up for the poor quality of the local troops. Dunsterville asked Bicherakov to help and the latter repaid his debt by sending down by boat such men as he could spare from his own operations against Petrovsk.

The Turks had meanwhile steadily built up their strength and on 26th August launched a major assault on the defences, the course of which is described by Ruston, who spent a hectic day with his command's machine-gun sections.

At 10 a.m., after a preliminary bombardment which considerably surprised us, such was its fury, the enemy attacked the centre of the line, his objective being the village and railway junction of Balajari – a most important strategical point. Around Balajari were the oil-fields of Griazni Vulkan, Binagadi and Balakhani. At the station itself were large quantities of rolling stock, tank waggons, etc.

Our defensive position consisted of four detached infantry posts with macine-gun support, the two posts on the right resting on the crest of Griazni Vulkan (the Mud Volcano). No friendly wire protected us, and no communication trenches existed from no fault of ours. The force at this point numbered 120 all told. On its left flank was a gap of half a mile, after which came an Armenian battalion, which ran after the first shot. On our right flank was another Armenian battalion, under a British officer. This battalion remained at their post, finding the logic of his service revolver irresistible until he stopped one in the leg and was unable to continue the argument.

The commencement of the attack was the usual thing. Guns, which up to now had remained hidden, rained shrapnel and high explosive on our positions with admirable accuracy, and later the enemy bore down on us in open order. They were no irregulars that we saw, but the pukka Turk – well-trained, well disciplined and well equipped. As they came across the open, we at once got onto them with machine-gun and rifle fire and for a while arrested their progress, in spite of the absence of artillery support – the gunners had apparently bolted also.

It was soon evident that the numerical superiority of the enemy would prevent us from hanging on indefinitely, but we would take our toil before retiring, we thought. Our fire tore gaps in the enemy ranks, but always they came on until at last they were on top of us, the machine guns going to the last. A short, sharp tussle, of which I remember little, ensued and we – what remained of us – retired, having held on for over three hours. The position taken up was roughly 400 yards in rear of the old one, and we were soon shelled out of it. We retired still further, taking up a position immediately in front of Balajari itself.

However, these details are tedious. Suffice to say that the Turk, after suffering heavy losses, failed to take Balajari, and a well-executed counter-attack by a company of North Staffords robbed him of almost all his gains. Our losses had been heavy, both infantry and machine-gun section suffering severely. Ted Titterington got a nasty wound in the shoulder but, using his revolver with great effect, he fought his way out and got away to tell the tale.

Ruston was awarded a DSO for his part in this desperate holding action.

During the initial assault, Sergeant Frank Round's car had operated on the left flank of the North Staffords. After covering the infantry's withdrawal the car began to retire towards the new line when its progress slowed to a crawl and the interior was filled with the unmistakable smell of burning clutch lining. The crew were old hands now and their reaction was instinctive. The first priority was to keep the vehicle moving, since it would remain immobile if once allowed to stop. Round and his fellow gunner tumbled out and pushed with all their strength while Turkish bullets clanged off the armour all round them. Simultaneously, the driver set to unbolting the clutch housing, tossing back his cap for them to fill with sandy soil. The clutch plates were then separated and the contents of the cap poured between them, providing just sufficient friction to get the car back the 400 yards required. The men's action had been cool and professional and, by some miracle, none of them had been hit.

For others, however, the results of the day's fighting had been far less fortunate. 'The position of our wounded was a pitable one,' wrote Ruston. No stretchers were available, and the nearest dressing station was fully two miles away. Those that could get away did so, and those that failed were undoubtedly bayoneted by the numerous hangers-on for which the Turkish Army is noted. Once arrived in the town they were conveyed to a hastily erected hospital and admirably treated by Maitland Scott, who throughout worked like a Trojan and stuck it almost single-handed until the final evacuation.

Desulory fighting continued in this locality for several days, but on the whole our positions were maintained. Unfortunately, the lessons the

Turk had taught us were passed over unheeded, and the Village Idiot took no steps whatever to strengthen existing positions or make alternative ones, relying on a handful of British troops, ravaged by dysentery, malaria and influenza, to drive back two divisions of Turks.

Thus things remained until the middle of September, when a flutter of excitement was caused one morning by the arrival of a Turkish officer in our lines. He was an Arab, and on this account had been insulted to such an extent that, unable to bear it any longer, he chose to give himself up, and his friends away. From him we got full information as to the Turks' plans, numbers and artillery dispositions, and naturally this was of great assistance to us.

The regular Turkish forces opposing us consisted of 7,000 of the best troops of the Ottoman Empire. In addition, Kurdish, Tartar and Georgian irregulars were giving their assistance to the enemy, who had grossly over-estimated our strength; had he but known what a handful of stalwarts in khaki stood between him and his goal, he could have taken Baku fully six weeks earlier.

On 14th September – the date fixed by our officer prisoner – daybreak began with artillery demonstrations all along the line. It was very soon evident that the Turks had the preponderance in artillery and, moreover, were well supplied with ammunition. The dark night was gently changing to dawn as they left their position on the ridge opposite Wolf's Gap and, ignoring the pitiful opposition of the local troops, they actually marched in column of route with artillery, etc, across the intervening valley and up the *chaussée* road through the Wolf's Gap, thus reaching the Armenian main position unopposed. Here they deployed in splendid order and were soon in possession of the entire ridge extending from Balajari to the sea, actually behind a company of North Staffords holding the coast. Taking their own time, and with the confidence of trained and tried troops, they next proceeded to shell the local troops who had re-formed on a ridge about 500 yards away and were making a stand in the very last defensive position before Baku. From this ridge an excellent field of fire was obtained whilst broken ground, a large cemetery and chalk pits considerably enhanced it value.

But so far the Turk was top dog, and, to prevent reinforcements coming up, he started demonstrations and side-shows all along the line. The battle raged the entire day with alternating success. Those sectors held by the British on the whole remained in our hands; but though the Armenians, scared by the knowledge that they had at last got their backs to he wall, put up a better fight, the mischief was done. The main line had been given up without a struggle and a second formed line, protected by barbed wire, did not exist. The opening fighting considerably favoured the well-disciplined troops of the enemy. In vain British reinforcements were sent to where the fighting was thickest; they fought like heroes and inflicted heavy losses on the Turks. The company cut off by the coast hacked their way through and, under able leadership, joined in the fray around the cemetery. Armoured cars darted hither and thither, spitting death at the advancing enemy. Many deeds of valour were performed but eventually sheer weight of numbers told and by six o'clock in the evening the Turks were on the outskirts of the town.

Dunsterville had foreseen the possibility of a hasty evacuation and some time previously he had asked Sergeant Round to set up a machine-gun aboard his headquarters ship, the *President Kruger*, to cover the final phases of this. It was clear as early as the morning of the 14th that Baku was doomed and throughout the afternoon the sick and wounded were moved aboard the *Kursk* and the *Abo*, which sailed for Enzeli that evening. In view of the marked lack of enthusiasm among the local troops for their own cause, Dunsterville was unwilling to demand further sacrifice of his own men, and as dusk put an end to fighting in the suburbs, he advised the Dictatorship that he was withdrawing that night. The Dictators blustered that if he tried to leave the harbour their guardship would blow him out of the water; he ignored the threat. After dark the weary rifle companies began filing down to the harbour, sniped at occasionally by their erstwhile allies. The armoured cars were driven onto the pier, rendered useless, and pushed off into deep water. The rest of the transport was similarly wrecked and the munitions in the Arsenal were loaded onto a small coaster, the *Armenian*.

The embarkation was completed by 2200 hours and an hour later the two vessels sailed. The *President Kruger*, crammed with over 800 men, was fired upon by the guardship, but was not hit; the much slower *Armenian*, with tons of explosive aboard, was hit seven times but escaped serious damage. Both ships reached Enzeli the following day, while Bicherakov's contingent arrived safely at Derbent in their own steamer.

Dunsterforce was disbanded and, superficially at least, it seemed that Dunsterville had failed in his mission. He was, however, the only commander of the Interventionist period actually to fulfil his brief, for the delays imposed on the Turks by Bicherakov during their advance on Baku, and by the stubborn defence of the British troops during the siege, meant that not one drop of Caspian oil reached the Central Powers before Turkey surrendered on 31st October. The 39th Brigade returned to Baku on 17th November to take over from the Turks, who told them that they had suffered 2,000 casualties during the siege. British casualties for the same period amounted to 71 killed

Machinery wagon in trouble.

Austin Armoured Car bogged down on the Enzeli road.

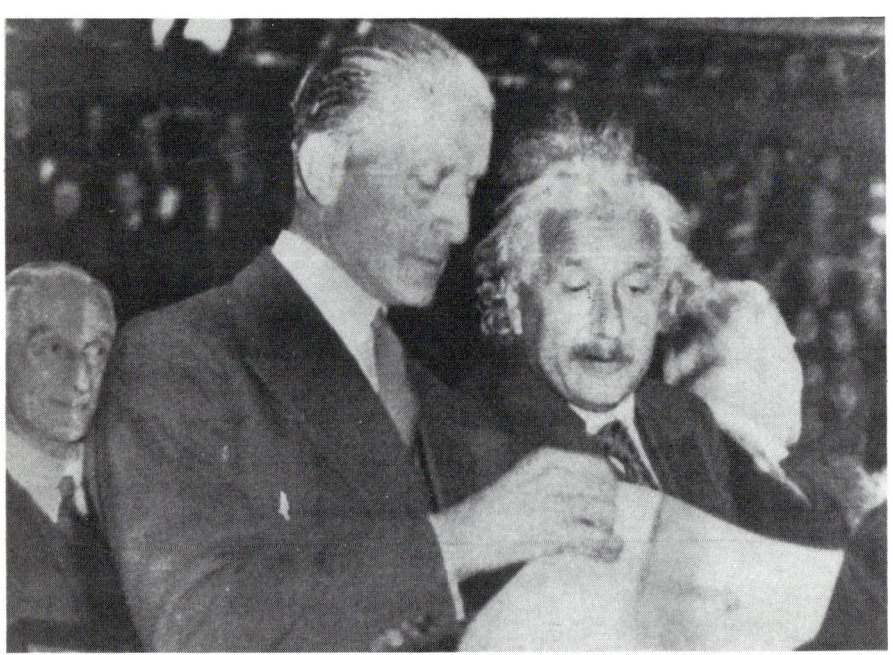

Locker Lampson's secretary, later Mrs Oliver Locker Lampson and then Mrs Mullholland, with a very young Prince Philip and Oliver Locker Lampson at a Horse Trials near Cromer.

Einstein and Locker Lampson at a Peace Rally in London.

Back to Russia

and 85 wounded, of whom 21 of the latter subsequently died in Persian hospitals.

Dunsterville published his own account of his operations in 1920, and it was not popular with the authorities. It was, after all, difficult to explain why British armoured cars had been sent to the aid of Bolshevik troops when, at various points around the perimeter of Russia, other British units were actually engaged in fighting them. Only those who had witnessed the Trans-Caucasion melting-pot at first hand would have understood.

On 11th November Germany concluded an armistice and the war was officially over. Duncars moved back by easy stages to Baghdad and then went down-river to await transport home. They embarked in mid-January and retraced the route of their outward journey, arriving at Southampton on 28th February. There was no doubt reflection that the Dunsterforce episode had cost the unit more deaths in action and through disease than the entire period they had spent in Russia with Locker Lampson.

It was, therefore, a tragedy that it should have been sent directly to the notorious Belton Park Camp, where the conditions were so bad that its administration was the subject of an official enquiry. The men arrived in freezing weather, many still wearing their thin tropical drill uniforms, to find that there were neither huts, heating, blankets nor food available for them, and the night was spent sleeping rough. The next morning they were found huts, thanks to a personal and extremely angry visit to the War Office by Major Sholl, but the damage had been done. Six men died of pneumonia and of the numerous frostbite cases one had a leg amputated and several others lost fingers.

Conscience-stricken, the War Office approved an immediate release and even sanctioned the wearing of Russian decorations. On 14th March 1919 the majority left for home in a snowstorm, and Wells Hood waved them off from Grantham station. The Czar's British Squadron had disbanded.

Not all its members had returned to the United Kingdom, however. George Bromley, the communications specialist, had been detached from the unit in Persia for various staff duties. He travelled home by the more direct route, crossing Turkey and the Balkans by rail, and at one stage of his journey found himself in Varna, Bulgaria, where he stopped the night with a unit responsible for the repatriation of British prisoners taken by the Bulgarians at Salonika and elsewhere.

During general conversation in the mess he mentioned that he had been in Russia with Locker Lampson and was surprised to be told that several members of the unit were present in the former prisoner-of-war camp. A small group of men was pointed out, still wearing the faded but recognisable uniform of the RNACD. They were Mitchell's and Ingle's crews, captured over two years previously in the Dobruja.

A Postscript

For much of 1918 Locker Lampson was attached to an intelligence organisation which was responsible for interpreting developments inside Russia; his slightly vague title was Representative for Russia of the Ministry of Information. His popularity was now at its height and when the first post-war election was held in December 1918 his Huntingdonshire constituents returned him with a clear majority of 4,344. In January 1919 he was appointed Parliamentary Private Secretary to Austin Chamberlain, Chancellor of the Exchequer, and held this post until 1921.

Once his men had been demobilised and their first euphoria at release had gone, they began to hanker for the comradeship which shared danger and experience alone can bring, and which has no parallel in civilian life. A reunion dinner was quickly organised and held on 23rd May 1919 in the Venetian Room at the Holborn Restaurant. The dinner ran to eight courses, and there was much for everyone to talk over. After all, they had covered more ground than any other armoured car unit before or since, and had served in France, Belgium, the Arctic, Russia, Turkey, Rumania, Austrian Galicia and Persia; they had fought with British and Gurkha infantry, with Frenchmen, Belgians, Russians, Rumanians and Armenians and, for reasons which still puzzled some, with White Russians *for* the Bolsheviks! They had fought against Germans, Austrians, Hungarians, Bulgarians, Kurds, Turks and Persians, and in their primitive cars they had overcome impossible terrain by their sheer skill and determination.

The principal guest was Winston Churchill, to whom the unit owed its existence, and he proposed the toast of 'The Russian Armoured Car Division, RNAS', to thunderous applause. The main event of the evening, however, was a presentation to Locker Lampson. It consisted of a beautiful sterling silver model of a Rolls Royce armoured car, complete in every detail; the base was **inscribed**: 'Presented to Commander O. Locker Lampson, CMG, DSO, RNVR, MP, by the men of the Russian Armoured Car Division as a token of regard and affection in which they held him as their Commanding Officer, 1914–18.' Arounnd the base were further silver plaques recording the countries in which the unit had fought. On accepting this most generous present he received a long standing ovation, and would have been less than human if he had not been very deeply moved.

As Treasury Representative for the government's Victory Loan he toured the country with armoured cars borrowed from the Army, joined by such officers and men as happened to live in the area of his visits; they, too, would have been less than human if they had not persuaded the regular drivers to hand over the wheel from time to time! One such Victory Loan Celebration Dinner, held at the Savoy Hotel, London, was given 'in honour of the officers and men of the British naval squads and the officers and men of the Anglo-Russian Armoured Car squads who have been helping towards the success of the Victory Loan.' When closed, the Loan had reached a staggering total of £700,000,000.

About this time he received an invitation from White Russian officers to return to Russia and command their armoured units. The financial inducements offered were impressive, and doubtless many of his veterans would have joined him had he chosen to go, but he declined and instead accompanied Chamberlain to the Peace Conference at Versailles. In 1921 he became Parliamentary Private Secretary to the Leader of the House, and later Lord Privy Seal. In 1922, at the pinnacle of his parliamentary career, he moved to the constituency of Handsworth in Birmingham, and held this seat until he retired from the Commons in 1945. During much of this period he was joined on the benches by Walter Smiles, who had eventually abandoned his tea planting career in favour of politics, sitting first for Blackburn and later for North Down, and earning a knighthood.

Locker Lampson's later parliamentary career was distinguished but never achieved real greatness. It would be simplistic to suggest that his war efforts had burned up his surplus energy, or that he had fulfilled his ambitions; in fact he remained a fighter, a champion of the underdog and of lost causes, a bitter critic of the Nazi persecution of the Jews and of the barbarities of Communism. He was one of very few public figures who agreed openly with Churchill that Hitler's rise to power inevitably meant a Second World War. Rather, it was the spirit of the times which changed. In a climate of increasing economic hardship, people wished to forget the trauma of the war, and were prepared to go to any lengths, including appeasement, to avoid a repetition. For all their clarity of vision, Locker Lampson's views would have been regarded as hawkish by his party's hierarchy, and out of sympathy with the electorate.

In 1923 he married Bianca Paget of Passadena, California. The ceremony took place at Cromer Parish Church and afterwards his Cromer ratings followed the old naval tradition of pulling the couple's car through the town. It was to be a tragically short marriage, for Bianca died on Christmas Day 1930. For a while Locker Lampson was heartbroken, but five years later he married his former secretary, Barbara Goodall, who outlived him. Amongst the many eminent visitors to Rowfant and Newhaven Court were Winston Churchill, Rudyard Kipling, Professor Einstein, Lord Birkenhead and the sculptor Epstein.

He made some unfortunate investments and after his retirement he devoted himself to writing, producing an uncompleted volume of memoirs, articles and stories; little, if any of this has ever been published, and much has disappeared. He possessed a large library and spent much time among his books. Always given to deep thought, he became increasingly introspective as he grew older.

His men travelled as many roads as there are to take. Some returned to the dominions, others went out to join them there, and a few emigrated to the United States. As the years passed, some prospered and others fell upon hard times; the latter could always rely on Locker Lampson to help them through their difficulties.

The last of them to see him alive was former Petty Officer S. Rule, who happened to be in London on business in 1954. 'I had about two hours to spare and as I was walking past Hyde Park Corner, I thought I would like to see again the garage where we prepared the armoured cars for Russia. I saw a policeman and asked him if by chance he knew a Commander Locker Lampson who I believed lived nearby. The constable replied that he did know him, though people rarely saw him now, and he gave me the address. Off I went, forgetting all about the garage for the moment, keen to meet the Commander again after all these years.

'I eventually found the house and rang the doorbell. At first there was no reply, then I heard shuffling and the door opened a crack. A voice I recognised as the Commander's asked me what I wanted, and I told him who I was and that I had come to see him as I was passing. He told me to wait, and shut the door.

'After a few minutes the door once more opened, this time fully, to reveal the Commander in bedroom slippers, uniform jacket, and an old pair of trousers. He looked tired and far from well, but he squared his shoulders as I recalled our association in Russia, although it didn't seem to convey much to him. At length he apologised, saying he had a lot of things to do, and closed the door again. I was greatly shocked to have seen the Commander like that, and I knew he was a very sick man.'

Some days later Rule read that Locker Lampson was dead, but he may unwittingly have performed one last service for his old commander. Now aged seventy-four, Locker Lampson was suffering from severe bouts of depression and in these circumstances the donning of his old tunic, bearing the ribbons of British, Belgian, Russian and Rumanian decorations, was a positive action. One can but wonder where the old man's thoughts led him after Rule had gone. To the early, exciting days when, with Churchill's approval, he had raised his first squadron? To the heaving deck of the *Umona* as she battered her way across the Arctic Circle? To the freezing wastes of Alexandrovsk? To his conversations with the Czar, the Grand Duke Nicholas, Alexeiev, the desperately worried Kerensky and the scheming Kornilov? Did he fight his way again across the sweltering Mush Plain, visit the palace at Jassy, or watch his cars fighting their epic rearguard action in Austrian Galicia? Or did he stand again at the top table in the Venetian Room with the silver Rolls Royce in front of him, looking down the lines of smiling faces, hearing their cheers and applause, feeling the pride rise in his throat and prick at his eyes? If so, the stern features now lined by time and care, would have softened, perhaps for the last time, into a reflective smile.

The last chapter of his memoirs was never written, but it was to have been entitled *The Lure of Life – A Final Appeal to the World to Live and Love and Laugh.* Those who knew him agree that no more fitting epitaph can be found.

Appendix

Awarded the St George Cross for 'Conspicuous Gallantry in Action' at Topalul, Dobruja, working under the orders of 4th Siberian Corps, Danube Army:

PO Rogers, R.
    Spencer, D.
    Watson, H. L.
    Hearsey, H. V.

PO Johnston, W. H.
    Whiting, H. G.
    Francis, W. A. R.
    Vaughan, K. M.

Awarded the St George Medaal for 'Bravery under Fire' at Topalul:

PO Allison, J. G.
    Smith, A. E.
    Armstrong, J.
    Deane, S.
    Savery, E. C.
    Henderson, W.
    Rodwell, A.
    Sanders, N. J.
    Milner, L. C. M.

PO Harrison, J.
    Stanfield, J.
    Hyams, I.
    Swan, W. D.
    Crawford, E. J.
    Robertson, E.
    Slade, J. F.
    Pepper, S. F.
    Etches, F.

Awarded the St George Medal (3rd Degree) for 'Bravery under Fire' at Topalul, (second mention):

PO Pursell, A. S.

Awarded the St George Cross for 'Conspicuous Gallantry in Action' at Braila, Rumania, working under the orders of 4th Siberian Corps, 6th Army:

CPO Common, R.
    Viane, E.
PO Radway, S. A.
    Dunbar, W. H.
    Graham, A.
    McCreadie, R.

CPO McFarlane, J.
PO Hassan, J.
    Fear, F. W.
    Classey, A. J.
    Pepper, S. F.
    Dempster, R.

Awarded the St George Medal for 'Bravery under Fire' at Braila, Rumania:

PO Babbage, W. H.
    Newman, H. M.
    Andrews, W.
    Wildbore, A. J.

PO Sinclair, J. D.
    Poland, A. S.
    Maynard, J.

Index

Abo (steamship) 170, 176
Admiralty, decisions re unit, 28, 152
 and Tank Development, 24
Alebei Chioi, 87, 88
Alexander, The Great, 59
Alexandria, Egypt, 103, 162
Alexandroff, 46
Alexandrovsk (Port of) 35, 36, 38, 39, 42, 43, 76, 99, 182
Alexeiev, Gen, 40, 74, 76, 107, 150
Algate, PO, 146
Alhovtse, 143
Allen G. & Sons (Tipton), 77
Allenby, Gen, Sir E. H. H., 25
Alyat, Harbour, 168
Antwerp, Belgium, 19
Ararat, Mount, 73
Archangel (Port of), 27, 42, 44, 48, 51, 52, 89, 148, 151
Archangel Herald, 33
Arges, battle of River, 87
Armenia, 50, 59
Armenian (Coaster), 176
Armenians, 171-3
Armoured Cars, *Ulster*: 22, 90, 91, 94, 95, 98, 128. *Londonderry*: 22, 90, 91, 97. *Mountjoy*: 22, 97
Armoured Car (Squadrons) No 1 : 23, 28, 59, 73, 81, 87, 88, 103, 115; No 2 : 24, 28, 59, 60, 68, 72, 81, 84, 86, 87, 115; No 3 : 24, 28, 59, 72, 81, 87, 115; No 4 : 24; No 5 : 24; No : 6 24; No 8 : 24; No 15 : 22, 23, 24, 28; No 17 : 24, 28; No 20: 25, 26; (General Terms) 159, 160; Special Service Sqdn : 'A' 90, 97, 98; 'B' 95; 'C' 97
Armoured Car Squadrons (Dunsterforce) Squadron 'A' 164, 165;

'B' 164, 170; 'C' 164; 'D' 164, 170; 'E' 164
Armoured Motor Batteries (Light), 25
Army (British):
 Royal Armoured Corps, 26
 Tank Corps, 26; (17th BTLn) 164
 14th Hussars (C Squadron), 167
 Royal Field Artillery (No 8 Battery), 168, 169
 Gloucestershire Regiment (9th Bn), 170
 Gurkha Rifles (1st/2nd), 168-70
 Hampshire Regiment (1st/4th Bn), 168-70
 Machine Gun Corps, 26, 162
 North Staffordshire Regiment (7th Bn), 170, 174, 175
 Royal Warwick Regiment (9th Bn), 170
 Royal Worcestershire Regiment, 170
 Army Service Corps, 20
Army (Imperial Russian):
 Imperial Guards, 107
 Armies, 6th : 87, 94, 97, 99; 7th : 115, 119; 8th : 119; 11th : 126, 130
 Corps, 4th Siberian : 81, 87, 101; 22nd : 140, 143, 146; 34th : 135, 141; 41st : 112, 115, 122, 124, 126
 Divisions, 2nd Cavalry: 142; 3rd and 5th Trans- Amur : 115, 116, 118, 119; 10th : 98; 74th Siberian : 115, 116, 117, 118, 119; 10th : 98; 74th Siberian : 115, 116, 117, 118; 76th : 119; 113th : 115, 119; 124th : 90, 97; Orenburgsky : 127; 'Wild' :

185

141, 150; Battalions of Death : 113, 118
Arctic Circle, 157, 182
Arctic Ocean, 52
Asadabad Pass, 166
Ash, PO, 92
Astrakhan, 171
Astoria Hotel, Petrograd, 106, 108, 159
Austin Armoured Car, 27, 164
Australians, 113
Austrian Counter Attack: 126, 127; Infantry: 128; Artillery: 128; Prisoners: 170
Bagge, Mr Picton, 75
Baghdad, 54, 72, 164, 166, 177
Baker, PO, WP, 32, 43, 55 81, 83
Baku, (Caspian), 75, 163, 164, 168, 171, 175, 176
Balajari Rail Junction, 173, 175
Balfour, A. J., 25, 26
Balgramo, Col, 90, 91, 92, 94
Baltic Fleet, 152
Barham, HMS, 80
Basra, Persia, 162, 164
Belgian Army, 18, 19; (Armoured Cars), 39
Belgian Squadron (Russia), 27, 39, 113, 140
Belt, Lt Cdr, FW,, 59, 74, 75, 81, 82, 83, 87, 88, 89, 97, 103, 104, 111, 146, 162
Belton Park, Camp, 177
Bendixon, PO, 52
Bengal Lancers, 73
Benson, Sub-Lt, 72, 98, 130, 143
Bessarabia, 149
Bicherakov, Col, 166, 167, 168
Bicherakov, Forces, 168, 169, 170, 173, 176
Bingham, Mr Justice, (Lord Mersey), 17
Birkenhead, Lord, 181
Bishop, 48
Bisotun, 166
Bitlis, 58, 59, 60

Bizerta, 103
Black Sea, 52, 80
Blackwoods Magazine, 170
Bolgrad, 80, 88, 89, 97
Bolshevik Party, 124, 125, 150, 152, 152, 154, 155, 158, 160, 163, 164, 168, 170, 171, 177
Bolton, PO, 102
Boot, CPO, 131
Boothby, Cmdr FLM, 24
Boutall, CPO, 146
Braila, 80, 88, 89, 90, 94, 95, 96, 97, 98
Brattianu, Prime Minister, 79, 80
Brest-Litovsk, 153, 158
British Consuls, (Tabriz), 73; (Resht), 170
British Naval Officer (Archangel), 34
Bromley, 2nd Lt G, 21, 29, 36, 43, 53, 162, 177
Brovari, 148, 151
Brusilov, Gen, (C-in-C), 40, 79, 80, 107, 115, 124
Bryars, PO, 102
Brzezany, 115, 116, 117, 118, 119, 130, 135, 146
Buchanan, Sir George, 151
Bucharest, 80, 87
Buczacz, 132, 134, 135, 139, 140
Bulgarians, 80, 85, 86, 87, 90, 92, 94
Bullard King & Co, 30
Burton Park (Lincolnshire), 25
Carpathians, 79
Carpentier, G., (Croix de Guerre), 33
Caucasus, 51, 52, 74, 75, 99, 101
Cernavoda, (Crossing), 81
Central Caspian Distatorship, 170
Champagne, SS, 39
Chappell, Charles, HM Trawler, 159
Checkley, CPO, 131
Cherbourg, 162
Chertkov, 134, 139, 140, 142

Index

Churchill, Winston, 16, 19, 25, 179, 180, 181, 182
Classey, PO, 91, 92, 102
Communication Between Vehicles, 20
Connick, de Lt, 61, 71, 118, 129
Constantinople, 28, 74
Constanza, 80, 81
Cossacks, 40, 54, 56, 58, 59, 60, 61, 65, 66, 70, 72, 98, 107, 109, 119, 122, 123, 127, 130, 133, 136, 141, 149, 166, 167, 168, 169, 172
Crawford, Col, 165, 173
Cromer, Norfolk, 16, 22, 23, 152, 181
Cromwell, Oliver, 149
Crossing, Capt, 66, 131, 143, 168, 169
Ctesiphon, (Ruins of), 164
Cuicei-Bismal, (Village), 95, 96
Czar, (The) Nicholas, 15, 29, 37, 39, 40, 41, 42, 45, 49, 75, 76, 106, 107, 110, 124, 125, 141, 182
Czar (Russian Liner) 42, 43
Czarevictch, Alexis, 42, 108
Czarina, (Empress) Alexandra Fedorovna, 56, 106
Czechoslovak, (Battalions), 113, 119
Daily Mail, 29
Daimler, (Armoured Car), 20
Danube, 80, 81, 88, 97
Darius, (Persian King), 166
Darakoov, 135, 136, 137, 138, 145
Dardanelles, 25, 50
Denisof, (Aerodrome), 131
Derbent, 75, 169, 176
Dniester, River, 110
Dobruja, 74, 75, 80, 87, 88, 97, 98, 99, 101, 103, 177
Donctz, (Basin), 149
Donnelly, PO, 51
Doobsche, 115
Dover Street, HQ-RNACD, 19, 21, 160
Dreadnought, HMS, 18
Dress, (Insignia), 21

Dukhonin, General, 153
Dundee, 152
Dunkirk, 18
Dunsterforce, 164, 166, 167, 169, 177
Dunsterville, Maj-Gen, E. L., 17, 163, 164, 165, 170, 173, 176, 177
Dvina, (River), 44
Dvinsk, (Russian Liner), 42, 43, 151
Dye, Lt Cdr, 97, 102, 159, 160
East Anglia, 22, 23
Eastern Front, 27, 28, 152
Ecbatana, *see* Hamadan
Edwards, Lt, 90, 92
Einstein, Professor, 181
Elburz, Mountains, 167
Elizabeth, (Grand Duchess), 47
Enver Pasha, 50
Enzeli, (port of), 164, 165, 166, 168, 170, 17; Road to, 167, 173
Epstein, (sculptor), 181
Erdelli, Gen, 11th Army, 119
Erzerum, 50, 58
Eton, 15, 16
Euston, 29
Everest, Mrs, 16
Excelsior, touring car, 18
Falkenhayn, Gen, Eric von, 80, 95
Fear, PO, 78, 102
Feodorchen, A, (39th Siberian Rifles), 87
Ferdinand of Russia, Prince (Royal Yacht), 97, 100
Fiat, Armoured Cars, 145
Foster, William & Co, Lincoln, 24, 25
Ford, Armoured, 89, 90, 91, 94, 98, 128
Ford, Lorries, 90
Ford 'T', Model Tenders, 77, 91
Franklin, Mr, 106
French, Aviators, 113, 132
GHO, Caucasian Front, 52
Gaden, Capt, 116
Galatz, 80, 89, 96, 97, 98, 100, 104
Galicia, 31, 74, 111, 112, 113, 140, 167

Gallipoli, 24
Gammages, (London Store), 29
Gardiner, PO, Australian, 118
Gardner, PO, 117, 146
Gawler, Sub-Lt, 83, 127, 129
Genoa, Italy, 103
George V, King, 26, 30, 39, 40, 76
Georgian, Military Road, 54
Girard, Capt, Baron de Contancon, 10th Novgorod Dragoons, 97, 100, 106, 116, 131, 133, 160
Gladushoff, (Scout), 86
Glory, HMS, 157, 158, 159
Glustenka, 143
Goodall, Barbara, 181
Goodier, PO, 84
Grabovoi, Capt, 89
Graham, LPO, 92, 102
Gregory, Cdr R., 28, 42, 43, 59, 75, 76, 77, 78, 80, 81, 87, 88, 89, 94, 95, 96, 97, 99, 100, 102, 103, 104
Gregson, PO, 146
Gusiatyn, 134, 140, 141, 142, 143, 150, 151
Gutor, Gen, Commander South Western Front, 115, 117
Gutteridge, L., CPO, 77, 89
Habsburgs, 80, 119
Hamadan, 166, 167
Hand, Capt, 116, 131
Hanna, Lt, 97, 100, 140, 146
Happy Valley, 65, 69
Harris, PO, 102
Harrison, LPO, 117, 146
Haskoi, (Village), 61
Hassan, PO, 102
Helenkuf, 127, 130
Henderson, Sub-Lt, 90, 92
Henley, Daniel, HM Trawler, 159
Hill, CPO, 26
Hills, 132 and 69, 83
Hills-Johnes, Gen, Sir James, VC, 30
Hinadia, (Camp), 164
Hindu-Kush, 59
Hirosova, 80, 81, 87, 89

Hitler, (Adolf), 126, 180
Home Rule Bill, (Irish), 22
Hood, Lt Cdr Wells, 38, 43, 84, 85, 86, 95, 97, 102, 115, 117, 130, 143, 146, 162, 177
Hornby Dock, Liverpool, 30, 31
Hotchkiss Landaulette, (car), 17
Hulls, Lt, 74, 133, 136, 142, 168
Hunniford, James, HM Trawler, 159
Hunter, Lt, 86, 94, 97, 98
Husk, PO, 102
Hyderabad, 73
Icon, (Russian), 45
Idema, HM Trawler, 159
Indian Ocean, 162
Indirect Shoot (AFV) 71
Ingle, Lt, 85, 100, 102, 177
Irish Insurrection, (results of, at Alexandrovsk), 43
Irregulars, (Kurds, Tartar, Georgian) 175
Isaksha, 88, 89
Ismail, 89
Italian, Armoured Cars, 19
Ivanov, Gen, 40
Izerna, (Town), 126
Jameson Raid, (Boer War), 94
Jangalis, 166, 167, 170
Jaroslav, 46
Jassy, 95, 104, 182
Johnson, PO, 52
Kaiser, (Wilhelm II), 40, 145
Kamiloovka, (Hamlet), 135, 137, 138, 139
Kandalaksha, (Station), 157
Kars, 56, 73, 74, 75
Kasbeck, Mount, 52
Kasvin, 166, 167, 170
Kemp, Adm, 158
Kerensky, Alexander, 15, 113, 114, 115, 117, 119, 123, 125, 126, 149, 150, 152, 153, 182
Kermanshah, 166
Keupri-keui, 59, 73, 74
Khabalov, Gen, Military Governor

Index

of Petrograd, 107
Khan, (Kuchik Mirza), 166, 167, 169, 170
Khartoum, Garrison, 25
Khurkur, Pass, 166
Kidd, Sub-Lt, 94, 97
Kiev, 131, 148, 149
Kipling, Rudyard, 30, 163, 181
Kitchener, FM, Lord, 26
Kluck, General von, 18
Kobelovloki, (Village), 142
Kola inlet, 35, 38, 42, 43, 45, 159 141, 145, 148, 149, 150, 151, 152, 182
Kootkovtse, (Forward Base), 143
Kopyczincze, 140, 142
Kornilov, Gen, 40, 119, 124, 132,
Kozova, 112, 122, 123, 126, 130, 131, 132
Kremlin, 47, 48
Kronstadt, 109, 125, 152
Krylenko, C-in-C, 153
Ksheeve, (Village), 131
Kuh-E-Alvand, (Pass), 166
Kuh-E-Safid, (Pass), 166
Kurds, 50, 59, 60, 61, 62, 64, 65, 66, 68, 73, 74, 168
Kuropatkin, Gen, 40
Kuropatniki, 126, 127
Kursk, 148, 151, 152, 154, 155, 156, 160, 161
Kursk, SS, 170, 176
Kut-al-Amarah, 54, 164
Landships, (Tanks), 24
Lambert, Cdre, Cecil Foley, 4th Sea Lord, 24, 25, 26, 28
Lamkert, Lt, 60, 88, 89, 97
Lampson, Sir Curtis, 16
Lampson, Jane, 16
Lanchester, Armoured Car: 19, 22, 29, 55, 60, 62, 73, 77, 85, 91, 95, 106, 143; Lorry: 90
Landships Committee, 24, 25
Lapland, 41
Lawrence, Col, T. E., 25
LeFroy, Sub-Lt, 82, 95, 116, 140

Lenin Vladimir Ilyich, 124, 125, 153
Liberal Party, 17
Lietyatin, 115
Ligne, Prince Baudouin de, 19
Liverpool, 29, 44
Lockhart, Bruce, 158, 161
Locke, CPO, 118
Locker, Frederick, 16
Locker-Lampson, Jonathan, 104
Locker-Lampson, Commander Oliver, RNVR, (MP), 15, 16, 17, 18, 22, 23, 24, 26, 27, 28, 29, 30, 31, 33, 35, 36, 37, 38, 39, 41, 42, 45, 46, 47, 48, 49, 51, 52, 53, 54, 55, 56, 58, 59, 60, 61, 62, 65, 68, 72, 73, 74, 75, 76, 77, 78, 79, 81, 94, 99, 100, 101, 102, 103, 104, 105, 106, 108, 110, 111, 113, 115, 117, 119, 122, 124, 125, 126, 129, 130, 135, 137, 138, 139, 141, 145, 146, 148, 150, 151, 160, 161, 164, 165, 177, 179, 180, 181, 182
Locul Sarat, 94, 97, 98
Lloyd George, David, 26
Lloyds Magazine, 41, 75, 145
Lucas, Harriet, 16
Ludendorff, General von, 164
Lvov, Prince, 124
Lyaskootse, 137
McEwen, PO, 117, 146
McIvor, PO, 102
McKeown, PO, 128
MacDowell, Sub-Lt, 90, 92
MacFarland, PO, 117
MacFarlane, CPO, 78, 90, 96, 102
Macedonia, 59
Macin, 97, 98
Malta, 103
Maluna, (Troopship), 162
Manchuria, 40
Marconi Wireless School, 21
Maria Louise, Princess of Schlewig-Holstein, 30
Marshall, W. R., Lt-Gen, Sir, 163
Martin, Sgt G., 43, 44, 48, 81, 84,

104, 165, 166, 167, 168, 169
Martini Henry, (Rifle), 64
Mastagi, 172
Maude, Gen, 164
Maxim, Machine Gun, 19, 20, 36, 37
Menjil, (bridge), 166, 169
Mewes, (Correspondent, *Daily Mirror*), 145
Michael, Grand Duke, 108
Milner, Lord, 155
Mimosa, HMS Sloop, 103
Minerva, (Touring Car), 18
Mitchell, Lt, 85, 86, 177
Mitchell, PO, 118
Mogilev, 7, 39, 7, 106, 107, 150, 153
'Moses Rock', 166
Moscow, 47, 48, 51, 52, 151, 161
Murmansk (Alexandrovsk), 36, 156, 158, 159
Mush, (Plain), 58, 59, 73, 75, 165, 166, 182
Namibia, (German South West Africa), 23
Newcastle, 152
New Haven Court, Cromer, 16, 181
Newport, Monmouthshire, 76
Nicholaivich, Grand Duke Nicholas, 56, 58, 60, 73, 74, 76, 101, 108, 182
Nile, (Steamer), 162
North, PO, 29
North Cape, 33
Norton-Griffiths, J., Col, 94, 95
Norway, 39, 42
Novikoff (39th Siberian Rifles), 86
Odessa, 15, 74, 75, 76, 80, 113, 149
Orloffsky, 160
Ostend, (Belgium), 18
Paget, Bianca, 181
Pai Tak, (Pass), 166
Palestine, 25
Pantilimon Ustin, (Village), 81, 84
Pantiloovka, (Hamlet), 136
Passchen, von, 166, 167
Paveloff, (2nd Lt), 86
Pearson, PO, 118

Perlita, (Hamlet), 91
Persia, 58, 74, 88, 165
Persian Gulf, 162
Peterborough Standard, 17
Petrograd, 38, 39, 42, 58, 74, 105, 106, 108, 111, 116, 123, 124, 131, 154, 156, 159; Garrison: 124, 125, 150, 152; Military Governor: 107
Petrov, 171
Petrovsk, 169, 173
Petrozavodsk, 38
Pickin, Oliver, HM Trawler, 159
Pierce-Arrow, Heavy Armoured Vehicle, 19, 95, 142
Pincott, PO, 102
Ploesti, (Oil Field), 95
Podgaitse, (English Hospital at), 131, 132, 133
Polish Regiments, 113, 115, 119, 123
Poole, Gen, 115, 155, 156, 160
Poznan, 119
President II, 29
President Kruger, (Steamship), 170, 176
Proskurov, 112, 132, 143, 148
Provisional Government, (Russian), 15, 111, 124, 140, 152
Prussian, (Guards), 149
Putilov, (Industrialist), 151
Radio, (Intercept), 53
Read, T., PO, 84, 156, 158
Reckitt, Sir James, HM Trawler, 159
Red Cross, (Russian), 53
Red Guards, 154, 159
Red Sea, 162
Red Square, (Moscow), 47
Reni, 80, 87, 88, 89, 90, 97
Reppmann, Lt, 88, 133, 160, 161
Resht, 166, 167, 169, 170
Resmilo, HM Trawler, 159
Reuters Correspondent, 159, 160
Riga, (City), 150
Ritchie, PO, 128
Robertson, H. S., Captain, 30, 32, 35

Robertson, Gen, Sir William, CIGS, 26
Rodway, PO, 128
Rodwell, PO, A., 47
Rogers, PO, 143
Rolls Royce, Armoured Car, 19, 21, 22, 25, 77, 85, 95, 117, 139, 182; Tourer: 55, 64, 85
Romanoff, (Village), 157
Roobla, 90, 94
Rostchavosky, Cdr, Imperial Navy, 37, 38
Rostov-on-Don, 51, 72
Round, F. Sgt, 32, 81, 110, 129, 174, 176
Rowfant, (Sussex), 16, 181
Royal Air Force, No 72 Squadron, 167
Royal Flying Corps, 28
Royal Naval Armoured Car Division, 19, 20, 22, 24, 26, 28, 177
Rubberine Tyres, 167
Rule, S., PO, 181, 182
Rumania, 79, 80; Warships: 81; Army: 88; Front: 99; Rumanian Royal Family: 74, 75, 76, 77, 78, 79, 104
Russian Armoured Cars, 39, 83, 87, 88, 89, 122, 139, 140
Russian Armoured Car Division, RNAS, 15, 28, 30, 39, 45, 56, 74, 177, 179
Russian Baltic Fleet, 28
Russian Brigade, (France), 27
Russian Imperial General Headquarters, (*see* Stavka)
Ruston, Lt Cdr, 104, 115, 117, 118, 130, 132, 133, 134, 135, 136, 138, 139, 140, 141, 143, 144, 162, 165, 168, 170, 173, DSO: 174
Ryan, Lt, RNR, 159
St Anne, (Order of), 146
St George, (Awards), 73, 99, 101, 132, 146
St Michael, (Icon), return of, 45; (Order of), 101
St Vladimir, (Order of), 101
Salsibury, PO, mentioned in despatches, 102
Sampson, C. R., Cdr, 18, 19, 24, 28
Sarikamish, 50, 56, 58, 59
Schmerinke, 75
Scott, G., Surgeon-Cdr, 35, 52, 84, 100, 102, 123, 131, 160
Scott, M., Surgeon Lt, 84, 174
Scott-Maxim, Motor cycle combination, 20
Scottish Women's Hospital, 88, 89, 97
Seabrook, Heavy Armoured Car, 19, 24
Sea Lords, 25, 35, 100, 103
Senussi, (Moslem sect), 25
Sergei, Grand Duke, 40
Sereth, River, 104, 105, 140, 142
Shadwell, L., Lt, 78, 90, 91, 92, 127, 128, 129
Sharafkhaneh, (Railhead), 73, 74
Shaw, PO, 129
Sholl, Major, 65, 69, 72, 73, 83, 99, 177
Siberia, 76
Sinn Fein, (Dublin rising), 43
Sirelius, Gen, 4th Siberian Corps, 81, 87, 88, 90, 95, 100, 101, 112
Sissons, H. A., PO, 21, 23, 25, 105, 106
Smiles, Lt-Col, Walter, D., 21, 78, 81, 90, 91, 92, 94, 95, 96, 97, 98, 99, 100, 101, 102, 104, 105, 110, 115, 116, 117, 122, 127, 128, 129, 130, 132, 138, 139, 140, 142, 143, 162, 180
Smith, PO, 111
Smith, C. J., Lt, 59, 159, 160
Smith, Masterton, 100, 101, 102
Soames, Lt-Cdr, R. J., 152, 153, 154, 155, 156
Southam, Sub-Lt, 138, 140
Southampton, 162, 177
Spencer, PO, D., 81, 151

Stanley, Adm, 153, 156
Stentor, HMT, 151
Stokes, Gun, 115, 116, 117, 124
Stavka, (Russian GHQ), 28, 39, 41, 49, 50, 53, 107, 150
Suchadol, 143
Swan, PO, W. D., 139
Tabriz, 72
Tanga, (Tanzania), 24, 25
Tank, Landship: 24; MkI: 25; Little Willie: 25
Tara, SS, 25
Taranto, Italy, 162
Tarnopol, 112, 119, 126, 127, 131, 132, 135, 142
Telyache, 132
Tennyson, Lord, (Alfred), 16
Terek, (Cossacks), 51
Terek, River, 52
Teyache, 131
Thornhill, Col, 160
Tiflis, 54, 55, 56, 58, 74, 168, 172
Tigris, River, 162
Tiraspol, 97, 99, 102, 103, 104, 105, 106, 110, 111, 112
Tithonus, HMS, 158
Titterington, Sub-Lt, 130, 142, 174
Tobolsk Militia, 161
Topalul, 81, 84
Trans-Caucasia, 49, 74, 165
Transylvania, 75, 80
Trezibond, 50
Trinity College, (Cambridge), 15
Trotsky, Leon, 15, 125, 158, 161
Tsarskoe Selo, 106, 108
Tudor-Tudor, Adm, Sir Frederick, 25
Tudor-Vladimirescu, 95
Tulchea, 8
Turkish-Caucasus Islam Army, 168
Turkish, (Cavalry), 168
Turner, PO, 47, 65
Turner, Sub-Lt, 65, 69, 70, 89, 118, 146
Ulster Volunteer Force, 22
Ulyanov, (Vladimir), *see* under Lenin

Umona, (SS), Natal Line, 30, 31, 32, 33, 34, 35, 36, 38, 42, 43, 151, 182
Unionist Party, 22
Urka, HM Trawler, 159
Urmia, Lake, 58, 73
Valei Canepei, 90
Valentine, Col, RFC, 131, 132
Van, Lake, 58
Varna, 177
Vaughan, PO, 85
Venisilovka, 130
Veronica, HMS Sloop, 103
Viane, PO, 118
Viboodov, 130
Vizurul, 90, 91, 92, 94
Vladikavkas, 51, 52, 54, 55
Vologda, 46
Vostoff, 46
Walford, Sub-Lt, 82
Wallace, Sub-Lt, 138, 139
War Graves Commission, 119
War Ministry, (Russian), 106
Watson, PO, 102
Wavell, A. F. M., (Viceroy of India), 76
Weller, PO, 63, 65
Western Desert, (Senussi Campaign), 25
Western Front, 24, 27, 79
Westminster, Duke of, 22, 25
White Sea, 27, 34, 43
Whiting, PO, 102
Wilton, Robert, (*Times* Correspondent-Petrograd), 145
Winter Palace, 152
Wolfs Gap, 172, 175
Woods, Sub-Lt, 118, 138
Wormwood Scrubbs, (Depot), 19, 22
Yudenich, Gen, N., 50, 56, 58, 163
Zavalinshevsky, Col, 39th Siberian Rifle Regiment, 86
Zbrucz, 143
Zurikoff, Gen, Commander, 6th Army, 95, 96, 97, 98

£3